CIVIL RIGHTS IN THE WHITE LITERA

CIVIL RIGHTS IN THE WHITE LITERARY IMAGINATION

Innocence by Association

Jonathan W. Gray

University Press of Mississippi / Jackson

www.upress.state.ms.us

The University Press of Mississippi is a member of the
Association of American University Presses.

First printing 2013

∞

Library of Congress Cataloging-in-Publication Data

Gray, Jonathan W.
Civil rights in the white literary imagination : inno-
cence by association / Jonathan W. Gray.
p. cm.
Includes bibliographical references and index.
ISBN 978-1-62846-054-4 (cloth : alk. paper) —
ISBN 978-1-61703-650-7 (ebook) 1. American literature—
White authors—History and criticism. 2. Civil rights in
literature. 3. Race relations in literature. 4. African Ameri-
cans—Civil rights—History—20th century. I. Title.
PS173.N4G68 2013
810.9'3520396073—dc23   2012031363

British Library Cataloging-in-Publication Data available

Contents

vii   Acknowledgments

3   Introduction
PERFECT UNIONS
Innocence and Exceptionalism in American Literary Discourse

14   Chapter One
"THE LOOK BACK HOME FROM A LONG DISTANCE"
Robert Penn Warren and the Limits of Historical Responsibility

44   Chapter Two
THE APOCALYPTIC HIPSTER
"The White Negro" and Norman Mailer's Achievement of Style

72   Chapter Three
"THE WHOLE HEART OF FICTION"
Eudora Welty inside the Closed Society

105   Chapter Four
"NEGROES, AND BLOOD, AND HORROR"
William Styron, Existential Freedom, and *The Confessions of Nat Turner*

133   Epilogue
PERFECTING INNOCENCE

139   Notes

155   Works Cited

161   Index

Acknowledgments

So many people helped me bring this book to fruition that I barely know where to begin. Back in the days when I was a teenager, Rosemarie Garland-Thompson got the ball rolling with love and patience. Around the same time Charles Verharen taught me that the perfect is the enemy of the good. Michael Szalay disabused me of a notion by asking a tough question, and suggested a path that led me to today. Louis Menand forced me to contend with the rich tapestry that is American culture and showed me the importance of writing clearly. He sets a high bar. Robert Reid-Pharr cajoled and encouraged me during the beginning and middle of this process, and taught me the importance of attention to detail, a lesson I have learned incompletely. Jon-Christian Suggs was calm, considered, and helpful with matters of literature and the law. Thanks for giving me a shot. David Blight provided me with the means to reorient this project and connect it more surely to the threads of race and history that run throughout the cultural life of the United States. Benjamin Talton blazed the trail, blessing me with his unwavering confidence, words of encouragement, and a stiff drink. Keota Fields ran with me step for step until out paths diverged, and I advance in large part due to the pace he set. Thank you. Minkah Makalani showed up suddenly and left too soon, but read a chunk of the manuscript and offered valuable feedback. Thanks, cousin. James de Jongh offered material and spiritual support throughout. Jeanne Theoharis helped me understand the changes the civil rights movement wrought in the North, and proved a generous presence. Glenda Carpio made putting the time in easier at the beginning, and remains a model and an inspiration. David Yaffe suggested a name for the project, and, once I flipped it, it sufficed. Thanks for that. Richard Perez nipped at my heels, keeping me focused on the finish line. Slow down! Baz Dreisinger provided the support that only a matey can. Good looking out. Ta-Nehisi Coates kept me at my desk by showing and proving every day. Damn son. Cheo Vidal was always full of ideas when it was time to kick back. Thanks for helping me keep the batteries charged. Ruth Wilson Gilmore showed up too late to help with this project, but serves as a lodestar. Thank you for reminding me the world can change.

I also want to thank the people whose presence in my life, tangential though it may often be, continues to instruct, inspire, and motivate. They include: Allistarr Durant, Lopa Basu, Juan Battle, Moustafa Bayoumi, Nikhil Bilwakesh, David Brothers, Janice Cable, Michael Cano, Dan Charnas, William Jelani Cobb, Zach Davis, Ashley Dawson, Michael Dumas, Jennifer Egan, Eric Falci, Allyson Foster, Mikhail Gershovich, Karen Green, Peter Hitchcock, Rachel Ihara, Bassey Ikpi, Candace Jenkins, Geoff Klock, L'Heureux Lewis-McCoy, Maha Malik, Anne McCarthy, Kevin McGruder, Koritha Mitchell, Anthony Morris, John Murillo, Greg Pardlo, Lisa Perdiago, Nick Powers, Sherie Randolph, Samuel Roberts, Corey Robin, Jack Shuler, Antonio Taylor, Jill Toliver-Richardson, Alia Tyner, Rebecca Wanzo, Ivy Wilson, and Jerry Watts. Thank you all. This couldn't have happened without your considerable contributions.

I want to thank all of my colleagues at John Jay–CUNY for their support and forbearance during this long process, particularly Marc Dolan, Nivedita Majumdar, Mark McBeth, Adam McKible, Allison Pease, and Margaret Tabb.

We lose so many people on life's journey, and I want to acknowledge four people whose absence tempers my joy: Shirley Cuffee Gray, Robert Cummins, Eve Sedgwick, and Diana Colbert.

This manuscript was completed with the support of grants provided by my union, the Professional Staff Congress–City University of New York. I want to thank the union for fighting on my behalf to make the PSC Research Award Program possible. An investment in scholarship is money well spent.

I want to thank Jay Barksdale, who administers the Wertheim Study and the Allen Room at the Forty-Second Street Branch of the New York Public Library for his generous support. Without access to the valuable resources for scholars available in those spaces, completing this manuscript would have been impossible.

I extend my deepest and most profound thanks to my family. My father, Charles Claxton Gray, gives me more love than I have any right to expect. I am forever in your debt. Thank you. My mother, Shirley A. Gray, welcomed an unruly adolescent into her home with patience and grace. Thank you for your love and patience. Deidre Cuffee-Gray insisted on a brother, gifted me with my name, and stuck with me through thick and thin. Thank you. Michael Sinclair thought he was teaching me basketball, but was really teaching me how to work towards a goal. Thank you. John Sinclair insisted on toughness and self-sufficiency, and I learned that lesson well. Dawn Sinclair exhibits a poise and discipline in all aspects of her life that I can only aspire to. Tina Sinclair showed me how a fiery will can overcome difficult circumstances. Cynthia Sinclair proves that perseverance can lead to redemption. You have been some of my best teachers and I thank you for the lessons.

I want to thank my children, Zola, Ellison, and Oliver, for pouting when I couldn't take them to the park, for complaining when playdates went unscheduled and movies unseen, for insisting on treats from the patisserie and walks for locally sourced ice cream. You understand what is really important. Don't ever let me forget it! I love you all far more than you can know.

I want to thank Valerie Ferguson Gray for her love, companionship, and support throughout this process. Without you I have nothing.

CIVIL RIGHTS IN THE WHITE LITERARY IMAGINATION

PERFECT UNIONS

Innocence and Exceptionalism in American Literary Discourse

This is a book about the intersection of literature, social reform, and American innocence, which is to say a book about the persistence of American exceptionalism as a metaphysical and metaphorical state of being. It began—and remains to a significant degree—as an examination of the literary output produced during the crucible of the civil rights movement by four liberal white writers: Robert Penn Warren, Norman Mailer, Eudora Welty, and William Styron.[1] This study extends from a premise which, in its easy acceptance, has almost been reduced to a cliché—that the civil rights movement transformed America—by seeking to ascertain how the events of the most significant American social protest movement of the twentieth century inspired these four very different writers to reorient their creative work in light of the nation's evolving recognition of Black American citizenship. There is, of course, a tradition of white writers critiquing America's democratic experiment by fictionalizing the nation's treatment of Black Americans, from Herman Melville and Harriet Beecher Stowe to Mark Twain and William Faulkner. However, although Mailer, Warren, Welty, and Styron produce important work during the period between the *Brown v. Board of Education* case and the social unrest that followed the assassination of Martin Luther King, two signposts that mark a beginning and an end to the civil rights movement,[2] each of these writers produced major work prior to 1954 that failed to question the racial order of the United States, and, in the case of Warren, demonstrated outright hostility to those who sought to challenge this status quo.[3] The events of the 1950s and '60s forced these writers to, in the words of Lionel Trilling, turn "their adverse, critical and very intense passions upon the condition of the polity" and produce work that allowed them to reorient their writerly selves in light of the new dispensation.[4]

3

That work—from Warren's *Who Speaks for the Negro?* to Mailer's "The White Negro" to Welty's "Where Is the Voice Coming From?" to Styron's *The Confessions of Nat Turner*—permitted these writers to explore the implications of America's changing social order due to the events of the civil rights movement. This writing helped to reshape the post–World War II consensus about race and social justice in America, and yet, even as these writers called into question the American ideology that limited Black Americans to second-class citizenship, each of them maintained some resistance, an unwillingness to embrace fully the various counternarratives being offered by the ascending civil rights movement and its adherents.[5] My project seeks to explain why these writers were reluctant to commit to what David Blight calls emancipationist narratives in the face of a persistent legacy of racial oppression. I argue in what follows below that this hesitancy recalls a similar reluctance displayed by white writers during an earlier period in the history of American literature about race, one that allowed for the preservation of American innocence by enshrining racial difference.[6]

The historical narrative of American innocence begins at the end of the Civil War, for, although the South lost the conflict on the battlefield, it won political and rhetorical control over the war's ultimate meaning after Reconstruction by encouraging a deliberate forgetting of the actual causes of the war.[7] As Warren would have it, "We may say that only at the moment when Lee handed Grant his sword was the Confederacy born; or to state matters another way, in the moment of death the Confederacy entered upon its immortality."[8] The South achieved this apotheosis, according to Blight, by carefully crafting a collective memory of the war that necessitated obscuring slavery as the central cause of the conflict. Blight identifies, in the immediate aftermath of the Civil War, "[t]hree overall visions of Civil War memory [that] collided and combined." Two of these three versions of cultural memory, "the reconciliationist vision" and "the white supremacist vision [that] locked arms with reconciliationists," conspired to produce the kind of ideological forgetting that enabled the rhetorical reunion of the United States at the expense of the former slaves. Blight notes that "by the turn of the century" these complementary accounts of cultural memory "delivered the country a segregated memory of the Civil War on Southern terms" capable of producing a national identity that—paradoxically—celebrated reunification as the war's central achievement while remaining hostile to full citizenship for African Americans. These dual visions of post-Reconstruction America accomplished this by marginalizing the "emancipationist vision" which sought to remember the war as a source for "the reinvention of the republic and the liberation of blacks to citizenship and Constitutional equality."⁹ The emancipationist narrative, which celebrated Black freedom and undermined the legitimacy of white supremacy by seeking to fold African Americans into the body politic, was forgotten in the name of national comity after the war. This post-Reconstruction period, memorialized by historian Rayford Logan as the nadir of Black American citizenship, is codified by *Plessy v. Ferguson*, the Supreme Court case that established de jure segregation as permissible just twenty years after the end of Reconstruction.

Blight describes this state of affairs as "a story of how in American culture romance triumphed over reality, sentimental remembrance won over ideological memory" (4). In other words, an ideological fantasy of post-bellum reconciliation—which, in order to produce and protect an innocent white identity, ignored both the emancipationist narrative and the abject material condition of black citizens that Reconstruction attempted to address—triumphed over an account that attempted to assess how a southern ideology of white supremacy nearly destroyed the nation as we know it. The sentimentalized fictions of the Lost Cause not only marginalized the existence of slavery as the reason for the Civil War, but also enabled the nation to ignore the consequences of the failed Reconstruction for more than seventy-five years. This post-Reconstruction amnesia occurred because overlooking continued southern intransigence and racial intolerance was preferable to acknowledging "a contradiction that menaced the legitimacy of [America's] perennial self-representation as the exceptionalist and 'redeemer nation.'"¹⁰ White Americans embraced the Lost Cause fantasy that the nation went to war over a disagreement that centered on differing interpretations of the proper role of government rather than confront the racial intolerance that continued to fester.¹¹

American innocence is born here, in the aftermath of a war fought to correct America's greatest injustice. This innocence was more than just metaphorical. It is, after all, almost impossible to hold citizens, soldiers, or politicians accountable for the injuries that result from (the legacies of) their actions if this violence is immediately and deliberately effaced.¹² The Lost Cause's successful reframing of individuals who went to war in defense of white supremacy and chattel slavery into agrarian cavaliers protecting a distinctive way of life allowed the South, and thus the nation at large, to regain its innocence. One of the chief legacies of the Civil War, then, was the recuperation of a forgetful (southern) innocence that

produces exceptionalism, but this postbellum innocence is always imperiled by other narratives contained within America's celebrated pluralism,
narratives associated with citizens whose very bodies present a challenge
to the Lost Cause's fiction of innocent partisans.

In "Memory and Identity: The History of a Relationship," John R. Gillis calls attention to the role that cultural memory plays in establishing the
grounds for both personal and national identity by noting that "memories
and identities are not fixed things, but representations or constructions of
reality, subjective rather than objective phenomena." Gillis identifies the
mutual dependence of identity and memory, locating the intersection of
memory and identity as the place where American innocence and thus
American exceptionalism is produced and internalized. "Memory work,"
Gillis observes, "is, like any other kind of physical or mental labor, embedded in complex class, gender and power relations that determine what is
remembered (or forgotten), by whom and for what end." It is by following
Gillis's admonition to "decode" the exceptional nature of American innocence "in order to discover the relationships [it] create[s] and sustain[s]"
that I shall illustrate how the literary figures above deploy American
innocence in their civil rights literature.[13] The literary revision of cultural
memory in support of civil rights attempts to reverse the earlier historical
moment where fictions of American innocence demanded an entirely different kind of postwar reinvention, but this revision is far from complete.

Ronald Fiscus calls this imperiled yet exceptional innocence, this
state of blamelessness, "the premise of innocence," and demonstrates
how it limits appeals to social justice.[14] Fiscus, a legal scholar, asserts that
when seeking to redress a societal injustice such as the legacy of racial
discrimination, "as long as whites are perceived [which is to say, perceive
themselves] as innocent, no degree of burdening will appear principled."
The premise of innocence, then, continues to determine the possibilities for social justice even in post–civil rights, postcolonial, postmodern,
post–9/11 America.[15] Fiscus offers a refutation of the premise of American
innocence that relies on a thoroughgoing analysis of post-*Brown* Supreme
Court cases, but the refutation I attempt below focuses on how the literature produced during the civil rights movement by the four writers under
consideration permitted the successful recuperation of the premise of
white American innocence at precisely the moment when a reinvigorated
emancipationist narrative—the civil rights narrative—challenged the basis
of that innocence. These writers embraced this ideological innocence in

part because each sought to maintain his or her own idiosyncratic idea of American exceptionalism.

The articulation of American exceptionalism is usually associated with American studies scholars from the post–World War II period like Perry Miller, Henry Nash Smith, and R. W. B. Lewis rather than writers of literary fiction from the same period.[16] But the sense of blamelessness that is American innocence is hopelessly intertwined with notions of American exceptionalism, and the literary writers above contribute to its maintenance. American exceptionalism is, in fact, a necessary corollary to the Lost Cause myths that create and sustain American innocence. As Donald Pease observes, American exceptionalism is a fluid concept because it "operates . . . as a fantasy through which U.S. citizens bring . . . contradictory political and cultural descriptions into correlation with one another through the desires that make them meaningful." This capaciousness extends even to the word exceptional itself, which "has been taken to mean that America is 'distinctive' (meaning merely different), or 'unique' (meaning anomalous), or 'exemplary' (meaning a model for other nations to follow)."[17] The malleability of American exceptionalism means that it can accommodate itself to a variety of cultural and political uses.[18] This indeterminacy, this forgetting of root causes, is the product of the blamelessness that is American innocence.

This is not to say, contra Pease, that notions of American exceptionalism exist purely as fantasy. The group identity of a persecuted religious minority did in fact gain a sense of divine purpose by embracing the metaphor of the city on the hill, the shining example for others to emulate. Thomas Paine secularized and extended that metaphor to colonists outside that religious community when he asserted in his best-selling treatise that American independence would usher in a "new era for politics . . . a new method of thinking."[19] Emerson did indeed fetishize individualism in "Self-Reliance" and elsewhere, and Tocqueville's observations about the fundamental differences between the United States and the Continent found a credulous audience both in the US and abroad. And, thanks to the writing of James Fenimore Cooper and others, one could understand the frontier as a shifting location that symbolized the possibilities for rebirth present in the lawless and liminal spaces of the United States. Cold War scholars like Perry, Smith, Lewis, and the other founders of American studies, building on the idiosyncratic work of Vernon Parrington, may have articulated and exported an ideology of American exceptionalism by foregrounding various elements of our literary and political history, but they certainly did not produce this culture out of whole cloth.

What I am trying to establish here is that American exceptionalism's very capaciousness depends on the kind of cultural forgetfulness, what Pease describes as "structures of disavowal" (6) inaugurated after the conclusion of the Civil War.[20] As American exceptionalism is reshaped to meet political and cultural demands at various moments during the Cold War period, it must also be retroactively constructed to erase its excesses, be they Jim Crow or Japanese internment, in order to reconcile the ideological inconsistencies present in that history.[21] This troubling malleability is visible in William Spanos's genealogy of American exceptionalism as

> an ontological interpretation of the American national identity whose origins lay in the American Puritans' belief that their exodus from the Old World and their "errand in the wilderness" of the New was, on the prefigurative analogy of the Old Testament Isrealites, divinely or transcendentally ordained and which became hegemonic in the course of American history with its secularization as Manifest Destiny in the middle of the nineteenth century and as the end of history and the advent of the New World Order at the end of the twentieth century.[22]

A national identity grounded in an ontology capable of such slippage threatens to become incoherent unless these systemic ruptures are continually confronted and corrected.[23] The practice of forgetting is a site where this cultural and historical maintenance takes place.

But, one might ask, why select these writers to illustrate this process? One reason, as stated above, is that they each produced major work before the *Brown* case signaled to the nation that Black Americans must be better integrated into mainstream society. This allows for a comparative approach that will illuminate how each addressed race before and after *Brown* and the Montgomery bus boycott unleashed the tumultuous unrest of the period. If these writers base their initial presentations of race on the settled expectations of the day, the literature they produce in support of civil rights must confront their earlier assumptions. What I hope to demonstrate is how their revision of cultural memory attempts to fashion a postwar reinvention entirely different from that which occurred at the end of the Civil War, but ultimately leaves important aspects of American exceptionalism intact. Since, as Phillip Barish would have it, American exceptionalism "is a stance, a posture—a template—for positioning and presenting oneself, simultaneously for one's own gaze and for the gazes of 'foreign' others," any attempt at ascertaining each author's use of American exceptionalism will also explore how they sought to reposition themselves to their various publics.[24]

INNOCENCE BY ASSOCIATION

My project opens with "'The Look Back Home from a Long Distance': Robert Penn Warren and the Limits of Historical Responsibility," which details the evolution of Warren's perspective towards the exceptionalist South. Warren's first two texts, a biography of John Brown and "The Briar Patch," a defense of segregation that was his contribution to the Southern Agrarians' *I'll Take My Stand*, explicitly support the Lost Cause mythos that grows out of the failed Reconstruction. These earlier works trouble Warren as his views begin to evolve after the *Brown v. Board of Education* case. His reorientation begins with *Segregation: The Inner Conflict of the South* (1956), originally a magazine piece that attempted to assess the mood of the South in light of the *Brown* decision. In a fascinating self-interview that concludes this text, Warren reveals his desire to maintain the premise of southern innocence, even as events make this increasingly untenable. In his self-interview Warren clings to the fiction that exceptional white southerners will emerge from this struggle better able to provide moral leadership for the nation, calling desegregation "one small episode in the long effort for justice." At this point he resembles the nineteenth-century reconciliationists so taken with the nobility and leadership qualities of the defeated southerners.

Warren strikes a somewhat different note in *The Legacy of the Civil War* (1961), though his ambivalence remains. Warren now asserts that the history of the United States properly begins with the Civil War, which places an added importance on the current effort to resolve the issue of race and democracy in America once and for all. Given the importance of the legacy of the war and the integration of African Americans in the United States, Warren here laments the myths that allowed both the North and the South to put off until now a proper resolution of the issue. This text seeks to warn both northern liberal and southern segregationist that without a fresh perspective, a change in national attitude, the mistakes of the Civil War—by which he means the failed Reconstruction—may repeat themselves. After criticizing the traditional northern and southern viewpoints on race and democracy, *The Legacy of the Civil War* offers a qualified endorsement of the emancipationist project undertaken by the civil rights establishment. By *Who Speaks for the Negro?* (1965), Warren's support of the emancipationist agenda is no longer qualified. Here Warren explicitly endorses the goals of Martin Luther King and the NAACP and warns that unless white America is truly willing to embrace an integrationist narrative a resurgent Black Nationalism exemplified by the Nation of Islam will attract enough adherents to make a just and fair resolution to the problems of race and democracy in the United States impossible.[25]

"The Apocalyptic Hipster: 'The White Negro' and Norman Mailer's Achievement of Style," details the forces that shepherded Mailer into a qualified embrace of the emancipationist project. During the early 1950s, Mailer imagined himself a progressive and anarchic artist stifled by the conformity of the times. His first two attempts to break through this sense of alienation, *Barbary Shore* and *The Deer Park*, were both critical and commercial failures that retroactively lessened the power of his debut, *The Naked and the Dead* (1948). *Barbary Shore* (1951) rejected both the celebratory materialism of the postwar period and the left-wing political movements that sought a middle ground between the US and the USSR, preventing both anticapitalists and anticommunists from embracing this ostensible novel of ideas. *The Deer Park* (1955) explores the psychosexual corruption of Hollywood, but does so primarily through two amoral characters: a director who recanted his past radicalism during a HUAC hearing, and a pimp. These wholly unsympathetic characters trivialize Mailer's attempt to dramatize the connection between political and sexual repression. In the wake of these failures, the Montgomery bus boycott inspires Mailer to explore the ways that African Americans struggle against American repression, and he discovers in the jazz clubs of the Village and Harlem an anarchic bohemianism that seems to him a more authentic rejection of American conformity than socialism or the orgone box.

His experiences in the clubs inspire Mailer to produce "The White Negro" (1956), a text that contrapuntally argues for African American equality by asserting that black Americans possess a kind of moral superiority derived from their talent for graceful living in the face of annihilation. Mailer finds this talent a necessary skill for modern life, one that would help white Americans better endure the threat of nuclear war between the USA and the USSR and the bilious hysteria spread by Senator McCarthy. To this end Mailer champions a language of hip, an interracial vernacular that rejects the sterility demanded by an escalating Cold War.

For Mailer, adopting the perspective of marginalized African Americans enables a critique of what he perceives as an increasingly disciplinary society that erodes autonomous notions of the self. This is the perspective that enables him to produce *An American Dream* (1965), a caricature of the consequences of middle-class conformity that finds both a receptive audience and critical approval despite its nihilism. Mailer's attention to African American discourse is ultimately qualified by his avowedly selfish desire to say something meaningful in a society where the accumulation of wealth and the existential threat of the Soviet Union muted criticism of society and idiosyncratic self-expression.

"'The Whole Heart of Fiction': Eudora Welty inside the Closed Society" focuses on the three texts Welty produced during the 1960s: the dramatic monologue "Where Is the Voice Coming From?" (1963), the essay "Must the Novelist Crusade?" (1965) and the short story "The Demonstrators" (1967). The assassination of Medgar Evers—like Welty a lifelong native of Jackson, Mississippi—inspires her to write "Where Is the Voice Coming From?" in protest. Unlike earlier stories like "Keela, the Outcast Indian Maiden" (1940), this story explicitly denounces the ideology of white supremacy that serves as the logic for segregation and Jim Crow and also enables an innocence that deforms the moral values of white men in the South. It remains one of the most powerful texts produced during the civil rights movement and perhaps the least ambiguous of Welty's career. The essay "Must the Novelist Crusade?" was a response to northern correspondents who urged Welty to take a bigger role in the civil rights movement, but it also represents Welty's attempt to protect southern innocence by defending inaction on the part not only of novelists, but of the "silent majority" in the South that stands by as others commit acts of violence to preserve their racial hierarchy. "The Demonstrators" sees Welty return to the indirect style of "Keela" as she depicts the structural violence endemic to small-town southern life through the perspective of the befuddled town doctor who finds himself increasingly unable to abide the tyranny of his community, yet remains both unwilling and unsure about how to agitate for change without endangering both his life and his livelihood.

While the shockingly widespread violence and repression in her native Mississippi initially inspired Welty to her very public endorsement of the goals of the civil rights movement, she resisted jettisoning narratives of innocence and exceptionalism. Her three civil rights texts reveal a profound ambivalence about producing narratives of emancipation. This is why in "Must the Novelist Crusade?" Welty, who was famous for her baroque and peculiar short stories, asserts a utopian color blindness that rejects the articulation of particularized difference in literature as grounds for reflection about political reform. Art can never take the place of political speech, she warns, rejecting art's ability to dramatize the everyday. Welty's reluctance to endorse the production of a politicized art that seeks to promote social reform is more than just the studied criticism of a writer committed to local color and place. It serves to mask her unease about texts like "Where Is the Voice Coming From?" that depict the ways in which segregation damages the very structure of southern society by insisting on the maintenance of white supremacy. She much prefers texts that present this in an indirect fashion, like "The Demonstrators."

I close my study with "'Negroes, and Blood, and Horror': William Styron, Existential Freedom, and *The Confessions of Nat Turner*." William Styron, whom Mailer considered among his chief competition for the mythical title of best living writer, possessed a curious perspective about the South. Like Warren, Styron could embrace the romanticized notion that increasing industrialization would compromise the unique character of the southern states without dwelling on why industrialization was so late in coming. As with Welty, Styron was personally progressive about matters of race, though like her he felt the need to defend those southerners unwilling to accept the American ideal of justice and equality for all. Styron also shared with Mailer a fascination with existentialism and a desire for his work to reveal something meaningful about the nature of American society. To this end Styron produced two existential texts, the novella *The Long March* (1953) and the novel *Set This House on Fire* (1960). The protagonists of these texts are faced with profound moral choices and each struggles to express his personal desires within the conforming milieu of the state. *Set This House on Fire* is particularly intriguing because its protagonist struggles to integrate several acts of violence, including murder and a racist assault on a sharecropper in his youth, into his self-identity as an innocent American. The novel ends with him at peace, having successfully reconciled his past violence into an authentic sense of self. Willing participation in a racially motivated attack, Stryon suggests here, does not disqualify an individual from possessing American innocence.

The way that Styron resolves *Set This House on Fire*, I argue, should inform any reading of *The Confessions of Nat Turner* (1967), Styron's brave but futile attempt at inhabiting an emancipationist Black sensibility. As the interviews he gave while he was writing the novel demonstrate, Styron finds himself increasingly unable to reconcile his existential beliefs with the facts of the case, even though a Black slave protagonist committed to a program of violence and murder in a futile attempt to overthrow slavery seems infinitely easier to justify to a reader in the late 1960s than a "hero" who destroys a sharecropper's home at the urging of a racist co-worker. Having devoted his previous two works to explorations of moral choice, justice, and ultimate transcendence, Styron fashions in *The Confessions of Nat Turner* a narrative that revolves around guilt, sexual frustration, and a crisis of faith.[26] *The Confessions of Nat Turner* fails in its attempt to establish an equivalency between the struggle for freedom during the antebellum period and the struggle for inclusion during the sixties, but it is a productive failure in that the text became a site for Black Arts and Black Nationalist critics to point out the hypocrisy of white liberals celebrating as racially progressive a text that simultaneously belittles the religiosity of emancipationist discourse and protects white innocence. Just as southerners' blandishments silenced emancipationist narratives during the late nineteenth century, allowing them to arrest the reforms begun during Reconstruction, the controversy over *The Confessions of Nat Turner* presaged the post-1968 splintering of the consensus pursuing racial equality as a societal goal.

As in the post-Reconstruction nadir, the post–civil rights moment's return to narratives of innocence stunted the pursuit of distributive justice. The nation again turned away from completing the work necessary to finally fully integrate people of color into the broader society as the white electorate lost patience with the ever-shifting goals of the civil rights movement. Nixon's attempts to recuperate white innocence with his articulation of a silent majority, premised as it was on fatigue with the demands of an emancipationist discourse (which unfolded *at the same time* that Styron was confronting his Black critics at conferences and in the pages of the *New York Review of Books*), signaled to various literary voices that the time to advocate for democratic reform was over. Still, the modern emancipationist narrative had succeeded in displacing much of the white supremacists' narrative, and the United States was profoundly better for it. Unfortunately, without a fiction committed to testing the boundaries of this new dispensation, some of the opportunities these reforms presented were squandered, both within literary circles and in the culture as a whole. While it is easy to understand the ways in which racism continues to circumscribe certain outcomes in our society, translating that knowledge into an action requires a renunciation of innocence, and acknowledgment that perfecting America's union requires actions as well as words.

Chapter One

"THE LOOK BACK HOME FROM A LONG DISTANCE"

Robert Penn Warren and the Limits of Historical Responsibility

Unlike the other authors considered in this project, early in his career Robert Penn Warren offered a full-throated defense of southern innocence, which is to say segregation. His first book, the biography *John Brown: The Making of a Martyr*, published in 1929 while he was at Oxford on a Rhodes Scholarship, treats the abolitionist radical not as a symptom of the polarizing force of slavery, but as a violently unbalanced man driven by an otherworldly megalomania to reckless acts of violence justified by his opposition to slavery. This text is of a piece with the continuing revisionist project of the Lost Cause, as is his next publication, a rationalization of southern exceptionalism titled "The Briar Patch" included in *I'll Take My Stand: The South and the Agrarian Tradition* (1930). Although Warren's views on the South evolve dramatically from the positions he stakes out in these initial pieces, he never fully rejects certain premises expressed therein, even as he finally discards the ideology of southern innocence. The opinions and observations Warren expresses in his three civil rights texts, *Segregation: The Inner Conflict of the South* (1956), *The Legacy of the Civil War* (1961), and *Who Speaks for the Negro?* (1965), remain qualified by elements of conservative Agrarianism not tied to matters of race but concerned instead with Cold War notions of exceptionalism.

Agrarianism was both an insular and catholic movement from its beginnings.[1] The introduction to *I'll Take My Stand*, subtitled "A Statement of Principles" declares that "no single author is responsible for any view outside his own article" although all "the articles . . . tend to support a Southern way of life against what may be called the American or prevailing way" (xix). Agrarianism, a defensive response to attitudes outside the South, was conceived in opposition to the Fordist society that came to dominate manufacturing during the Roaring Twenties. The Agrarians considered the cosmopolitan, proindustrial, urban society produced by the assembly line as inappropriate for their region, and by extension, much of the nation. Although *I'll Take My Stand* offered a strong critique of industrial capitalism, the Agrarians rejected Communism as a suitable alternative on the grounds that both systems were equally committed to a technological development they found relentless and alienating.

Rather than endorsing capitalism or Communism, *I'll Take My Stand* attempts to articulate a humanistic way of life tied as closely as possible to the land, "not an abstract system, but a culture, the whole way in which we live, act, think, and feel. It is a kind of imaginatively balanced life lived out in a definite social tradition. And, in the concrete, we believe that this, the genuine humanism, was rooted in the agrarian life of the older South" (xxvi). This argument subordinates economic productivity to the restricting necessities of regional culture. The Agrarians felt that only in the South could one escape the hastening tempo of modern life in a society that provides more and more material goods, but fails to deliver the time or the means to integrate these goods into "the life pattern of the community" (xxix). Agrarianism celebrates the contemplative leisure necessary to achieving balance between the economic, social, and cultural phases of life and scoffs at the notion that rising wages or increased productivity are worth the sacrifice of man's speculative time.[2]

"The Briar Patch," Warren's contribution to *I'll Take My Stand*, concerns itself with Agrarianism's capacity for permitting the development of the Black community in the South, for, if "the Southern white man feels that the agrarian life had a certain irreplaceable value in his society, and if he hopes to maintain its integrity in the face of industrialism . . . he must find a place for the negro in his scheme" (263). Warren's paternalistic assertion that Agrarianism must account for the status of its minorities if it hopes to maintain legitimacy was simultaneously conservative—since Warren conceives of Black southerners as serfs, dependent for the foreseeable future on the largesse and equanimity of a white southern gentry—and progressive, because, as Warren is painfully aware, many southerners would happily "keep the negroes forever as a dead and inarticulate mass" instead of permitting a course of action that allows for their gradual economic development (248). Acknowledging Black Americans' second-class status in the former Confederacy demands an account of how this state of affairs came about, and "The Briar Patch" offers one designed to preserve (white) southern innocence.

Warren claims that after emancipation "the negro was as little equipped to establish himself in it as he would have been to live again . . . in the Sudan or Bantu country" (247). In Warren's view, Reconstruction offered a fleeting opportunity for social integration between the races, but Black southerners could not seize this chance in part because "people in the North thought that the immediate franchise carried with it a magic which would insure it success as a cure-all and fix all for the negro's fate" and thus wasted their resources promoting suffrage without providing an economic base from which Black southerners might preserve their vote (249). Unfortunately, after "the bluecoats and bayonets disappeared, when certain gentlemen packed their carpet-bags and . . . scalawags settled down to enjoy their profits or sought them elsewhere, the . . . negro found himself in a jungle as puzzling and mysterious, and as little answering to his desires, as the forgotten jungles of Africa" (247). This hostile state of affairs was not, in Warren's view, the result of continuing racial prejudice and economic exploitation on the part of southern whites, but instead stemmed from "Reconstruction [which] badly impaired the white man's respect and gratitude. The rehabilitation of the white man's confidence for the negro is part of the Southern white man's story since 1880" (248). Reconstruction, then, cruelly deceived Black southerners by nourishing an unrealistic hope of political efficacy that served to deny them their proper place in southern society, a place they have struggled to find since.

For Warren in 1929, segregation in the South is a natural consequence of Black people's economic and social inferiority and the northern insistence on the franchise for Blacks at the close of the Civil War, an interpretation that fails to acknowledge the massive resistance to Reconstruction carried out throughout the South in order to return former slaves to a subordinate position.[3] Only by excluding this narrative can Warren posit that "Reconstruction did little to remedy the negro's defects in preparation" for life after slavery, or that the Black politicians who held office during Reconstruction were, in effect, "used as an instrument of oppression" by northern carpetbaggers (248). Segregation is, Warren suggests here, simply the penance that Blacks must pay in order to regain the esteem of the white community lost during Reconstruction. That Warren ascribes the abject condition of southern Blacks to historical circumstance rather than being the result of some genetic defect or biblical decree is the only saving grace in this articulation of the logic of white supremacy and white innocence, because it demands that Warren put forth a program through which African Americans might improve their lives in the South.[4]

Warren cannily incorporates language from Booker T. Washington's 1895 Atlanta Compromise into his assessment of a Negro way forward, arguing that it is futile to permit Blacks to vote in the South if they lack the education necessary to properly discharge the responsibilities of citizenship.[5] Like Washington, Warren assumes educational advances for the Negro masses will eventually result in their full participation in society, but "the end [i.e., Blacks being granted full citizenship via some demonstration of educational achievement] is far from sight . . . [and] to realize this one has only to see the negroes in the deep South, or even in the middle South, sitting before the cabin, stooping over the cotton row or tobacco hill, or crowding the narrow streets of a town on a Saturday night in summer" (249). Warren's argument here—which refrains from commenting on the forces keeping southern Blacks in a state of peonage—conceives of southern Blacks as immutably tied to the land, a trope that appears again and again in every genre of Warren's writing even as the realities of Black life in the South underwent tremendous change.[6]

Black educational achievement, Warren insists, will prove beneficial only within "a separate negro community or group...which is capable of absorbing or profiting from those who have received this higher education." The creation of this self-sufficient community is vital, for if "the negroes in the South cannot support their more talented and better equipped individuals...the educated negroes will leave the South to seek his fortune elsewhere" (251).[7] Indeed, while Warren laments these departures, he considers the idea of a white man hiring a Black lawyer, doctor, or architect "to say the least, a little eccentric" and approvingly cites Washington's metaphor of separate fingers on a hand as a justification for continued segregation in the South (254). According to Warren, highly educated Black Americans should expect to be rewarded for their professional and intellectual ability "when, and only when, the negro is able to think of himself as the member of a group which can afford an outlet for any talent or energy he may possess" (255).

Warren's Agrarian program grants Black southerners few options. Industrialization would seem to represent the best hope for the emergence of a Black professional class able to realize a living within their own community, since factory workers, regardless of race, enjoyed far larger disposable incomes than their rural counterparts, but Agrarianism opposes industrialization and so Warren rejects this argument with an interesting twist of logic. The new factory "come[s] to profit from the cheap labor, black and white, which is to be had" in the South, but this enterprise threatens segregation because the presence of cheap Black labor serves as "a tacit *threat* against the demands which white labor may make later of the factory owner" (256, emphasis added). Warren acknowledges that Black workers might compete successfully for spots on the assembly line because their exclusion from organized labor in the South permits them to accept lower wages. Warren fears that economically insecure whites would seek to erase the competitive advantage that derives from racism and segregation in the South through lynching and other acts of intimidation. These acts threaten southern innocence by calling attention to the violence inherent in the maintenance of Jim Crow.

In response to this potential hazard, Warren proposes "an enlightened selfishness on the part of the Southern white man . . . encourag[ing] the well-being and possibly the organization of negro, as well as white, labor" (258). Warren hopes that if labor organizes southern workers regardless of race it would remove an incentive for companies to seek locations in the South and thus slow the pace of industrialization. Moreover, this prescription supports his assertion of equal protection under the law as a precondition for a palatable segregation, for "white workman must learn . . . that he may respect himself as a white man, but, if he fails to concede the negro equal protection, he does not properly respect *himself* as a man" (260, emphasis added). Granting Blacks equal protection in the courts and access to unions benefits white southerners not only by slowing the spread of industrial capital in the South, but by removing much of the guilt that might burden southern whites benefiting from a segregated society. Thus, though Warren's essay sought to describe a program of Black southern development, his plan also preserves white innocence.

Warren's treatment of the past demonstrates his need to elide historical responsibility. Nefarious carpetbaggers, bluecoats, lazy Negro politicians, and scalawags populate "The Briar Patch," but the pro-segregationist politicians that forced the withdrawal of federal troops from the South in 1877 and enacted the Black Codes are entirely absent. Warren submerges southern agency with these omissions, turning the establishment of the segregated South into an inevitable phenomenon caused by a series of unfortunate historical events precipitated by northern hubris. Forrest Robinson notes that Warren sought to "dissipat[e southern complicity in oppression by using] essentially determinist constructions of history and human will" throughout his career, and we can detect one of the earliest manifestations of that tendency here if we look past Warren's surprising suggestion that whites permit Blacks limited political rights.[8]

More than twenty-five years would pass between the publication of "The Briar Patch" and Warren's next essay on race and southern society, *Segregation: The Inner Conflict of the South*.[9] During the interim, several events conspired to alter Warren's attitudes about segregation. According to Warren, the most important change in his evaluation of history was the fact that he started writing novels.[10] Prior to "The Briar Patch," excluding his biography of John Brown, Warren's only publications were poems in little magazines. Warren composed "The Briar Patch," at Oxford "at about the same time [he] began writing fiction, the two things were tied together—the look back home from a long distance."[11] Writing fiction changed Warren's perceptions about society and, shortly after he returned to the South from England, he realized that the sentiments he expressed in "The Briar Patch" conformed to southern tradition, but failed to represent his "subjective [self], yours truly, in relation to the objective fact" of racial subjugation.[12] Tellingly, Warren castigates himself for being unable or unwilling to explore his discomfort with the system he was defending in print, but not for making the defense itself.

While Warren grappled with the shift in sensibility brought about by his turn to fiction, he migrated from the South to the Midwest and eventually to New York City and its surrounding environs, a change that further altered his particular notions of place and pace. Warren moved from the English department at Louisiana State University to the University of Minnesota–Minneapolis due to a salary dispute with the administration at LSU. He would never make his home in the South again. As his biographer notes, Warren had never lived in such a large city as Minneapolis before, "a metropolis of nearly four hundred thousand individuals," but this prepared him for his next move, which was to New York City and then to the Connecticut suburbs and a long professional association with Yale.[13] In New York, Warren participated in the New York intellectual salon scene that placed him in intimate contact with Black writers Ralph Ellison and James Baldwin. Ellison and Warren, and their wives, became friends and the couples sought out each other's company, dining together in Italy, New York, and Connecticut.

While Warren's personal accommodations changed significantly, the nation experienced an epochal transformation between 1930 and 1956. In those years the United States faced depression, enacted the New Deal, fought World War II, birthed the atomic age, began the postwar process of suburbanization, nervously witnessed the rise of the Soviet empire and Red China, and endured a demagogic McCarthyism that exploited the fears of an anxious American public. The Black community also gained in economic power and political prestige during this period. Franklin Roosevelt issued executive order 8802 banning segregation in the military-industrial complex in 1941 in order to avert a strike called by A. Philip Randolph's Brotherhood of Sleeping Car Porters. Six years later Randolph's union successfully pressured Truman into issuing executive order 9981 banning segregation in the military.[14] The two executive orders challenged the southern way of life, but the Warren court's *Brown v. Board of Education* decision fundamentally undermined southern traditions as nothing had since 1877. As if emboldened by the court's decision, African Americans organized the Montgomery bus boycott to challenge their subordinate social status in the South shortly thereafter. White southern backlash against both the *Brown* decision and the efforts of the Montgomery Improvement Association led Jack Jessup, a friend of Warren's family and an editor at *Life*, to suggest Warren produce "an article for *Life* on desegregation in the South."[15] *Segregation: The Inner Conflict of the South* emerged from that article.

Segregation is an interesting piece of what would come to be understood ten years later as the New Journalism.[16] Though most people associate Norman Mailer, Truman Capote, Joan Didion, and Tom Wolfe with this genre, Warren's reflections on the various challenges to southern tradition emerging after the *Brown* decision is an early example of the form.[17] Warren records events for this article as an implicated observer, permitting his interior reactions to various incidents to shape his novelistic presentation of the facts. Warren organizes *Segregation* thematically, shifting the narrative backwards and forwards through time, digressing to treat different subjects and abruptly shifting locales. *Segregation* is divided into six sections, beginning with a fragmentary opening that places him in a South both familiar and tantalizingly different from that of his youth. The next three sections revolve around several questions Warren asked of his subjects, white and Black: "What are the white man's reasons for segregation?," "What does the Negro want?," and "What's coming?" While he rarely uses names when reporting his subjects' responses to these queries, Warren reveals enough about several of the speakers so that their voices recur in a dialogic fashion throughout the text, despite the pretense of anonymity. The fifth section of *Segregation* serves as a conclusion of sorts, as Warren attempts to frame the political and social implications of his respondents' answers to his questions. *Segregation* closes with a self-interview where Warren reveals his own hopes and fears regarding integration in the South, which he now welcomes and admits is inevitable.

Warren opens *Segregation* by manipulating time, exaggerating the length of his absence in order to convey how fundamentally the South has changed since he departed. As such, Warren has not been absent from the South since 1942 when he left LSU, a period of less than fourteen years. Instead it has been

> a thousand years since I first drove that road, more than twenty-five years ago, a new concrete slab then, dizzily glittering in the August sun-blaze, driving past the rows of tenant shacks, Negro shacks set in the infinite cotton fields. . . . Last week, I noticed that more of the shacks were ruinous, apparently abandoned. More, but not many, had an electric wire running back from the road. But when I caught a glimpse, in the dark, of the interior of a lighted shack, I usually saw the coal-oil lamp. Most shacks were not lighted. I wondered if it was too early in the evening. Then it was early no longer. Were *that many* of the shacks abandoned?" (285, my emphasis)

Warren would assert to Ellison in 1957 that when he made his defense of segregation "in 1929—the South wasn't ready for [change], the North was not ready for it, the Negro wasn't,"[18] but he seems truly astonished upon his return that so many Black people seemed to have escaped what he once thought were incontestable social conditions for parts unknown.[19] Later, the refined speech of one of his Black respondents "surprises me the way my native ear used to be surprised by the speech of a Negro born and raised, say, in Akron, Ohio" (295). Warren finds these changes—the shanty left behind, the unself-conscious display of proper diction—unnerving since they fly in the face of his understanding of historical circumstance and imply the possibility of increased Black agency.

It is with palpable relief that Warren encounters a scene that seems to conform to his expectations. As he continues south along 61, Warren spies

> the figure, suddenly in our headlight . . . ris[ing] from the roadside, dark and shapeless against the soaked blackness of the cotton land: the man humping along with the croker sack on his shoulders (containing what?), the woman with a piece of sacking or paper over her head against the drizzle now, at her bosom a bundle that must be a small child, the big children following with the same slow, mud-lifting stride in the darkness. . . . They will move on, at their pace. Yes, *they are still here.* (285, my emphasis)

This tableau both comforts Warren and serves as a signpost that allows him to reorient himself in this strange new South. However, while Warren takes this family as indicative of a kind of social permanence, this family might be among those hoping to escape the privations of the rural South. They might be taking slow strides towards freedom. That is, after all, how the shacks came to be abandoned in the first place. Warren ignores this possibility.

The fragmented style of *Segregation* allows Warren to make these observations and then flash back to earlier historical events. Indeed, the paragraph after Warren notes the family along the roadside finds him contemplating the battle of Shiloh, one of the bloodiest of the Civil War. The battle of Shiloh was a daring assault by Confederate troops desperate to halt the advance of Union soldiers at the Tennessee-Mississippi border. Both of Warren's grandfathers fought in this battle for the Confederacy and it proved a costly defeat for the South. Still, to many, Warren included, the Confederate Army's willingness to attack a larger force in the hopes of transforming impending defeat into victory signified the gallant daring of the southern forces. Having established this idiosyncratic historical context, Warren takes stock of a contemporary battle currently testing the mettle of the South: the admission of Autherine Lucy into the University of Alabama.[20] By juxtaposing the lost battle at Shiloh with his brief comments on the unfolding Lucy case, Warren establishes the persistence of the Lost Cause's narrative in the South.

Warren next presents two episodes that he identifies as clichés: an interview he conducted with a Black woman, and a chance encounter with a teenaged boy from Atlanta. The woman is a victim of racist violence: an intoxicated white man has killed her husband and she suspects he will be cleared of any wrongdoing. The widow reveals to Warren that when she visited a store shortly after the murder and was recognized as the wife of the victim, the clerk asked her if "that man up yonder is still in jail for killing a nigger?" When the wife cautiously informed the clerk that her husband's killer was indeed still in jail, the clerk replies that "they can't do anything to a man for something he does drunk," a declaration of innocence that completely devalues her husband's life (313). She tells Warren, in a southern dialect that he reproduces faithfully, that these events have carried her to her wit's end. If the town "try him and 'quit him, doan know as I kin stay heah. . . . He git 'quitted, that man, and maybe I die, but I die goin." Warren dismisses this episode as "the cliché of fear . . . come fresh and alive," curiously refusing to contextualize the racial violence that continues to characterize life in the South (288).

The next clichéd episode occurs in Nashville where Warren meets a youth who, with his "tattered brown leather jacket, blue jeans . . . faded blue stocking cap [and] a mop of yellow hair," seems to emerge fully formed from Warren's imagination (289). After exchanging pleasantries, the teen acknowledges that he hates Black people. When he asks Warren if he feels the same and Warren replies, "[C]an't say that I do," the boy "utters the sudden obscenity, and removes himself a couple of paces from me" (290). Warren characterizes this display as "the cliché of hate" (290) and declares these episodes "thing[s] the uninitiated would expect" (288). Warren hopes to conduct an examination of southern society that reaches past these clichés, since, despite such events, "in the end people talked, even showed an anxiety to talk, to explain" (293). Warren's reluctance to connect these two events with continuing resistance to desegregation protects southern innocence by refusing to draw seemingly obvious conclusions about the pervasive blamelessness that permits these utterances.

As Warren makes his way through Mississippi, Alabama, Arkansas, Kentucky, and Tennessee, he encounters a profound mistrust of outsiders, even expatriate southerners like himself. Ironically, native southerners now view Warren the way he, in "The Briar Patch" perceived Black southerners gone North: as an exile unable to comprehend the society he has abandoned. Warren connects this "suspicion of the outsider, or of the corrupted native . . . with suspicion of the New York press, but this latter suspicion may exist quite separately, on an informed and reasoned basis" (292). This statement simultaneously forgives southern insularity and condemns the national media for presenting a clichéd (which is to say accurate) view of the South. Indeed, throughout the text Warren sympathizes with southerners who reject the depictions of the South in the mainstream press, including "a Southern newspaper man of high integrity and ability" who, despite being an integrationist, exclaims that "it's not in them not to load the dice in a news story" about the South (292–293).[21] These statements grant *Segregation* an iconoclastic authenticity by positioning it between what Warren maintains are extremes of southern and northern prejudice. Still, taking this position demonstrates Warren's continued, if increasingly qualified, support of southern exceptionalism.

Warren calls attention to the southerner's liminal positionality when he relates a joke he shared with a northern compatriot before returning South. The friend complained that southerners were like Jews, "exactly alike . . . so damned special," to which Warren replied, "Yes . . . we're both persecuted minorities." Now mingling among "black Southerners, a persecuted minority, too," Warren begins to reevaluate his earlier tongue-in-cheek statement (293). Although Warren recognizes white southern hegemony in the South, that he even facetiously equates southerners and Blacks as persecuted minorities demonstrates the lengths to which he is willing to go to preserve southern innocence. This equivocation, combined with Warren's refusal to closely examine what he considers the clichés of the region and his antipathy for the northern media, reveals his readiness to protect the South from blame. *Segregation* positions all members of southern society as innocent victims of history, persecuted in some fashion and therefore not responsible for their individual shortcomings. While this is a sentiment very different from that expressed in "The Briar Patch," it falls well short of rejecting southern exceptionalism.

Warren reports that few of the whites queried in *Segregation* defend Jim Crow, invoke the Civil War, and promise resistance. One of the respondents, however, expects "to fight this bogus law [the *Brown* decision] . . . based on social stuff and progress" (316). His response troubles Warren, and not simply for the violence implied in its expression, but because his fear of change extends to the notion of progress and he "wonder(s) how deep a cleavage the use of that word indicates" (316). Flying out of Memphis, Warren regains a measure of "relief," but recognizes this absence of tension as "the relief from responsibility" (320). Safely ensconced in the North, where the segregation is de facto and not de jure, Warren is no longer required to listen to genial bigots declaim about the cranial capacities of whites and Blacks or forced to contemplate a nonviolent protest being met with mob violence. Circumstance has transformed Warren into a kind of carpetbagger willing to flee the scene in the face of a mounting resistance to change, despite his earlier intentions to commune with the land of his youth.

Warren identifies many "lines of fracture" among southerners struggling between defending segregation and accepting reform. Some of these include the southerner's "social views and his fear of the power state . . . his allegiance to organized labor and his racism [though, in the Lucy case, the latter won out rather easily] . . . his own local views and his concern for the figure America cuts in the international picture" (322). Warren assumes that most southerners will eventually reconcile these fractures by concluding that integration is the proper course of action for the South and the nation. To advance this possibility, Warren presents subjects who are struggling to accommodate themselves to the idea of Black equality throughout this section of *Segregation*. One of the respondents, from Kentucky, admits that a "man can hate an idea and know it's right, and it takes a lot of thinking and praying to bring yourself around. You just have to uncover the unrecognized sympathy in the white man for the Negro humiliation" (325). This presentation of a submerged sympathy signals the potential for the peaceful accommodation of both races in a New South, and is remarkably similar to what Martin Luther King (whom this volume curiously ignores) insisted to the boycotters in Montgomery existed in the hearts of southern whites.

Of all of the fractures the text identifies, however, one stands out because it reveals the source of Warren's continued protectiveness towards the South. Warren claims that there exists in some southerners a dichotomy between their "own social idealism and [their] anger at Yankee Phariseeism. (Oh yes, he remembers that in the days when Federal bayonets supported the black Reconstruction state governments in the South, not a single Negro held elective office in any Northern state)" (321). Although Warren imbeds this statement amongst a list of reasons for the South's struggles with integration, this assertion recalls his argument in "The Briar Patch" that Black elected officials served as agents of northern oppression, and is too historical and specific to represent anyone's position but his own. Indeed, on the previous page, as Warren describes his flight from the South as an abdication of responsibility, he admonishes those who

> eat the bread of the Pharisee and read in the morning paper, with only
> a trace of irony, how out of an ultimate misery of rejection some Puerto
> Rican school boys—or is it Jews or Negroes or Italians?—who call them-
> selves something grand, the Red Eagles or the Silver Avengers, have stabbed
> another boy to death, or raped a girl, or trampled an old man into a bloody
> mire. If you [northerners] can afford it, you will . . . send your child to a
> private school, where there will be, of course, a couple of Negro children on
> exhibit.

In this passage Warren castigates northern liberals who criticize the South and send money to the NAACP and the Montgomery Improvement Association without lifting a finger to address the inequalities present in their local communities. He scoffs at the notion that things are better in the North simply because some Jews, Italians, or Puerto Ricans live in the same miserable conditions as poor Blacks, or because there exist in northern cities a few Black families with the wherewithal to send their children to private school. Warren maintains that without addressing these structural flaws northern liberals lack the moral standing to criticize affairs in the South.

While his criticism of northern liberals has merit (indeed it is redolent of Baldwin), Warren's use of the phrase "Yankee Phariseeism" reveals his continuing antipathy to emancipationist narratives. The theologian Robert Lewis Dabney, a Civil War veteran who served as a Confederate chaplain and as Stonewall Jackson's chief of staff, provides one of the earliest print references to "Yankee Phariseeism" in his *A Defense of Virginia* (1867).[22] In this text Dabney attributes the spread of slavery in the South to northern shipbuilders and financiers, while asserting the innate inferiority of the Negro based on a convoluted reading of the Bible. Dabney, a widely read figure in the postbellum South, helped transform "the Union Theological Seminary at Hampton-Sydney [Virginia into] a leading educational institution of Presbyterian clerics."[23] Dabney authored the first authoritative biography of Stonewall Jackson in 1866, a text Warren's dear friend and fellow Agrarian Allen Tate consulted when he was researching his own 1928 biography of Jackson.[24] Tate, of course, helped secure Warren's contract to write a biography of John Brown.[25] It is therefore almost a certainty that Warren discussed Dabney with Tate and scoured Dabney's papers for references to John Brown's raid on Harper's Ferry, since Dabney kept an extensive diary.[26] It is from this influential conservative theologian, an apologist of the plantation tradition who "defended the bygone values of an *organic society* based on social conservatism and slavery" that Warren almost certainly took the phrase Yankee Phariseeism.[27] Throughout *Segregation*, Warren alludes to events like the battle of Shiloh and the presence of "pale eye[d] lean-hipped men . . . like the men who rode with Forrest," but Warren's gratuitous evocation of Dabney's unique take on northern disingenuousness indicates a continuing investment in southern innocence (288–289).

During his self-interview Warren admits that he believes "the Northern press sometimes distorts Southern news [i.e., the South's history because] they like to feel good," a claim that bases northern exceptionalism on southern guilt (328). Warren's assertion that "responsibility is a seamless garment. And the northern boundary of that garment is not the Ohio river" protects southern innocence by implicating the North in the maintenance of segregation (329). Ultimately, Warren states his support for integration by recommending "a process of mutual education for whites and blacks. And part of this process should be in the actual beginning of the process of desegregation" (330). Still, Warren declares himself "a gradualist" when it comes to matters of reform, for "gradualism is all you'll get. History, like nature, knows no jumps" (330). So, despite a firsthand observation of the disorienting changes occurring in the South, Warren's view of historical progress remains essentially unchanged.

Segregation marks the first attempt by Warren to record and interpret contemporary history as a mature writer, and it received enthusiastic reviews, selling about twenty thousand copies, impressive for a sixty-six-page pamphlet that took a nuanced position on a controversial subject.[28] Warren would next address issues of race and history in 1961's *The Legacy of the Civil War: Meditations on the Centennial. The Legacy of the Civil War* could not be more different from *Segregation*. While the earlier text is a piece of impressionistic journalism that subsumes Warren's thoughts on the topic in order to better record the responses of his subjects, *Legacy* is an ambitious intellectual history that attempts to identify the continuing psychological cost of the nineteenth-century conflict. If *Segregation* serves as Warren's qualified attempt to revise the arguments he advanced in *I'll Take My Stand*, then *Legacy* seems designed to broaden Warren's earlier examination of the psychological genesis of John Brown's attack on the South. As with *Segregation, Life* magazine played a role in this text, publishing an excerpt three weeks before the full study was published on March 17.[29]

Warren opens his assessment of the psychological effects of the Civil War by noting its singular centrality in the nation's history. He declares the conflict "the great single event of our history" and claims that prior to "the Civil War we had no history in the deepest and most inward sense" of the concept (3). Warren claims that the Civil War inaugurates American history, serving as "our only 'felt' history—history lived in the national imagination. . . . It is an overwhelming and vital image of human, and national, experience" (4). *Legacy* also attributes the emergence of a strong national identity to the fundamental changes enacted during the Civil War. Warren claims that while the objective of the Civil War was to preserve the Union, the conflict in fact created a bond far more powerful than Lincoln could have envisioned. Prior to the Civil War the nation could negotiate the terms of its federation, but after the war unionism became "the overriding, overwhelming fact, a fact so technologically, economically, and politically validated that we usually forget to ask how fully this fact represents a true community" (6). Warren questions this sense of belonging to a large and disparate nation rather than to a local community.

Warren claims the Civil War's legacy continues to be felt in part because it "demanded the great American industrial plant, and the industrial plant changed American society" (10). The Civil War allowed the North to embrace the mercantilism and manufacturing that was to transform the nation's economy, complete the transcontinental railroad, establish "a national banking system in place of the patchwork of state banks, and the issuing of national" currency, and inaugurate "Hamilton's dream of a national debt to insure national stability . . . including the new income tax" (11–12). The war restored the southern states to the nation, but it also domesticated frontier states like "Ohio and Minnesota [both] claimed so effectively that for generations the memory of the Bloody Shirt and the GAR would prompt many a Middlewestern farmer to vote almost automatically against his own interest" (13). Warren's Agrarianism manifests itself in his emphasis on the changes manufacturing wrought on the nation, the lack of choice in the South as to the direction of the nation after the war, and the concern that the pro-business Republican Party doesn't truly represent the values of Agrarian midwesterners. These sentiments would not be out of place in *I'll Take My Stand*.

If the Civil War provided the nation with the sense of national unity that pertains today, a "second clear and objective fact is that the Civil War abolished slavery, even if it did little or nothing to abolish racism" (7). Warren does not use this as a point of departure, which might be expected given his approach in *Segregation*. Instead, he focuses on something else the Civil War helped produce, pragmatism, the uniquely American philosophy of thought that William James called "a new name for an old way of thinking" (17). Warren notes that "more than one historian has found in Lincoln the model of the pragmatic mind" who was forced by circumstance to "make a rule for the practical matter in hand than to decide a general" principle (17). Oliver Wendell Holmes, "thrice wounded" in the war (18), used his experiences in battle to help him determine, later in life, "that the process of seeking truth through the free collision, coil, and jar of ideas is more important than any particular 'truth' found" (19).[30] Warren portrays Holmes's legal "philosophy as being a reaction [against] two types of . . . opposing absolutes, 'higher law' and 'legalism'" (20). These opposing forces were, in Warren's opinion, responsible for quickening the disagreements that surrounded slavery into civil war. Warren's admiration for Holmes is not difficult to credit, given Warren's own attempts at resolving opposing and seemingly incompatible "extremes" in "The Briar Patch" and again in *Segregation*.

Legacy asserts that when abolitionists began appealing, in the hopes of ending slavery, to a "higher law" than the democratic government of consensus and compromise enacted by the Constitution, they articulated an extremist position. Unable to persuade their fellows as to the moral repugnance of slavery, the abolitionists quickly abandoned democratic principles in their quest to eradicate what they felt was the most pressing evil in the nation. *Legacy* quotes William Lloyd Garrison, Theodore D. Weld, Wendell Phillips, Charles Sumner, Emerson, Thoreau, and, of course, John Brown, demonstrating that their uncompromising morality left no room for the negotiation that one expects in a representative democracy. Warren feels that the abolitionists were drawn to slavery because poverty, "the most obvious abuse in that new society," failed to excite the passions of these scions of the wealthy New England gentry (28). A subtle cause like eradicating poverty, with its relative ends and means and ceaseless negotiation between factory owner and worker seemed tedious, but "with slavery all was different. One could demand the total solution, the solution of absolute morality; one could achieve the apocalyptic *frisson*" (29). *Legacy* condemns the transcendentalists who advocated abolition for abnegating the Aristotelian pragmatism offered by leaders like Lincoln and other realists on the issue of slavery. Warren believes that this strain of northern idealism still fails to grasp the necessity of a gradualism that works towards social justice realistically.

What distinguishes *Legacy* from Warren's earlier writing on race is that southern apologists for slavery and segregation receive as vigorous a condemnation in the text as their northern counterparts. *Legacy* maintains that if the abolitionists were ready to sacrifice democratic principles to achieve their goals, "Southern constitutionalists and philosophical defenders of slavery did not deny the concept of society. But the version of society which these egregious logicians deduced so logically from their premises denied, instead, the very concept of life" (33–34). Southern apologists accomplished this with their "defense . . . of bondage" and their "refusal to allow . . . for change, for the working of the life process through history" (34). *Legacy* laments "the Nat Turner insurrection" because in the South, after this uprising "the possibility of criticism—criticism from the inside—was over" (35). At that point "the only function then left open to intellect in the South was apologetics for the closed society, not criticism of it; and in those apologetics there was little space for the breath of life, no recognition of the need for fluidity, growth, and change which life is" (39). Apologists for slavery suffocated the intellectual and moral culture in the South, *Legacy* claims, in order to preserve the "profits to be had from the slave system" (35).

Warren carefully insists that he has "not intended to imply that the Civil War was 'caused' by the extremists on both sides"; he is merely trying to ascertain why American society after the war rejected extremism to produce a more pragmatic temperament (40). Through this rhetorical sleight of hand, Warren places those committed to ending slavery and those committed to preserving it on the same moral ground. This is in keeping with his belief that the best use of history lets those living in the contemporary moment identify the claims the past makes on the present.[31] Warren claims that the two-party system settled into place after the war, in part because this tends to muzzle groups on the outer fringes of political thought. The Civil War taught voters in the United States "that logical parties may lead logically to logical shootings, and they had had enough of that" (43) because Americans "have an instinctive distaste for being made martyrs themselves to the admirable convictions of a politician who happens to have won an election" (44–45). Unfortunately, according to Warren, in addition to establishing a pragmatic and political conservatism the war also "gave the South the Great Alibi and gave the North the Treasury of Virtue" (54).

Despite Warren's earlier pronouncements about pragmatism, he feels that the "Great Alibi" and the "Treasury of Virtue" remain the most deeply felt legacies of the Civil War in their respective regions and each of these is a form of exceptional innocence. Warren asserts early in his essay that defeat "made [the South] more Southern" (14), claiming that "only at the moment when Lee handed Grant his sword was the Confederacy born; or to state matters another way, in the moment of death the Confederacy entered upon its immortality" (15).[32] If, prior to the war, the South stifled serious intellectual debate about the nature of its society, the Great Alibi worsened this tendency. "By the Great Alibi," Warren writes, "pellagra, hookworm, and illiteracy are converted into badges of distinction. Laziness becomes the aesthetic sense, blood-lust rising from a matrix of boredom and resentful misery becomes a high sense of honor, and ignorance becomes divine revelation" (54–55). The Great Alibi may allow a southerner to think of himself as "an innocent victim of a cosmic conspiracy," but Warren remembers the populist accomplishments of Huey Long, and so perceives the typical southerner as "trapped in history," unable to realize his potential because he is too busy "parrot[ing] the sad clichés of 1850" (56). Warren finally rejects southern innocence here, answering definitively the question left undetermined at the conclusion of *Segregation*.

The Legacy of the Civil War dismisses southern resistance to integration as "a debasement of [Southern] history, with all that was noble, courageous, and justifying bleached out, drained away" (57). Confederate soldiers were willing to die for their beliefs, not just kill for them, and they openly faced a formidable foe armed with that conviction. The contemporary "mob . . . howling vituperation at a little Negro girl being conducted into a school building" dishonors "those gaunt, barefoot, whiskery scarecrows who fought it out . . . at the Bloody Angle at Spotsylvania, in May, 1864" (57). Bloody Angle was one of the most savage battles of the Civil War, a conflict that played out over two weeks with heavy losses on each side. Warren mentions Bloody Angle, perhaps, because the battle began by accident, with Union and Confederate forces colliding as each marched to reinforce the frontline. The conflict in Arkansas in 1957 between the so-called "Little Rock nine" and Arkansas Governor Orval Faubus seems as circumstantial a battlefield as Spotsylvania, Virginia, a town of questionable importance. However, if the southern partisans acquitted themselves with valor at Spotsylvania by trying to hold the line, the forces confronting the Little Rock nine dishonor their memory, for there is little honor in abusing children to preserve segregation.

There was little indication that in September of 1957 the Little Rock nine's attempt to enroll in Little Rock's Central High would precipitate an international crisis. Governor Faubus used that state's National Guard to effectively void a decision reached by local school officials and a federal district court the previous year to integrate the schools. The impasse between Faubus and the students lasted three weeks, attracting headlines across the nation and around the world. Yet, after Eisenhower convinced Faubus to withdraw the Guard, the situation deteriorated as a mob encouraged by Faubus's speeches attacked the Little Rock nine as they tried to enroll on September 23.[33] Eisenhower responded by literally sending in the Marines, as "paratroopers from the 101st Airborne Divison . . . ringed Central High School on the morning of September 25."[34] For the proponents of southern innocence, this Yankee invasion revealed the program of integration initiated by the *Brown* decision as a pretext to reoccupy the South and extract further punishment for the Civil War by denying southerners their constitutional right to assembly and association. Warren, as he indicates by comparing the standoff at Little Rock with one of the greatest battles of the Civil War, finds this line of reasoning contemptible.

Despite *The Legacy of the Civil War*'s rejection of interposition and mob violence, Warren's position remains remarkably consistent with his earlier claims. Immediately following his renunciation of Faubus, Warren wonders if the Arkansans exhorted to mob violence understand that "whatever degree of dignity and success a Negro achieves actually enriches, in the end, the life of the white man and enlarges his own worth as a human being" (58). This statement recalls assertions in both "The Briar Patch" and *Segregation* that insisted that white southerners must grant Blacks respect in order to realize their own self-worth. *Legacy* supports integration while granting that the dismantling of Jim Crow creates tremendous logistical and personal problems. Warren rejects southern apologists because they "rus[t] away the will to confront those difficulties, at either a practical or an ethical level" (58). One may hold out hope, as Warren did at the conclusion of *Segregation*, that the South may assume a position of moral leadership by working out its race problems, but after "the events of Tuscaloosa, Little Rock and New Orleans" *Legacy* does not seem to place much stock in this happening.

Still, according to *Legacy*, while the innocence of the Great Alibi causes southerners to devalue the memory of their forefathers and robs them of the will to solve the problems inherent with integration, the Treasury of Virtue lends northerners an innocence that allows them to forget their own history of racism. Warren asserts that, in their interest to forget their own history, northern fabulists recast the war "as a consciously undertaken crusade so full of righteousness that there is enough overplus stored in Heaven . . . to take care of all small failings and oversights of the descendents of the crusaders, certainly unto the present generation" (64). For Warren, the southerner who invokes innocence via an appeal to his forefathers is as misguided as the self-righteous northerner who maintains a sense of innocence by refusing to seriously consider the difficulties inherent in any reform. This desire for the righteousness of innocence produces untenable situations like the standoff in Little Rock, where neither the governor nor the president demonstrated moral leadership, and the condemnation of the international media only served to reinforce regional identities.

According to Warren, northern exceptionalism prevented a serious discussion of the moral quandary produced by the North's abandonment of Reconstruction. The South found itself in an entirely different circumstance, according to the text, victims of "a confused and aimless Reconstruction ending in the Big Sell-Out of 1876" (67). In a slight shift from Warren's earlier essays, *Legacy* attributes the failure of Reconstruction not to the ex-slaves vaulted into positions of leadership after the war, but to corrupt northern Republicans, uninterested in completing the difficult tasks left to them by Lincoln and uncaring about the tenuous status of the Negro in the South. Warren asserts that the Republicans ignored the recommendations of the Freedmen's Bureau to provide freed black men with forty acres and a mule because a program of massive land redistribution was not "acceptable to sound Northern business sense in that heyday of rambunctious young capitalism" (68). This perspective conveniently overlooks intense southern resistance to the goals of the Freedmen's Bureau. Warren suspects that such a redistribution might have changed the course of American history, perhaps by making an Agrarian program feasible in the South.

In the wake of the Civil War the North created a society where "prosperity was clearly a reward for virtue. In fact, prosperity *was* virtue" (69). The equation of wealth with moral standing allowed the North to ignore issues of social justice, and even today a northerner "casts a far more tender—or at least morally myopic—eye on the South Side in Chicago or on a Harlem slum than he does on Little Rock, Arkansas, and when possible insulates himself from democratic hurlyburly by withdrawing into penthouse, suburb, or private school" (70). This unreflective willingness to ignore the failings of our democratic principles permits America to uncritically perceive itself "as the Galahad among nations" (71), exhibiting a "moral narcissism" that "gets us into the wars" of the twentieth century (72). The northern tendency to embrace moral causes without reflection produces righteousness, and "the man of righteousness tends to be so sure of his own motives that he does not need to inspect consequences" (74), not even the "obligation of our 'inclusiveness'" (73). The civil rights movement would finally force the North to align its version of an exceptional society with one that accounted for its less successful members.

Legacy attempts to assign the nation's current difficulties with integration to the self-division that sustains segregation in the South and a misguided sense of exceptionalism in the North. In contrast, the heroic participants of the Civil War were "individuals; that is, by moral awareness they had achieved identity." This heroic achievement of a moral sense of self through resolute struggle with the great issues of the day could not be more unfamiliar to "our age of conformity, of 'other-directedness', of uniformity and the gray flannel suit, of personality created by the charm school" (90). Contemporary men, faced with the twin challenges of the civil rights movement and the Cold War, hearken back to the Civil War "to define clear aims and certain commitments in the complexity of life" (89–90). "In our world of restless mobility," *Legacy* claims, "we look back nostalgically on the romantic image of some right and natural relation of man to place and man to man, fulfilled in worthy action" (92). That this natural relation of man to place and man to man recalls arguments about society made in *I'll Take My Stand* in 1929 should by now come as no surprise.

The nation's simultaneous engagement in a global struggle against totalitarianism and a domestic movement that often precipitated violence merely by demanding social justice foregrounds the need for a healing of the divisions that separate the North from the South. Such a rapprochement might allow the nation to apply the unheeded legacy of the Civil War to the internal divisions revealed by the civil rights movement. This is imperative, for, despite the emergence of the United States on the world stage, "we have not yet achieved justice. We have not yet created a union which is, in the deepest sense, a community. We have not yet resolved our deep dubieties or self-deceptions . . . we are sadly human" (107). Exceptionalist narratives obscure the limits and imperfections of this fallen humanity, and it is only by acknowledging our shared communal being-with (to invoke Heidegger) that we can create a society with a deep understanding of our moral and political obligations. That the United States has assumed a position of leadership in the world without having done this work gives Warren pause, and he hopes that the US might begin to understand "the powerful, painful, grinding process by which an ideal emerges out of history" (108). Warren also hopes that in contemplating the legacy of the Civil War "some of that grandeur, even in the midst of the confused issues, shadowy chances, and brutal ambivalences of our life and historical moment, may rub off on us." Despite a consumer culture that creates false desires, the elevated sense of identity that comes from serious contemplation of moral issues "may be what we yearn for after all" (109).

Surprisingly, *The Legacy of the Civil War* ignores the longstanding dispute between the northerner W. E. B. Du Bois and the southerner Booker T. Washington as to the way forward for the Black community, a dialog he enthusiastically referenced thirty years earlier in "The Briar Patch." *Legacy* makes several passing references to the events of the civil rights movement without pausing to consider how the seemingly contradictory program of nonviolent confrontation embodied by Martin Luther King's SCLC might have emerged from the intellectual culture and lived experience of Blacks in the South. And, despite its fetishistic use of Justice Holmes, Warren makes no attempt to reconcile his juridical opinion that the law must respond to "the felt necessities of the time" with Thurgood Marshall's successful exploitation of this legal perspective.[35] As in *Segregation*, Warren was willing to cede the point that racial discrimation was unjust, yet he seemed unable to understand that the moral leadership that he hopes for has, by 1961, already emerged in the Black leaders of the civil rights movement in the post-*Brown* South. Warren seems blind to the elevated sense of moral identity possessed by civil rights workers, from King to the lowliest maid walking to work, and thus fails to appreciate what the nation has already begun to learn from these battle-tested civil rights veterans.

Warren's reluctance to connect the civil rights movement with the Civil War was probably a deliberate act of restraint. Still, when faced with a hostile review of *Legacy* in *The New Republic*, a review that claimed Warren exhibited the same racial biases he displayed in *I'll Take My Stand*, his response presages his next consideration of the topic. In a letter to the magazine Warren declares "Martin Luther King a great man, and . . . the sit-ins conducted according to his principles are morally unassailable and will win."[36] This reply only serves to underscore the absence of any meaningful discussion of Black leadership and the implications of their moral stand in *Legacy*, yet also alludes to Warren's fear, hinted at in *Segregation*, of what might occur if Black southerners began meeting violence with violence. Warren also refers in his letter to an "explicit repudiation, some time back, of what I said in 1929." Warren may have been referring here to the interview conducted by Ralph Ellison and Eugene Walter published in *The Paris Review* in 1957, although for a man concerned with the deliberate march of history, four years does not seem a sufficient duration to justify his use of the phrase "some time back." This is, as far as I can tell, the only place where Warren explicitly rejects in print the views advanced in "The Briar Patch" prior to 1965. Still, Warren's response to *The New Republic* demonstrates his approval of what many whites continued to perceive as a homogenous civil rights movement led by King, which makes his reluctance to identify the intellectual tradition that produced King—a southern gentleman if there ever was one—more baffling.[37]

Turning his attention back to the contemporary moment, the incredibly productive Warren accepted an assignment with *Look* magazine for an article based on a series of interviews with the leaders of the civil rights movement. He traveled around the South during the semester break in January of 1964, interviewing many prominent figures associated with the movement.[38] During the Spring semester, Warren conducted a series of interviews with Black leaders and intellectuals based in the North, such as Adam Clayton Powell, Carl Rowan, Ralph Ellison, and Malcolm X. The article, titled "The Negro Now," appeared in the 23 March 1965 issue of

Look, with the book that grew from this project, *Who Speaks for the Negro?* appearing in May of that year. It is here that Warren finally confronts the principles of the civil rights movement.[39]

The nation's understanding of the civil rights movement changed in an important way between the publication of *Legacy* and *Who Speaks for the Negro?* Thanks to increased activism in the North, agitation that met with as much resistance and resentment as in the South, if not as much violence, the general public was now aware that racial injustices were in no way limited to one side of the Mason-Dixon. Prominent northern Blacks like Malcolm X and James Baldwin helped focus attention on the problems that existed in places like Harlem, the South Side of Chicago, and West Philadelphia, problems that were certainly not the product of southern-style segregation. That this perspective was just taking hold, a decade after the rise of the movement in Montgomery, confirmed Warren's longstanding criticism of northern myopia about race. While Warren was working on a draft of the text and reviewing his first series of interviews, the Harlem riots erupted in July of 1964, further confirming that the web of responsibility indeed reached north. The riots were precipitated by a Brooklyn police officer killing a Black youth on his way to night school, an act as contemptuous of Black life as those committed by Bull Connor. The somewhat hysterical tone of the New York press corps covering the story revealed entrenched misgivings about racial harmony.[40] If, as Michael Szalay claims, *Who Speaks for the Negro?* "is without doubt Warren's most heartfelt denunciation of Southern bigotry," this is in part due to the fact that the nation finally recognized bigotry as more than just a southern trait.[41]

Who Speaks for the Negro? is one of the 1960s' finest achievements in nonfiction journalism and cultural criticism, a comprehensive and sophisticated examination of the leaders of the civil rights movement, the implications of their goals on the politics and culture of the nation, and the movement's effect on liberalism in the North. *Who Speaks* combines the narrative and analytical styles of *Segregation* and *Legacy*, blending long interviews with prominent civil rights figures, historical background, analysis of contemporary scholarship, and other digressions. As in *Segregation*, Warren utilizes journalistic techniques that call attention to himself as an implicated observer. Indeed, he admits in his foreword that his "reader, were he more than the silent spectator which he must here be, would put more probing questions than mine, and would have other, more significant reactions," foregrounding his role as interlocutor (ix).[42]

Warren's observations, asides, and scholarly musings throughout the text provide further evidence of the evolution of his view about innocence and exceptionalism. As such, this analysis will focus on three important sections of the text, the first being Warren's reassessment of "The Briar Patch," the second a revealing discussion about John Brown, and finally the amazing "Conversation Piece," Warren's critique of the white response to the civil rights movement.

Warren, sensitive to accusations that he remains a segregationist at heart, denounces "The Briar Patch" early on in *Who Speaks*, claiming to have never read the essay since he produced it due to "some vague discomfort, like the discomfort you feel when your poem doesn't quite come off, when you've had to fake, or twist, or pad it, when you haven't really explored the impulse" (10–11). This discomfort emerges even though the "essay envisaged segregation in what I presumed to be its most human dimension" (11), because "even then, thirty five years ago, I uncomfortably suspected, despite the then prevailing attitude of the Supreme Court and of the overwhelming majority of the United States, that no segregation was, in the end, humane. But it never crossed my mind that anyone could do anything about it" (12). Reminding his readers that he was in England at Oxford when he wrote "The Briar Patch," Warren admits that "the image of the South I carried in my head [while in Britain] was one of massive immobility in all ways . . . an image of the unchangeable human condition, beautiful, sad, tragic" (12). The South has changed radically since the publication of "The Briar Patch," and Warren now ascribes his earlier pessimism to a failure of the imagination. Interestingly, during this elaborate repudiation of "The Briar Patch" Warren never provides its title, identifying it instead as "an essay" or "that essay." Warren does not want to call attention to the text, perhaps fearful that contemporary readers might draw their own conclusions about him after reading it.

By engaging with civil rights leaders throughout the nation, Warren exemplifies the evolution of his views. But during his conversation with Dr. Kenneth B. Clark, the famous psychologist trained at Howard and Columbia universities, the old Agrarian rears his head.[43] During their discussion, Dr. Clark (deliberately?) compares John Brown to Christ, an association that makes Warren apoplectic. Pressed by Warren, Clark maintains that "Christ was clearly a person committed to values other than those prevailing in his time" as was John Brown (318). Warren attempts to dismiss John Brown as a madman, but Clark reminds him that "it isn't always easy to differentiate between a madman and a martyr, or a person who irritates the status quo" (319). Warren wonders if we "must trust the madmen to be our moral guardians," refusing to accept Clark's claim about the metaphorical import of John Brown while begrudgingly granting that Brown's perspective was ultimately proven right by history (319). Searching for a way to foreclose this discussion of Brown, Warren then asks Clark if he would "judge the morality of an act by its consequences." When Clark carefully responds that in certain cases "morally valuable . . . consequences might be contaminated by the immorality of the act" Warren advances "John Brown [as] almost a test case for" a noble cause despoiled by an immoral act (320). Exasperated, Clark can only marvel at Warren's obsession with Brown.[44]

Warren uses this conversation as an occasion to revisit his earlier text, *John Brown: The Making of a Martyr*, providing contemporary readers insight into his fascination with the historical figure. Unlike his reflection on his controversial early essay, Warren identifies his first book, indicating, perhaps, a willingness to test the ideas contained within against the contemporary moment. As with "The Briar Patch," Warren regrets that the "book was shot through with Southern defensiveness," claiming that *John Brown* is "far from the book that I would write now (320). Warren also admits to oversimplifying his psychological presentation of Brown, but declares "the work on the book . . . my real introduction into some awareness of the dark and tangled problem of motives and values" (320). The problem of motives and values occurs so consistently throughout Warren's oeuvre that "a French novelist and critic . . . remarked that the mythic Brown figure recurs again and again in my fiction [as] the man who at any cost, would strike for absolute solutions—a type toward which, I suppose, I am deeply ambivalent" (320–321). Warren's lifelong discomfort with political actors possessed of moral certainty informs his treatment of Willie Stark/Huey Long in *All the King's Men*, abolitionists in *Legacy of the Civil War*, and his dogged insistence on the conflicted nature of the average southern white in *Segregation* and *Who Speaks for the Negro?*

Warren ends his digression and returns to Clark, who maintains "that major social changes toward social justice in human history have almost always come—if not always—through irrational and questionable methods" (322). Warren replies to this observation by wondering if the more privileged in society exploit those who are less able to abide the cruelties of American life in order to advance social justice. Clark responds by reminding Warren that "apparently rational, reasonable men, who are for making a change in the status quo, are generally ineffectual. Changes . . .

are more likely to come from irrational, unreasonable, questionable men" (322). The dispassionate Clark seems most concerned with an accurate apprehension of how social change occurs in the US, while Warren again worries about the ramifications of the reality that Clark has identified. Warren frets over the necessity of conflict, but Clark, even as he deplores violence, recognizes that "horrible things have to be done to prepare the way for the possibility of a little bit of change, or justice" (322). Warren does not immediately comment on Clark's fatalistic observation, which the violence in Mississippi and elsewhere supported as a kind of negative example, though he might have pointed out that Dr. King's program of nonviolence, still the dominant method of dramatizing the inequities of the nation, seemed to refute this claim. Warren, however, wonders how long the nonviolent center can hold, and worries that if the political structure does not begin to respond in some meaningful way to the grievances of Black people, "terrorist organizations, like the Russian nihilists or the Stern Gang [might] emerge among Negroes" (407). Warren fears for the nation's future if this is allowed to happen.

"Conversation Piece" revisits Warren's hopes and fears for the future of the nation, and it is here that one can see, despite the Agrarian origins of his political thought, Warren's full evolution. Warren shifts from investigative reporter to cultural critic in this concluding section, and by naming it "Conversation Piece" suggests that the issues detailed throughout deserve serious consideration from his (presumably) white audience. With this conceit, one purpose of the section becomes clear: Warren's final critique of American innocence. "Conversation Piece" locates culpability for the northern riots in the white community's reluctance to attend to the demands of the civil rights movement in good faith. This continued lack of good faith on the part of the white Americans North and South undermines the maintenance of an orderly society by granting credence to militant Black claims that white people, at least those in power, only respect violence or the threat of violence.[45] Warren fears that an outburst of Black violence would blunt the impetus for reform. This is why, throughout the text, Warren takes such pains to denounce Black Nationalism, for he has seen what southern nationalism has led to. Indeed, Warren is amazed that the Black leadership dating back to Douglass has been able to blunt a nationalist appeal to self-defense in the face of continuing violence, but fears that this cannot last.

Warren, who spoke in 1956 of being a gradualist, and who throughout the preceding sections of *Who Speaks for the Negro?* privileges the historical process, now dismisses the sentiment that "a certain condition of heart must generally and ideally prevail before a social change can occur" because this claim suggests "that no social change can ever come except in the Sweet Bye-and-Bye" (413). However, Warren understands that integration is no panacea, and cautions his audience to think of it as an expression of the democratic process, a "process by which we exercise our will to realize and explore, individually and institutionally, in the contingencies of life, that ideal of mutual human recognition and appreciation" (413). To understand how completely Warren has shifted his understanding, consider his reevaluation of states' rights, which in 1929 he had evoked by implication while asserting an Agrarian defense of regionalism. Now Warren perceives states' rights as a tool that "has frequently been used, and is being used today, as an alibi and a screen for some very unworthy proceedings—often quite cynically used and only for some special ad hoc advantage, with total contempt for the principle itself" (418). With this statement, Warren extends to his analysis of southern demagogues the same moralistic separation between principle and intent that he used to implicate John Brown. Warren recognizes that perverting a democratic tradition in the service of perpetuating injustice imperils the democratic experiment in the US, and he now refuses to endorse this behavior.

Warren suspects that some measure of reluctance to embrace integration stems from an unwillingness to embrace the unknown. "The word *integration*," he declares, "does not refer . . . to one thing. It refers to a shifting, shadowy mass of interfusing possibilities. It refers, in short, to the future" (415). While as recently as 1956 Warren sympathized with those southerners unable to accommodate change, he now supports this transformation. Ending segregation "will mean a great change; and change, however deeply willed, is always shocking; old stances and accommodations, like the twinge of an old wound, are part of the self, and even as we desire new life and more life, we must realize that a part of us . . . has to *die* into that new life" (415). This passage suggests that Warren's decision to return to the South again and again and again from 1956 to 1965 can be perceived as his desire to reconnect to his region in order to understand the possibilities of its future. As with the spread of industrialism in the South, Warren wants a potentially wrenching change to be well thought out and monitored so that the nation can realize its fullest democratic and spiritual potential. Any undertaking of integration that does not address these psychic demands, Warren feels, is doomed to failure or, worse, to incompleteness.

Warren traces the reluctance to embrace integration to conflicting desires. Some white Americans wish to maintain an unjust society in order to preserve their status, while others avoid responsibility out of the uniquely American desire to continue to perceive one's self as innocent. Civil rights workers have attained some modicum of political power by exploiting this contradiction, and Warren feels that a better society might be built through solving it. Warren's observation that "[t]here is one kind of power Negro leaders feel they have which is not relative [i.e., hegemonic or dialogic]. It is moral power. For, by the American white man's own professed standards the Negro is in the right, and enough white men know it to create a climate in which the Negro can proceed with his nonviolent Revolution" (410).

Warren is ultimately less concerned with the so-called "Negro problem" than with the white problem. Whites can only "deal with the 'Negro problem' [after they have] learned to deal with the white man's 'white man' problem . . . [which] is . . . to distinguish between whatever 'de facto superiority' he may, in fact, have and whatever notion of inherent superiority he may cherish" (431). If this is the primary stumbling block to social progress, it remains in Warren's view primarily a liberal problem. Southerners are very aware of their de facto superiority, due to the lengths to which they have gone to defend it. As such, they don't find the murder of Schwerner, Goodman, and Chaney shocking; they find white integrationists shocking because "the Southerner knows that [racial murder], evil as it is, is implicit in the structure of the society in which he lives" (425). This diagnosis is quite a change for a writer who cavalierly dismissed the "cliché of violence" just eight years before.

Warren fears whites' sentimentality will undermine their ability to recognize the claims of citizenship demanded by Negroes, in part because their protests function as moral rather than intellectual appeals. He suggests that "rather than depend on our spontaneous and uncriticized feelings we had better consult our intelligence, fallible as it is, to see what is reasonable, decent, socially desirable—and even just—and then, as best we can, act on that" (432). Whites must be willing to confront dispassionately their failure to live by the rule of law because the civil rights movement has not, as Warren acidly notes, "been mounted exclusively for the purpose of giving [white men] a spiritual cathartic" but to create a more just society for all US citizens (433). Despite this reality, when Warren interacts with northern liberals he detects "a strange sort of sentimentality . . . like all sentimentality it is ultimately self-centered, but here the self-centeredness is obscenely cloaked in selflessness, a profound concern for the rights and feelings of others" (434). Warren does not make this statement simply to demean liberals, but to suggest that achieving a just society will demand more than innocent sympathy and the occasional monetary donation. Warren wonders if, despite a decade of demonstration, whites are truly ready to bear the cost of integration.[46]

In making this argument, the influence of Ellison on Warren seems clear. Ellison was, at this time, beginning to come under fire for his decidedly cool stance on integration and his refusal to embrace the nascent Black Arts Movement that privileged the naturally poetic sensibilities of America's oppressed minority.[47] During the interviews conducted while compiling *Who Speaks*, Warren often detected an urge by his respondents to assign to all Black people some inherent nobility of spirit. Warren categorically rejects any notion of Black superiority here, and resists any attempt by whites to buy into the notion of superior Blackness out of guilt or a desire to accommodate difference. "If any man," Warren asserts, "black or white, isn't content to pass up a notion of group superiority . . . and to be regarded and judged as an individual man, with individual virtues and defects, [then] there is something wrong with him" (440). White and Black Americans must reject a self-conception based on notions of innocence and exceptionalism without attributing those qualities to a racial other.

Warren closes the argument in "Conversation Piece" as he did "The Briar Patch," with an appeal to the self-interests of whites. Having disabused them of the notion of thinking of Blacks as intellectually inferior or morally superior, Warren demands the creation of a society that would accept them almost as an afterthought. Such a society would benefit all, for

> [i]t is self-interest to want to live in a society operating by the love of justice and the concept of law. We have not been living in such a society. It is self-interest to want all members of society to contribute as fully as possible to the enrichment of that society. The structure of our society has prevented that. It is self-interest to seek out friends and companions who are congenial in temperament and whose experiences and capacities extend our own. Our society has restricted us in this natural quest. (443)

This sentiment resembles the "enlightened selfishness on the part of the Southern white man [that] must prompt him to encourage the well-being and possibly the organization of negro" in "The Briar Patch," but Warren has moved beyond a defensive argument in the service of a single racial group in one region of the United States. *Who Speaks for the Negro?* dramatizes how the self-interest of Black people coincides with the self-interest of white Americans, and argues for a reflective criticism that might produce a society capable of speaking to the needs of all its citizens. Although Warren had left the South twenty-three years earlier, it is not until he produces *Who Speaks for the Negro?* that he completes his evolution from being an Agrarian, for with this text Warren's public, writerly self embraces the true legacy of the Civil War, the civil rights movement.

Chapter Two

THE APOCALYPTIC HIPSTER
"The White Negro" and Norman Mailer's Achievement of Style

Robert Penn Warren wrote out of a southern tradition, treasured the distinctiveness of the South, and sought, throughout his literary career, to reconcile the contradictions between southern deed and the American creed. Warren considered himself an academic as well as a writer, serving on the faculty of various colleges and universities throughout his career. Norman Mailer was, in many ways, the antithesis of Robert Penn Warren. Mailer rejected conventional schools of thought, sought to provoke as much as he did to enlighten, and avoided the staid responsibilities of the academy. Mailer's fascination with race in the 1950s derived not from lived experience but from his study of the media accounts of the Montgomery bus boycott. From this consideration, Mailer concluded that white Americans could regain the moral standing they had lost during World War II by identifying with Black Americans. This identification would, Mailer felt, radicalize American innocence by aligning exceptionalism with a life that demanded meaningful action instead of conformity. Mailer arrived at this point by linking racial protest and American innocence with his negotiations with his own ethnic identity as he sought to transform himself into an American archetype, a process that intensified after the publication of his first novel.

Early success is a curious thing for a writer to experience, especially in the United States during that fifty-year period in the twentieth century when producing a best-selling first novel granted celebrity as well as wealth. Fame can hinder an author, for writing is a solitary vocation, and even the most socially integrated writer feels some measure of isolation while crafting a novel or collection of poetry. Ironically, success often deepens that sense of isolation, for, as Norman Mailer observed, as "a node in a new electronic landscape of celebrity, personality and status, [the newly successful writer] has been moved from the audience to the stage."[1] Some writers consider their newfound notoriety liberating and continue to create their art secure in the knowledge that they have earned a place in the literary market. Other writers seem intimidated by the sensation their breakthrough novel occasions, and find themselves either desperate to duplicate that achievement or determined to preserve their authenticity as a struggling artist by challenging their public with a narrative designed to be as difficult as possible. Some, like Harper Lee, simply abandon their literary careers altogether.[2] Norman Mailer, whose debut novel, *The Naked and the Dead*, was arguably the most successful of the period immediately following World War II, distinguished himself by acting upon each of these impulses before the protests of the civil rights movement led him to the insight that would shape the bulk of his career.

The iconoclastic Mailer is simultaneously one of the most idealistic and one of the most cynical writers in the post–World War II period. In *Advertisements for Myself* (1959), his autobiographical review of his literary career to date, Mailer reports that "before I was seventeen I had formed the desire to be a major writer."[3] Whether this claim serves as a self-fulfilling recollection or is an accurate representation of his adolescent desires, Mailer pursued this goal when he matriculated to Harvard by participating in various literary activities, though he was nominally an engineering major. While he flourished there, when Mailer arrived at Harvard from his Jewish enclave in Brooklyn he found himself on the margins for the first time. According to Adele Morales Mailer, Norman's second wife, "[H]e . . . felt like a fish out of water [at Harvard]. It was probably a combination of his family not having a lot of money and being Jewish."[4] Mailer recognized during his senior year at Harvard that there would be great demand in the literary marketplace for fiction about the war, and he volunteered for the army after graduating so that he could acquire the material he needed for such a novel.

Mailer's experiences in the army reinforced his outsider status, this time not because of religious or class differences. Mailer discovered that, despite his intellect and Ivy League education, "when it came to taking care of myself, I had little to offer next to the practical sense of an illiterate sharecropper" (91). This is an important moment for Mailer, because it taught him that outsider status is not the inevitable result of ethnic identity but can also be produced by an ignorance of cultural practices.[5] Outsider status is performative, not just perceptual. This was a valuable lesson for Mailer, who often effaced his Jewish identity after he returned from the army. As something of an interloper both at Harvard and in the army, he had to learn to discern and adjust to the expectations of the dominant group. Mailer refined this talent for discerning and then adjusting to the presuppositions of his audience throughout his literary career, but it wasn't until he produced "The White Negro" that he achieved the contrapuntal sensibility that would enable him to fully exploit his dichotomous perspective.

After he was discharged from the military, Mailer crafted his war novel *The Naked and the Dead*. He wrote well, if derivatively, and *The Naked and the Dead* (1948) sold two hundred thousand copies in its first nine months alone. Everything proceeded according to Mailer's plan, but when "it became obvious that *The Naked and the Dead* was going to be a best seller . . . a depression set in on me. I was twenty-five, living in Paris with my first wife" (91). It takes a uniquely perverse sensibility to resolve to be a writer, devote years of creative energy developing the skills necessary to realize that desire, formulate a plan—the execution of which demands that you risk your life as an infantryman in the Pacific Theatre—so that your first novel would find a large market, and then become despondent just as your strategy succeeds beyond your wildest expectations. To his credit, Mailer realized fairly quickly after *The Naked and the Dead* that while he could fashion a respectable career out of his sensitivity to literary, political, and cultural trends and his devotion to Dos Passos and Dostoevsky, this might make him a respected and well-compensated writer, but not a literary great.[6]

Mailer recognized that his artistic achievement to that point was not commiserate with his ambition, and so he spent the next ten years "gobbling up the experiences" that he hoped would enable him to become a truly great writer—Hemingway was his model—as well as a prosperous one (92). While Mailer was struggling in Paris with his unmitigated success, his verve for new encounters and ideas drove him into the arms of Jean Malaquais, a French socialist thinker. Interestingly, *The Naked and the Dead*, written before his encounter with Malaquais, closes with a meditation on the possibility of a totalitarian bureaucracy infecting a democratic society, represented in the novel by the army platoon, with Major Dalleson embodying "the postwar triumph of the bureaucratic mentality."[7] With this coda Mailer anticipates the conservative reversals that accompanied the onset of the Cold War in the US. Mailer's deep mistrust of state coercion and conformity announces itself at the conclusion of *The Naked and the Dead*, and this hostility to cultural group-think—no matter how well intentioned—would remain throughout his prodigious body of work.

Mailer moved quickly through the political culture of the Left in his search for insights that could ground his writing. Upon his return to America Mailer became infatuated with the democratic socialism offered by the Progressive Party and campaigned for Wallace in 1948, quickly became (thanks to Malaquais) disenchanted with the pro-Soviet progressives in the United States that sought to normalize relations with the USSR, began work on *Barbary Shore*, a novel that tried unsuccessfully to blend social realist and modernist literary styles, and was beginning to arrive at the conclusion (to Malaquais's consternation) that dialectical analysis was impotent and therefore dangerous.[8] Many left-leaning authors and artists who began working during the 1920s and '30s would reach similar conclusions by the early 1950s.[9] Mailer, of course, made his debut in 1948 and, in a hurry as always, arrived at this point by 1952.

Although *Barbary Shore* (1951) is a more ambitious novel than *The Naked and the Dead*, Mailer was not trying to diminish his readership. If anything Mailer wanted more people to read his second novel than had read his first. Ever sensitive to the demands of the literary market, Mailer knew that in response to the continuing deterioration of the relationship between the US and the USSR, "[a]nybody who worked and wrote for newspapers, magazines, television, movies and advertising was discovering (if he were still innocent) that the natural work of his pen was to hasten our return to chastity, regularity, pomposity and worship of the lifeless, the senseless, and the safe" (105). Once again, Mailer correctly diagnosed the direction of the literary marketplace, but this time, emboldened by the large audience he earned with his debut and the trenchant analysis that concludes that novel, he deliberately, and courageously, chose to challenge his readers by presenting them with a critique of the innocent conformity of the emerging middle-class society and the cold warriors who enforced that conformity. Yet in order to do this, Mailer needed the proper form, for, as Godfrey Hodgson observes, "[T]o dissent from the broad axioms of consensus [in the 1950s] was to proclaim oneself irresponsible or ignorant. That would risk disqualifying the dissenter from being taken seriously, and indeed from being heard at all."[10] Unfortunately for Mailer, this is precisely what happened.

Barbary Shore is perhaps Mailer's least personal book.[11] The milieu that Mailer created for his second novel emerged from "Jean Malaquais . . . the books I had read, and the aesthetics I considered desirable" (94). There is very little of Mailer's lived self in the novel, because, as he was acutely aware, he had not accumulated enough experiences to ground his fiction.

This wouldn't have posed such a problem for another writer, but Mailer was searching for a style that could reduce the artificial wall of language that separates narrative from actual experience. Mailer wanted *Barbary Shore* to demonstrate to his readers the need for skepticism and independence of thought in the face of the ideology of the Cold War. *Barbary Shore* depicts a terrifyingly (in?)competent government agent, Hollingsworth, who pursues something once possessed by a disaffected Marxist spy named McLeod. Both McLeod and Hollingsworth attempt to coerce Lovett, the innocent everyman protagonist of the novel who may or may not be in possession of the unnamed item, into accepting their view of history and thereby divulge the location of the artifact. In *Advertisements for Myself* Mailer describes *Barbary Shore* as "this first of the existentialist novels in America," but it seems instead an attempt to blend the psychological interiority of the modernist novel with the thinly disguised political polemics of the social realist novel (106).[12] Mailer admits as much when he complains that "the end of the novel collapsed into a chapter of political speech and never quite recovered" (94). *Barbary Shore*, flawed in its execution, failed in a literary marketplace that sought reassurance in the face of disorientating change, and received emphatically scathing reviews.

If most people seemed unaware or unconcerned about the "partially totalitarian society" that the US was slowly becoming, Mailer hoped his second novel would enlighten them.[13] Yet not only was the novel a commercial failure; it seemed to offend many of the critics assigned to review it. The hostility of the critics derived in part from the historical circumstances that pertained when the novel was published. Mailer himself regretted that "*Barbary Shore* showed its face in the worst of seasons, just a few months after the Chinese had come into the Korean War and set [the country] off [on] another of our clammy national hysterias" (105). What Mailer derides as hysteria might be more charitably viewed as legitimate concern. After all, in less than a year the Soviets successfully tested an atomic bomb, China fell to Mao Zedong and his Communist army despite massive USA aid to prevent this, a hot war broke out in South Korea, and Alger Hiss was convicted of perjury and imprisoned. Right-wing fearmongers, led by Richard Nixon, J. Edgar Hoover, and Joseph McCarthy, created a narrative of creeping Communist infiltration that exploited the looming threat of both the Soviet Union and China. With the benefit of hindsight, Mailer attempts to dismiss the historical circumstances surrounding the publication of his second novel, but even he recognized that any single novel that attempted to swim against this national current would have to be perfectly executed, and *Barbary Shore* was far from that. Given this reality there is little wonder why critics found *Barbary Shore*'s muddled critique of US ideology not just irrelevant but perverse. Mailer's decision to willfully ignore the contemporary mood was admirable, but his awkward marriage of high modernism and social realism demonstrates a lack of command in his writing style. He sought to produce a style that could be his alone, but this self-conscious aping of previous methods was not it.[14] With his disappointing second novel Mailer found himself behind the times literarily, politically, and stylistically, yet he was also racing headlong towards a stance that would soon place him in the avant-garde.

McCarthyism frustrated Mailer's desire to challenge the middle-class assumptions of his audience. The fearful conformity of the early 1950s made a serious hearing of Mailer's ideas—which would be difficult under the best of circumstances—almost impossible. McCarthyism's repression of the American Communist Party, left-leaning labor unions, and Hollywood creative talent dismayed Mailer even as he negotiated the politics of the Left. Writing about this period in *Advertisements*, he laments that "radical political life in America has become difficult, and to hold the position of a libertarian socialist is equivalent to accepting almost total intellectual alienation from America, as well as a series of pains and personal contradictions in one's work" (202).[15] Mailer was unwilling to accept intellectual alienation from America; indeed, he wanted nothing more than to export his idiosyncratic (and oxymoronic) brand of libertarian socialism—which he would call radical conservativism in *Armies of the Night*—to the American people. As Louis Menand notes, whatever he calls himself Mailer fears a "conservative liberalism" (a phrase he first coins in *The Naked and the Dead*), where individuals adjust to the failings of their society rather than confront them.[16] The inspiration Mailer drew from the protests of the civil rights movement seems entirely in keeping with his concerns.

Alienated both from the US and the prevailing critiques of the US as articulated by disillusioned Communists or *Partisan Review* liberals, Mailer began exploring how society disciplined its outsiders.[17] Mailer, who had by this time befriended anti-Communist liberals like Lionel and Diana Trilling, Irving Howe, Dwight Macdonald, and Norman Podhoretz, realized that the rhetoric of these New York intellectuals limited itself to critiquing the various iterations of Marxism and capitalism and sterile reviews of culture, but failed to address the ramifications of the conformity that Mailer sensed coursing throughout American life. Casting about for a lens through which to understand his society, Mailer, like many from his generation, became fascinated with psychology, although Mailer's interest was far from typical. Befriending the psychiatrist Robert Lindner after reading his *Rebel without a Cause: The Hypnoanalysis of a Criminal Psychopath* (1944), Mailer would often journey to Baltimore during the fall of 1951 to deepen his understanding of the "psychosocial motivations behind alienation and aggression."[18] Lindner's approach to understanding the psyche was distinct from the doctrinaire Freudianism that was sweeping the nation.[19] Mailer was at this point desperate to maintain the outsider status that had propelled his early success and sought out other contradictory perspectives to inform his perceptions.

To this end Mailer once again moved to challenge an audience. When the *Partisan Review* invited Mailer to contribute an essay for a symposium titled "Our Country and Our Culture" that sought to determine the proper role of the artist in the face of the Cold War and American consensus, Mailer delivered a stinging rebuke to those in attendance, rejecting the notion that any artist should ever consider himself integrated into his culture. Mailer felt that "the writer does not need to be integrated into his society, and often works best in opposition to it," rejecting identification with a nation that "threatens, suggests, nudges and promises" in order to achieve the broad consensus that promotes the American Century (188). Mailer had not yet produced a cogent oppositional stance, but he recognized that to accept the logic of the current status quo was to reduce literary work to sophisticated cultural propaganda. Mailer denounced an artistic community where "[o]ne does not ever say that total war and the total war economy predicate a total regimentation of thought. Rather, it is suggested that society is too difficult to understand and history impossible to predict" (189). Mailer knew this to be untrue because he had twice identified the sociocultural trends at work on his audience and tailored his texts accordingly. He believed that the writer who uncritically concerned himself with "a strapping participation in the vigors of American life" forfeited his opportunity to create an art that might introduce a new perspective (190).

Still struggling to find his own style, Mailer reports in *Advertisements* that he woke one morning with an ambitious premise: an eight-part novel where the protagonist "would travel through many worlds, through pleasure, business, communism, church, working class, crime, homosexuality and mysticism" (154). This audacious plan indicates how badly Mailer struggled with the limits of discourse associated with McCarthyism.

Despite the failure of his earlier attempt to find an audience, Mailer decides to engage the themes contained in *Barbary Shore* on a far larger scale, to repeat his attempt at a kind of reorientation and reinvigoration of the national discourse. He composed "The Man Who Studied Yoga" as the overture to his eight-part masterwork, and this story casts a harsh light on the well-adjusted suburban lifestyle born of prosperity and a fear of dissent that was transforming the nation. Mailer completed this prelude in 1952, and it is of interest in part because it encapsulates his discontent with post–World War II America's embrace of conformity. Although this story does not yield a new style for Mailer, it demonstrates what, in his view, was wrong with the audience *Barbary Shore* had failed to reach.

In "The Man Who Studied Yoga," Mailer reproduces the middle-class society for whom "nothing less than a revolution in the consciousness of our time" is necessary (17). A disembodied narrator relates the story, a character privy to the desires and inner thoughts of the protagonist, Sam Slavoda, a frustrated writer of comic books. Sam, a former member of the American Communist Party, lives with his wife, Eleanor, and their two children in a middle-class housing development in Queens, New York. Before Sam speaks, the narrator reveals several telling bits of information about him. Sam, we learn, "never [attempts his endeavors] with a whole heart"; longs for new experience but fears people, especially the homeless; and possesses a sincere desire to better understand himself through psychoanalysis (157). He is, with these characteristics, a depressingly typical member of his class. Worse, particularly for a writer of lowbrow media who longs for a broader forum for his ideas, Sam contentedly expresses himself in the empty idiom of the day.

The story opens at the Slavoda residence the morning after a party that granted Sam, his wife, and their coterie of post-radical friends a temporary escape from the ennui which plagues them. The narrator suggests that the novelty of the situation granted the Slavodas this breakthrough: "Last night at the party, there were perhaps half a dozen people whom [Sam] met for the first time, and he talked animatedly with them, sensing their reactions, feeling their responses, aware of the life in them, as they were aware of the life in him" (160). That moment of connection has passed, however, and Sam wakes to the sound of his wife making breakfast feeling depressed and hung over. Sam and Eleanor immediately begin to reprise their experiences from the previous night in an attempt to restore their fleeting vitality. Quickly, however, their recollections revert to sterile Freudian psychobabble, with Sam clinically observing that his friend

Charles "hates women . . . almost everything he says about them is a discharge of aggression" (161). Later in the conversation they wonder if an attractive woman at the party was a hysteric or merely compulsive. Sam and Eleanor cannot evade the empty and comfortable psychoanalytic jargon of the day, even as they attempt to re-create the moment when they felt authentic and alive. The couple, formerly bohemian representatives of the political Left, have traded in their Marxist discourse for secondhand and inexpert Freudian analysis.

After breakfast, settling back into his armchair—that symbol of suburban status and isolation—Sam begins to question the direction his life has taken. He longs to reject the dull employment that leaves him empty even as it provides for his tastefully appointed apartment complete with its own "television-radio-and-phonograph cabinet" (163). Although "writing for the comic strips seems to exhaust his imagination," Sam sabotages any serious attempt at creative art, placing the security his job affords him and his family above personal fulfillment. Looking through the Sunday paper, Sam rails against the "dishonesty, at the smooth strifeless world which [the media] presents" (163), even as he participates in this deception by writing vapid comic strips. Sam seems unaware or unwilling to act upon the disconnect between his feelings of outrage and his middle-class lifestyle.

Deprived of the programmatic analysis of the Communist Party, Sam seems incapable of generating an idea that must be carried through into action. In fact, Sam has fled so far from his former self that he has begun to wish for the relative ignorance of the working class, dreaming of a life where "to be happy it was necessary only to have more money, more goods, less worries" (165). Genuine human interaction like the sort that occurred at last evening's party, connections that seem to somehow transgress the notion of organized leisure, ease the disquiet that Sam feels, but he experiences such contact too infrequently for it to soothe him completely. Unlike the supposedly blissful working class, Sam experiences unhappiness that stems from ontological rather than material conditions, forcing him to seek vitality in others lest he face the feelings of impotence and betrayal that lurk within.

Luckily, Sam's friend Marvin Rossman provides an opportunity for stimulation when he asks Sam to screen a pornographic film in his apartment, a request that Sam quickly accepts. Sam, however, cannot revel in his anticipation of this event, clinically noting that his excitement possibly betrays an anal fixation (166). The friends that assemble to watch the film represent a cross section of postwar middle-class occupations:

staff writer for a mass media outlet, dentist, lawyer, schoolteacher, painter, social worker, and homemaker. Their impassioned conversation prior to watching the movie demonstrates their attempt to escape the conformity of the middle class by maintaining a faux-critical stance to the society at large. In their discussion of the day's prominent issues (the Negro question, the uncertain future facing their children), they all seem intent on proving to the others that they remain progressive and bohemian despite their comfort and safety. As the narrator observes with a disdain that suggests Mailer's voice, "[t]hey are all being the most unconscionable hypocrites," equally so for their feigned detachment towards pornography as for their seemingly radical stances.

Despite the group's stultifying performance of respectability, the frankness of the movie, a fantasy of seduction and domination, invigorates them, pushing Sam in particular towards another moment of vitality. Flush and stimulated from the film, Sam muses on the differences between eighteenth-century and twentieth-century uses of power:

> [During the eighteenth] century men sought wealth so they might use its fruits; this epoch men lusted for power in order to amass more power, a compounding of power into pyramids of abstraction whose yield are cannon and wire enclosure, pillars of statistics to the men who are the kings of this century and do no more in power's leisure time than go to church, claim to love their wives, and eat vegetables.

The pornographic seduction of the innocent presented on screen suggests to Sam an understanding of power that is personalized, concerned with mastering the flesh and with human conquest. Sam lives in a different, more impersonal era, the century of the Holocaust and Hiroshima, where bureaucrats mass-produce the means for faceless destruction in exchange for an upper-middle-class lifestyle and a façade of respectability. Sam's musing suggests that power in the eighteenth century was humane in that it sought to dominate life, while the merciless yet sterile power of the twentieth century searches for increasingly efficient means to mass-produce death. Still, Sam remains unable to conceive of a meaningful response to this state of affairs. For Sam, as for Mailer, the loss of personal autonomy, the reduction of men into mindless consumers attempting to ignore the Damoclean Cold War, represents the biggest threat to creative individualism.

None of Sam's cohorts seems able to posit a meaningful alternative to the contemporary life of conformity. This becomes evident when Sam and

Marvin speak about Jerry O'Shaugnessy, a former member of the Communist Party. Marvin reports that O'Shaugnessy, once a working-class hero in the Party whom Sam idealized, has become a wino. This comment begins a reverie that locates Sam's ontological angst in his loss of faith in the transformative potential of Communism. Sam's knowledge of the USSR's prison camps, show trials, and corrupt bureaucracy has marooned him "between the loss of a country he has never seen, and his repudiation of the country in which he lives" (179). This loss of faith plunges Sam into his "friendly depression" (179), the feelings of impotence and isolation that result from his struggle to find a place in the McCarthyist present. Indeed, as Mailer would later observe, "The average American Communist held to the myth of Stalin for reasons which had little to do with the political evidence and had everything to do with their psychic necessities" ("The White Negro," 356–357). This is why it is possible for Sam, who really does know better, to wish for the blissful ignorance of the working class. There seems no way out for Sam; he is every inch a one-dimensional man.[20]

After the company leaves, Sam and Eleanor have sex while watching the movie, consummating the intimacies they have felt over the past day. Psychological conceptions of sexuality emerge in Sam's mind as he couples with Eleanor, causing him to wonder about his latent homosexuality while he is penetrating his wife (181–182). Later, as their postcoital connection fades and he learns that Eleanor was pleased by his lovemaking, Sam castigates himself for his inability to lose himself in the experience, for wasting his life and talent, for abandoning his novel, the one thing that "would lift him at a bound from the impasse in which he stifles" (183). Sam's final thoughts before sleep concern a former friend of Eleanor's, a woman whom society has tossed aside as contemptuously as Jerry O'Shaugnessy. The unnamed woman has been institutionalized and claims, when Sam and Eleanor visit, that the orderlies sexually assault her during the night. Eleanor and Sam, unsure of the legitimacy of her claim, choose not to act, and when they next visit her she is less lucid than before. Uncomfortable at their silence in the face of another person's (possible) mistreatment, Eleanor and Sam subsequently put her and her claims of abuse out of their minds—except that, years later, the memory of this woman returns unbidden to Sam.

That Sam recalls Eleanor's unnamed friend on the same day that he learns of Jerry O'Shaugnessy's fall from grace is surely no coincidence. Troubled by the memory of his inaction in the face of institutional mistreatment, which suggests that Sam lacks the power to shape events, he makes an inevitable association: "the mental hospital. A concentration camp . . . Perhaps it would be the world some day" (185). Sam's lack of faith in the future of the USA or the USSR causes him to imagine that the world will soon become an inhumane expression of the totalizing statistical power of bureaucratic destruction. Sam justifies their refusal to help Eleanor's friend by evoking the monolithic power of the state, yet their refusal to investigate the woman's claims of abuse belie their self-image as radicals or reformers. When given an opportunity to challenge the authority of an institution, the couple turns uneasily away. Sam's reverie reveals that he suffers not from depression or a loss of faith but a failure of the imagination due to his loss of innocence. The story suggests that Sam and his cohorts once derived their identity from their commitment to reform the US via the Party; the failure of the Left to produce a viable alternative to current US policy combined with the material success made possible by the postwar boom undermines their reformist sense of self.

"The Man Who Studied Yoga" offers an eloquent illustration of the coterie that Mailer desperately wished to inform, the post-radical middle-class intellectuals cowed by McCarthyism who despaired the loss of the progressive movement that shored up their sense of self. This class, for Mailer, possessed an inert transformative power stifled by the failures of the Popular Front, the threat of nuclear war, and their seemingly effortless achievement of a prosperity that made it easy to conform. Yet, like the various authors of *The God That Failed*, the members of this group found it difficult to replace Marxist schemas in their epistemological frame. Due to their skill at dialectical analysis, this class recognized the flaws of US policy but seemed unable to use this information in any productive way. Instead, they relied on psychoanalysis to assuage the anxiety and guilt that derived from their rejection of American exceptionalism and their inability to turn this disavowal into transformative action.

In "The Man Who Studied Yoga," Mailer confronts the yawning gap between insight and purposeful action, and he demonstrates that any critique that concludes without a call for direct action is useless. Yet, just as the last section of *The Naked and the Dead* signaled Mailer's attitude toward bureaucratic capitalism, so does "The Man Who Studied Yoga" foreshadow the importance he placed on sexual conquest. In light of Marxism's increasing irrelevance to his class and generation, Mailer searched for another oppositional position that challenged the mores of Eisenhower's America, and sex was it. Sex, as fetishized by Mailer, was more than merely a reproductive act; it remained one of the few areas his contemporaries would not submit to regulation by society. But if sex offered individuals one of the few remaining opportunities for an unmediated connection with another person, Mailer remained uncertain as to how this connection might help one resist conforming to the demands of the coercive state outside the bedroom. Mailer would investigate this theme in his next novel, *The Deer Park*.

Mailer attempted to achieve a balance between the political and the sexual in *The Deer Park* (1955), the first of the eight novels that were to follow "The Man Who Studied Yoga." *The Deer Park* featured a cast of dissolute men living in and around Hollywood and Palm Springs, attempting to find meaning in their lives through exploitative or titillating relationships with women. Mailer's depiction of sex here is markedly different from "The Man Who Studied Yoga," where sex offers Eleanor and Sam the possibility for a genuine connection. Sexual relationships abound in *The Deer Park*, but because none of the participants is ever sure of their standing in their relationships, couples break apart and reform throughout the novel. Sex in the novel, while subtly depicted, serves as a proxy for power rather than a method of affiliation, demonstrating how coercion can deform even the most elemental of connections. In *The Deer Park* sex serves both as a way of keeping score—a way to determine who currently has the power to coerce whom—and a means to cope with one's artistic failings.

Sergius O'Shaugnessy (abandoned son of Jerry from "The Man Who Studied Yoga"?), a newcomer to California and one of the two protagonists of the novel, comes to understand that Hollywood is an elaborately socialized world where knowing when to transgress is as important as the talent that permits that transgression. Charles Eitel, the other protagonist of the novel, loses his artistic integrity through the machination of Hollywood's studio system and, after being blacklisted for refusing to testify before HUAC, pines away isolated from the community he needs to sustain him as an artist. Neither Sergius nor Eitel is quite what he seems, a claim that could extend to all the characters in this novel, but both men lose their sexual potency and place in society after confrontations that expose weaknesses they had hidden from themselves and others. The sexual politics of *The Deer Park* displaces the inert competition between socialism and capitalism of *Barbary Shore*, and Mailer augments the philosophical sexuality in the former novel by linking it throughout to a kind of social ambiguity typical of Hollywood.[21]

In *The Deer Park*, Marion Faye, a bisexual pimp whose mother hosts a popular Hollywood salon, seems the only character unaffected by the need to prove his sexual worth. Indeed, because Faye finds sex worthless, he is free in an anarchic sense and delights in humiliating the women and men who place themselves under his power. Interestingly, the rebellious Faye, unlike other characters in the novel, rejects the respectability that comes with material success. Faye descends from questionable stock; he never knew his father (although his mother claimed Faye's father was a nobleman) and his mother was "a call girl, a gossip columnist . . . a celebrity, a failure, she had been born in Chicago and discovered in New York, her father had been a drunk and died that way, her mother had disappeared with another man" (6). Despite these roots Faye's mother achieved wealth, stability, notoriety, and the parvenu notions of propriety that often accompanied such upward mobility, and Faye seemed to inherit a world-weary cynicism from his grandparents that resisted her attempts at sophistication.[22] Faye finds his place on the margins of society and refuses to rationalize his extralegal behavior, which grants him a kind of nobility in spite of himself.

While sexual negotiations play a central role in *The Deer Park*, Mailer also exploits ethnic ambiguities in the novel. Sergius is an orphan who passes, admittedly, as a "fake Irishman," claiming his identity after surviving the fights that occurred at his orphanage (20). Like the protean Jay Gatsby, Sergius presents himself as more accomplished than he is, and so he constantly seeks to understand other people's places in the social pecking order so that he can better exploit his position. For example, when Sergius meets Charles Eitel, he hears "more than one accent. I could hear New York in [his voice], and the theater, and once in a while if he was talking to somebody from those parts, a trace of the South or the Middle-West came into it, and with all of that it was a controlled voice—most of the time he sounded like society" (29). Mailer extends the notion of white ethnic ambiguity further, revealing that Faye's family name is actually O'Faye, a play perhaps on the Black vernacular "ofay," a term used to disparage whites. In light of Sergius's manufactured ethnic identity, the ambiguity he detects in Eitel, and the central role played by the sexually ambivalent pimp of unknown ethnic stock, *The Deer Park* can be represented as Mailer's first attempt to fashion characters who establish an authentic sense of self through sexual conquest, resistance to coercion, and adopted ethnicities.

Nevertheless, Mailer remains unsure what to make of Faye's resistance to the empty value system of the coercive bureaucracy represented by Hollywood, despite Faye embodying the ideals and tone of Robert Lindner's rebel without a cause. So, while Eitel and Sergius are both defeated by their vulnerability to various forms of coercion, Faye, who ends the novel imprisoned for carrying a gun without a license, fails to offer a meaningful alternative. Although Mailer intends Sergius to be a representative type, a modern man lost in the society that has emerged out of World War II, he remains a reworking of F. Scott Fitzgerald's Gatsby, without Gatsby's quixotic devotion to the idea of redemptive love. Indeed, none of the female characters in the novel are as fully realized as Fitzgerald's Daisy, and the relationships the women in *The Deer Park* have with men bring none of them much happiness. Marion Faye represents the kind of contemporary man that would come to interest Mailer, but at this point he was reluctant to place a pimp at the center of his narrative, choosing an innocent self-made man over the knowing libertine. Although Faye's attitude may transcend contemporary sexual mores, Mailer resists granting him moral authority in the novel. Try as he might, Mailer cannot yet conceive of the rebellious Marion Faye as a heroic exemplar around which one might found a movement.

Seven publishing houses found Mailer's novel unfit to publish due to its sexual content. Yet when Walter Minton at G. P. Putnam agreed to bring forth *The Deer Park* with minimal changes, Mailer realized that the form and the content of his third novel did not align. While the novel's narrative still pleased Mailer, he concluded that "the style was wrong . . . I had been strangling the life of my novel in a poetic prose which was too self-consciously attractive and formal" and "came out of nothing so much as my determination to prove I could master a fine style" (*Advertisements*, 235). Against the wishes of Minton, Mailer forced himself through a manic rewrite where "for the first time . . . I was able to color the empty reality of [the] first person with some real feeling of how I had always felt, which was to be outside, for Brooklyn where I grew up is not the center of anything" (237). This new style that emerged from his rewrite allowed Mailer to link the insights into alienation he had gained via his studies with Linder with his personal history and his own self-conception as an artist. For the first time since he began gobbling experiences, Mailer realized that he must arrive at a better understanding of himself and how he related to the various artistic, social, and political communities he belonged to in order to find his style. In the eighteen months that followed Mailer's epiphany, he experimented with drugs, systematically ended (or seriously tested) his friendships with WASP contemporaries like James Jones and William Styron, and threw himself into the jazz scene in New York. Jazz, especially the bebop modes that were currently *en vogue* in the downtown New York scene, seemed to Mailer to be outlaw music. Mailer was right in a limited sense: although it was sufficiently popular to have a large and devoted following, bop lacked the mainstream respectability of swing and big band music, to say nothing of Frank Sinatra. Mailer combined feelings of outsiderness with his embrace of a combative first-person narration to reorient his self-perception, and this was a crucial step in his development as an artist.

After publishing *The Deer Park*, Mailer would rehearse his newly confrontational style as a columnist for *The Village Voice*, the alternative newspaper he helped found.[23] While the *Voice* would eventually earn a reputation as a weekly that offered a decidedly progressive perspective on the events of the day, during its first few years the most radical content in the paper was its free-form reviews of off-Broadway shows and art house cinema. With the paper losing money, Mailer, recovered from the intense rewriting of *The Deer Park*, decided to contribute a column to the paper, trusting that this would bolster circulation. So, when Mailer began writing his column for the *Voice* at the end of December of 1955, less than a month into the Montgomery bus boycott that was to catapult Martin Luther King onto the national stage, the paper was more concerned with surviving the winter than chronicling the storm brewing in the South.[24] At the very moment that Mailer was searching for a literary form to shatter the smothering national conformity, the civil rights movement brought forth a social protest movement that promised to do just that, and Mailer was soon to take notice.[25]

Mailer mentioned the Montgomery bus boycott in his eighteenth and final column for the *Voice* (actually a full-page advertisement intended to rectify an earlier, and in his opinion, wrong-headed meditation on *Waiting for Godot*). In this column Mailer referred to "the mysterious and exciting phenomenon of the White South terrified of the Birmingham bus strike and the growing power of the Negro" (325). Of course, Mailer meant Montgomery and not Birmingham, but this statement demonstrates his newfound interest in the protests occurring in Alabama, which he perceived as a possible break in the wall of conformity established by McCarthyism and the fear of nuclear death. Epochal events like *Brown v. Board of Education*, the national outcry over the murder of Emmett Till, and now the Montgomery bus boycott suggested that Black Americans, at least, did not accept the status quo. These stirring events must have reminded Mailer of Lindner's assertion that "the resources of human salvation can be found more abundantly among that very group whom we have been instructed latterly by every possible means to despise and dismiss as lost than among the thronging shadows of the so-called 'adjusted'" (*Prescription for Rebellion*, 107). While Lindner was referring to the psychopath whom society excludes, Mailer understood that southern Blacks, like Jews at Harvard, intellectuals in the army, and daring writers in an age of conformity, might also form an excluded group.

While seeking to predict how the events in the South would transform the social and political and thus the literary sensibility of the nation, Mailer had also begun to investigate events closer to home that would also emerge in "The White Negro." Indeed, Mailer's sixteenth *Voice* column, "The Hip and the Square" offers his first attempts to define hip.[26] Hip "is an American existentialism. Profoundly different from French existentialism because Hip is based on the mysteries of the flesh, and its origins can be traced back into all the undercurrents and underworlds of American life, back into the instinctive apprehensions and appreciation of existence which one finds in the Negro and the soldier, in the criminal psychopath and the dope addict and jazz musician, in the prostitute, in the actor, in the—if one can visualize such a possibility—in the marriage of the call-girl and the psychoanalyst" (314). Note that Mailer articulates an underground consensus somehow hospitable to performers, disaffected military, criminals, and Negroes. He felt that these groups, whether they knew it or not, formed an anticonsensus that he hoped could appeal to a significant segment of the national population once they understood and appreciated its vitality as such. Indeed, Mailer believed that the jazz clubs in the Village and house parties in Harlem that he frequented demonstrated that the various groups of his anticonsensus were already beginning to come together to some degree. What this new disposition lacked was a prophet, someone to popularize and explain it. This new scene energized Mailer, and he promised "to continue writing about it for at least the next few weeks" (315). He ended his column at the *Voice* two weeks later, but he eventually kept his promise.

Mailer's *Village Voice* column "Hip" presages many of his points in "The White Negro," but at this point he had not written about the emerging civil rights movement in any meaningful way. This was to change in the winter of 1956. Responding to a challenge by Lyle Stuart, Mailer wrote four paragraphs on integration in the South to be published in Stuart's *Independent*, a monthly newsmagazine with a small following. According to Mailer, "Everybody who knows the South knows that the white man fears the sexual potency of the Negro" (332). Whites could not allow Blacks to attain social equality because "the Negro already enjoys sensual superiority" (332). Following this tortured calculus, if the sensually superior Blacks attained social equality they would surpass the sexually inferior whites in the South. Mailer sees justice in this impending turnabout, but "like all poor winners and small losers the Southern whites are unwilling to accept the reversals of history" (332). This is a ridiculous argument for many reasons, but the bloody history of segregation, emblematized most recently in the public imagination by the murder of Emmett Till for supposedly whistling at a white woman, made white fear of Black sexuality plausible to Mailer.

Stuart loved the provocative piece and decided to send it to William Faulkner for comment before publishing it. Faulkner's reply was withering: "I have heard this idea expressed several times during the last twenty years, though not before by a man. The others were ladies, northern or middle western ladies, usually around 40 or 45 years of age. I don't know what a psychiatrist would find in this" (333).

Mailer was devastated by this reply. Not only did Faulkner fail to take Mailer's ideas seriously; he compared him to a middle-aged middle-western lady, which the chauvinistic Mailer simply could not accept. Faulkner also implied—correctly—that Mailer did not know the South, and, worse, that Mailer should seek psychiatric counseling so that he could come to terms with his fascination with Black masculinity. Faulkner's reply was so condescending and dismissive that in that moment Mailer must have felt like an interloping outsider again. Although Hemingway was the writer that Mailer then admired most, Faulkner was also a Nobel laureate and this insult must be returned.

In his rejoinder to Faulkner, Mailer acknowledged his "extraordinary body of work" but wondered why his most stimulating conversations occurred with middle-aged midwestern women. Mailer then claimed to have learned of white men's fear of Black sexuality from "a most intelligent Negro carwasher . . . a mulatto sneak-thief and pimp, [and a former] madam of a whorehouse in South Carolina" (333). So there. Faulkner's insult reminded Mailer that despite his friendship with the Arkansan writer Francis Irby Gwaltney and his experiences with southern whites while enlisted, he really had no firsthand experience with southern racism. Even Mailer's fascination with the Montgomery bus boycott—which ended the very December that Mailer composed his thoughts on racial integration—was secondhand knowledge, delivered through the filter of the media. What Mailer did know was the New York jazz scene where hipsters frolicked. Indeed, in order to properly research "Hip," Mailer had gone off on "that happy ride where you discover a new duchy of jazz every night and the drought of the past is given a rain of new sound" (234), an experience that allowed him to realize that amoral pimps and idealistic preachers weren't the only people rejecting the conformity of the 1950s, and that something life-sustaining might be made from that rejection.

Stuart, a crusader for free speech who loved a good controversy, sent copies of Mailer's letter, with Faulkner's reply and Mailer's rejoinder, to Eleanor Roosevelt, W. E. B. Du Bois, William Bradford Huie, and Murray Kempton, among others. While the Faulkner-Mailer exchange generated denouncements of various intensities, Mailer realized that he had not done his topic justice, that he "would have to do a good deal better, because if I did not, I might lose one emotion and gain another, an exchange I was in fever to avoid, since the first emotion included no less than my faith that I was *serious*, that I was *right*, that my work would give more to others than it took from them" (334, emphasis added). If his four-paragraph meditation on sex and race was the best he could do on this topic, Mailer feared, perhaps he was not an important writer after all. "The White Negro," the essay that grew out of Mailer's attempt to revise and expand his initial thoughts on southern racism and Black masculinity, became, for him, a demonstration and confirmation of his talent. Mailer fails to explicitly mention southern protests in "The White Negro," instead using jazz to establish a conceptual link between southern and northern Blacks.

As recently as 1998 Mailer anointed "The White Negro" his most important piece of writing, a comment that seems at odds with the publishing history of a writer who won two Pulitzer Prizes and a National Book Award after publishing this essay.[27] The essay was initially published in *Dissent* by Mailer's friend Irving Howe, was made available as a pamphlet, and saw its widest dissemination in *Advertisements for Myself*. When "The White Negro" initially appeared it was derided by figures as diverse as James Baldwin, Ned Polsky, and Jean Malaquais, and Howe reportedly had second thoughts about publishing it.[28] Worse for Mailer, many of the intellectual heavyweights of the time thought his essay beneath notice, with the notable exception of Diana Trilling. Despite its troubled reception, Mailer remained convinced that he had successfully realigned his sensibility and was now in touch with the underground currents in American life and culture.

Although "The White Negro" celebrates the hipster, the essay opens with a bewildering section that seems to have little to do with bohemian culture. The fourth sentence of this famous précis, which follows below, is especially informative in light of my discussion of the role of innocence in the formation of a collective American identity. Mailer posits that

> if tens of millions were killed in concentration camps out of the inexorable agonies and contractions of super-states founded upon the always insoluble contradictions of injustice, one was then obliged also to see that no matter how crippled and perverted an image of man was the society he had created, it was nonetheless his creation, *his collective creation* (at least his collective creation from the past) and if society was so murderous, then who could ignore the most hideous of questions about his own nature? (338, emphasis added)

This fragment presents directly the fears that Mailer alluded to in *Barbary Shore* and "The Man Who Studied Yoga." As the ideals of the progressive movement atrophy, weapons proliferate that lessen human agency because they implicate the weak and indifferent alongside the bold and daring, rendering choice, even the choice to flee, meaningless. Worse, much of this technology lies in the hands of two dehumanizing bureaucracies, the USA and the USSR, each dominated by a politics of personality and seemingly inured against compassion or caution. We are always already implicated in this situation, always already guilty, because as a society our seemingly life-affirming choices have driven us inexorably to this point. In the face of this knowledge, conformity at least allows one to escape the despair occasioned by a serious contemplation of this impending conflict.

Mailer asserts that the hipster, the "white Negro," intuits a way out of the triple bind of concentration camp, nuclear destruction, and mind-numbing conformity. The hipster is for Mailer "the American existentialist . . . [who] accept[s] the terms of death, [who] live[s] with death as immediate danger" and as such erases his guilt by accepting potential destruction as a condition under which life is to be lived (339). Rather than cower in the face of eradication, the hipster embraces "the psychopath in oneself . . . in that enormous present which is without past or future, memory or planned intention" (339). Life as a Western and American subject, Mailer asserts, burdened by the memories of such rationally inhuman endeavors as Dresden, Auschwitz, Nagasaki, and the Stalinist purges, and the fear of an impending nuclear war, demands an embrace of psychopathic irrationality. If the Cold War and McCarthyism on the one hand and sterile liberalism on the other represent the contemporary existential choices of Western men, then the only sane choice is to abandon the ways of the West and forge a new path, as Mailer claims the hipster has done. That decision places the "white Negroes" into a sympathetic relationship with Blacks, who have faced death and destruction as a fact of life for over three hundred years as outsiders within the United States.

Obviously, the symbiotic relationship between Blacks and whites lies at the center of this text. Mailer claims that "the source of the Hip is the Negro" (340) and that one might avoid the conformist traps of 1950s America by "absorb[ing] the existential synapses of the Negro" (341). Once this occurs the hipster will be able to "accept the terms of death . . . as immediate danger. . . . divorce oneself from society . . . [and] exist without roots" (339). There is freedom and innocence in this social arrangement, Mailer feels, perhaps the only freedom possible for many in the wake of the crushing conformity of the 1950s justified by the rise of the USSR and Red China. Mailer realizes that US society has begun to demand of its white citizens what it has always expected of Blacks: silence in the face of policies that are unjust and inhumane in exchange for a promise of safety it cannot hope to guarantee. Such silence is inimical to the kind of critique of the US that Mailer desperately wished to offer, and to the creation of a truly free nation. Mailer's notions about the origins of hip depend on the unequal relationship that Blacks have with mainstream white society, their existence between what he calls "totalitarianism and democracy," but what might more accurately be termed the space between white supremacist conservatism and a naive liberalism that believes in incremental progress (340).

While Mailer was certainly never an apologist for segregation or institutional racism, he believed that the Negro's tenuous existence on the margins of society granted him a valuable perspective, just as his own presence on the margins did. Negroes, to their credit, had long ago ceased subscribing to the myth of American exceptionalism that presupposed a prelapsarian American subject. Conversely, clinging to this myth allowed white Americans to endure the mendacity of Senator McCarthy's House Un-American Activities Committee and the many loyalty boards that his work inspired. Mailer thinks that the racist exclusion of Black Americans from mainstream society grants them greater ethical insight by virtue of their skepticism about the American creed, and whites would benefit, indeed the hipster has already benefited, from adopting "a black man's code to fit their facts" (341), the rebellious worldview that "in a bad world there is no love nor mercy nor charity nor justice unless a man can keep his courage" (340). This would certainly be a radical thing for a well-adjusted suburban commuter to believe in the 1950s, but Mailer asserted that without a critical perspective of this kind, American discourse would remain toothless.

Despite the essay's embrace of violence and interracial sex, discourse is finally what "The White Negro" is all about.[29] The white Negro is born of "a ménage à trois" between "the bohemian . . . the juvenile delinquent [and] the Negro" and in the mouth of this infant hipster "was the language of Hip [which] gave expression to abstract states of feeling which all could share, at least all who were Hip" (340). The language of hip is, according to Mailer "a set of subtle indications of their success or failure in the competition for pleasure" (349). And so, Mailer predicts that a universal and critical language of protest and pleasure will emerge out of a nascent counterculture involving those excluded from the dominant discourse of the day, "a language of energy, how it is found, how it is lost" (349). Mailer felt that "Hip [is] a special language . . . that cannot really be taught—if one shares none of the experiences of elation and exhaustion which it is equipped to describe," but in an age where everyone lives on edge as Sputnik orbits the globe, few can rationally be free of the elation and exhaustion he describes (348). Mailer hopes he has discovered at last a truly American discourse that knows of Marx yet is not bound by him, that comprehends Freud yet finds him absurd, that enjoys a privileged outsider status in a revelatory culture that one can only truly understand by experiencing it.

For Mailer the most important aspect of the language of the hip is neither the common vocabulary this subgroup shares, nor that vocabulary's potential application to the society at large, but the kind of interpretations made possible by that language. Mailer invents a scenario to demonstrate his point, invoking the word "swing," an example that allows him to return, in a roundabout fashion, to the issues he first raised in his four-paragraph first draft.[30] Mailer claims to have witnessed an illiterate "Negro friend" having an intense conversation with a white girl who had graduated from college a few years before. Mailer's unnamed Black friend possesses "an extraordinary ear and a fine sense of mimicry" that allowed him to "respond to one or another facet of her doubts" (350). Mailer concludes that example by claiming, "The Negro was not learning anything about the merits or demerits of the argument, but he was learning a great deal about a type of girl he had never met before. . . . Being unable to read and write, he could hardly be interested in ideas nearly as much as in lifemanship, and so . . . he sensed her character (and the values of her social type) by swinging with the nuances of her voice" (350–351). Mailer avoids mentioning just what the illiterate Negro's swing accomplished, but his example suggests that the white girl took the Black man to bed and received some valuable lifemanship of her own.[31] Mailer suggests here that the language of hip enables innocence by equipping the hipster with the skills necessary to deconstruct the dominant discourse in order to produce a counternarrative. Even if the only content of that counternarrative is a racially transgressive coupling, once expressed it permits further destabilizations.[32]

The hipster achieves a Nietzschean kind of freedom by refusing the standards of society and embracing all the radical potentialities of his existence, which are simultaneously denied and permitted by the repressive language of American society. There are limits to this freedom, however, for "Hip sees the context as generally dominating the man . . . because his character is less significant than the context in which he must function" (353). The language of hip does not, then, grant an anarchic critical freedom, but an exploratory and testing freedom, eager to ascertain what real and imagined limits each context presents.[33] The language of hip enables greater expression than the empty dialog permitted by the conformist 1950s, and this expressiveness is theoretically available to all who are willing to "get with it."

Mailer's various literary, philosophical, and psychological fascinations are distilled into "The White Negro," which blends ideas about marginalized communities that Mailer gleaned from Lindner, Kerouac, and Wilhelm Reich with his rather muddled understanding of existentialism and his impression of the historical realities of the times.[34] But mostly "The White Negro" concerns itself with articulating a new philosophy of performative innocence that would permit whites to escape the repressive bonds of their society. Black Americans, Mailer realized, faced far worse coercion and a more serious and imminent threat of death than anything McCarthyism or the emerging arms race had impressed on whites, and they had endured this oppression for decades. Indeed, sexual expression was one of the most policed aspects of Black masculinity, as the very public murder of Emmett Till demonstrated, yet despite this Negroes (at least the ones Mailer hung out with inside jazz clubs) seemed to be more comfortable with their sexuality than the denizens of the middle class that Mailer derided in "The Man Who Studied Yoga." Black Americans also seemed to embrace artistic expression, from the way they spoke to the bebop jazz that, to Mailer's perception, exhibited a virtuosic yet improvisational performance style.

Mailer realized that the bohemians who flocked to bebop shows in the Village, and the even more intrepid hipsters who followed jazz uptown, were embracing performances that defied conformity, indeed that typified the creative potential of committed artists by their very being. Unlike Sartrean existentialism, which Mailer rejected as too rational, the American existentialism of jazz improvisation freed its practitioners from doubt and fear through embodied practice. Mailer now understood that the way to escape the pressures of conformity and attain a truer understanding of the self lay in performance, and the ultimate performers were the jazzmen who created new musical fugues at every show. Equally important were the sexual appetites of these jazzmen, their (seeming) ability to take a different woman, white or Black, every night. The bebop jazzmen, who existed in a haze of drugs, sex, and masterful music, must have seemed like Zarathustran *Übermensch* to Mailer, and he synthesizes a vocabulary of performative resistance out of the refreshing originality of bop-jazz players, his strong aversion to Freudian psychoanalysis, and his limited experience with the language of existentialism.[35]

Much has been made about the racism at the center of "The White Negro," and with good reason. Jazzmen may have been, as Mailer supposes in the essay, "the cultural mentor[s] of a people" (348) in the 1950s, but there were other cultural mentors (Jackie Robinson and Langston Hughes to name but two), and of course most Black people during this period paid far more attention to the victories of Martin Luther King, Adam Clayton Powell, or Thurgood Marshall than to the exhortations of Bird Parker. Further, a cursory glance at the traditions surrounding the African American church, particularly in the South, reveals that despite Mailer's pronouncements to the contrary, African Americans do indeed possess "the sophisticated inhibitions of civilization" although these inhibitions are often both different from and expressed differently from those of whites (341). The bohemian jazz that Mailer celebrates in fact rises out of the individual Black artist's negotiations with the particular conservatism of African American culture, a negotiation that begins with Duke Ellington, if not before. Indeed, Mailer's appreciation for bop musicians, his favorites being Thelonious Monk and Miles Davis, reveals his basic misunderstanding about jazz improvisation. While Mailer thought that bop solos were expressions of the anarchic impulse that underlies every act of self-creation, the performers themselves understood the highly formal and coded nature of bop improvisation. Mailer's misunderstandings reveal more about his own prejudices than they do about the Black people he came into contact with.

Despite the manifest flaws in "The White Negro," it remains an important example of a white writer attempting to animate the emancipationist tradition submerged in the wake of the Lost Cause's rhetorical triumph. "The White Negro" proceeds from the assumption that African Americans have a truer understanding of the values of democracy, some inherent grace deriving from their negotiations with slavery and racial segregation. The rising Civil Rights movement allows Mailer to refract his ambitions through the prism that it provided. That the novel that followed "The White Negro," *An American Dream*, earned him his best notices since his debut by fictionalizing what Mailer had asserted in his essay demonstrates his success at deriving a compelling literary perspective from the observations that went into crafting that piece. "The White Negro" does not accurately represent how New York bohemians actually interacted with each other, nor does it properly diagnose how decades of discrimination might have lessened Black Americans' inhibitions. Scrutinizing Mailer's essay, however, does allow us to note the stylistic development permitted by his recognition and simultaneous repudiation of what he understands to be mainstream white conformity and logic. Mailer's musings on race offer little understanding of subjects other than Mailer.

Having articulated the revolutionary possibilities of a new sensibility possessed by this emerging multiethnic subculture, Mailer returns to themes he explored in his final *Voice* column and attempted to clarify in his four-paragraph first draft. For, while Mailer has demonstrated the emancipatory potential of hip's language, there remains no guarantee that the governing forces in American society would permit hip to flourish. Indeed, according to Mailer, "[T]he future of the hipster . . . [and] the organic growth of Hip depends on whether the Negro emerges as a dominant force in American life" (355–356). Mailer's next point is plainly a refinement of the crude soliloquy that so upset Faulkner:

> Since the Negro knows more about the ugliness and danger of life than the white, it is probable that if the Negro can win his equality, he will possess a potential superiority, a superiority so feared that the fear itself has become the underground drama of domestic politics. Like all conservative political

fear it is the fear of unforeseeable consequences, for the Negro's equality would tear a profound shift into the psychology, the sexuality, and the moral imagination of every white alive. (356)

Given the potential shift represented by the full integration of the Negro into society, Mailer suspects that liberal expectations, which are simply another form of conventional discourse, might prove false because "for the average liberal whose mind has been dulled by . . . the professional liberal, miscegenation is not an issue because he has been told that the Negro does not desire it" (356). The many evenings Mailer spent in jazz clubs and the language of hip that derives from this experience suggests to him that the opposite may in fact be true. Indeed, Mailer feels that the desire to experience a forbidden sexuality must either continue to "vent itself nihilistically or become turned into the cold murderous liquidations of the totalitarian state" (357) through systemic repression. With his knack for forecasting political and cultural life in the US, Mailer speculates on the final shape of American society once Blacks have achieved parity, hoping that when this occurs "the mean empty hypocrisies of mass conformity will no longer work . . . and Hip would end up being absorbed" into the dominant discourse (356). By asserting that Negroes were more in touch with their sexuality, Mailer unwittingly supports a southern discourse that suggests that African Americans were inherently sinful creatures. His brilliance lies in his asserting that it is only through embracing the carriers of the original sin can white Americans preserve their innocence and avoid hell on earth.

Mailer concludes his essay by wondering if "it is perhaps possible that the Negro holds more of the tail of the expanding elephant of the truth than the radical" and it seems clear where he falls on this issue (357). For Mailer the philosophy articulated in "The White Negro" enables him to complete his reorientation by abandoning his liberal whiteness to achieve an existential solidarity with other marginal groups by becoming a hipster. Mailer rejects the incremental progress preferred by liberals, instead espousing a philosophy of contact, conflict, and genuine confrontation, a grappling that could be sexual, intellectual, or physical in nature. This is his theory of the psychotic, of men (and presumably Mailer is one of these men) so committed to testing the possibilities of themselves and their society that they risk the destruction of both to achieve its, and their, highest expression.[36] This is also, tellingly, the sort of statement that one might have expected to hear from radical abolitionists one hundred years prior. Like those earlier exemplars, Mailer believes that the United States can only justify its self-conception society through the achievement of some sort of social equality for its Black citizens.

With this essay, Mailer identifies for a nation of Sam Slavodas a method of defying American conformist power that challenges the logic of that society through disengagement as well as confrontation. Indeed, Mailer alludes in "The Man Who Studied Yoga" to a generation sensitive to the ethos of the hipster, the "kids" who "merely drift" yet have enough savvy to wonder of their parents "why are you so anxious?" (170–171) What the respectable middle class perceives as purposeless wandering, Mailer understands as a determination to escape the strictures of an increasingly conservative society. According to Mailer this radical potential was evinced in the hipsters' sexual attitudes and appetites which placed them into intimate relationships with one another, involving them in a contest of desire that evokes Sam's eighteenth-century notion of power. Indeed, Sam and the hipster function as reflections of one another, with Sam relishing superficial public interactions at parties but unable to experience communion with his wife, while the hipster viewed public mingling as merely a preliminary step for the greater intimacy to follow. Mailer trusted that the hipster's inversion of the public/private sphere presaged other inversions to come and hopes that the children of Sam Slavoda will mature into psychotic "white Negroes" who refuse to be cowed into a useless anxiety by the crushing circumstances of their existence.

With the publication of "The White Negro" Mailer created a perspective that matched the masculine style that he had excavated during his revisions of *The Deer Park*. For Mailer, the psychopath, both internal and external, became his muse and he would devote the next twenty-two years, from 1957's "The White Negro" to 1979's *The Executioner's Song*, to varied (though invariably first-person) considerations of this character. Mailer became over this period the primary celebrity writer of the era in that many more people knew his face and one or two details about his life than had read his books. This tendency made it difficult for his contemporaries to get ahold of his writing, for there was always the temptation to match the content of his prose with his latest exploit. Mailer, I think, deserves better, and his flaws and strengths as a writer are more readily appreciated if one divorces them from the public persona he created, a persona that often threatened to supersede the other Norman Mailer, the literary iconoclast determined to make his public understand America in a strange new way. With "The White Negro" Mailer finally discovered a program that he could articulate to his readership, a provocative point of view that could guide his own political and sexual performance while rousing his audience from their middle-class obsessions with comfort and the Cold War to pursue a radical and racial innocence that might truly transform the nation.

Chapter Three

"THE WHOLE HEART OF FICTION"

Eudora Welty inside the Closed Society

Eudora Welty, an incredibly productive writer for most of her career, published very little between 1955 and 1970, a period that coincides almost perfectly with the emergence of the civil rights movement as the dominant political and social narrative in the United States. These fifteen years contrast with the fourteen-year period from the debut of her first story collection in 1941 until 1955, when Welty produced a major work every two years, three novels and four collections of short stories in all, as well as dozens of book reviews and other essays.[1] The only manuscript Welty produced between 1955 and 1970, during an increasingly trying time in her life, was a brief children's story called *The Shoe Bird* to free herself of her commitment to Harcourt Brace.[2] Welty neglected her writing during this period in part because her two brothers and her mother lost their health, and Welty, unmarried and childless, devout daughter and sibling, felt obligated to assist her ailing family in every way that she could.[3]

Welty was unable to accommodate her work because her family, particularly her demanding mother, Chestina, who invariably drove off the homecare nurses Welty retained, was difficult to care for.[4] Despite this, Welty refused to place her mother in a nursing home unless she was called away from Jackson to lecture, which she did extensively throughout this period to make ends meet. Twice Welty submitted to the concerns of her friends and sent her mother to the Martha Coker Convalescent Home in Yazoo City, Mississippi, fifty miles from her hometown of Jackson, but she squandered any time that she gained from this arrangement by making the one-hundred-mile trip to visit her mother several times a week. As a result of her daughter's devotion, Chestina Welty spent much of the final decade of her life at home, while Eudora's production slowed almost to a halt. Despite Welty's faithfulness to family, tragedy struck repeatedly during this period: her brother Walter died on January 9, 1959, her mother on January 20, 1966, and her brother Edward four days later on January 24.[5] Freed from her familial duties, Welty threw herself back into her work, producing her two finest novels, *Losing Battles* (1970), which she had worked on intermittently while caring for her family, and *The Optimist's Daughter* (1972), for which she won the Pulitzer Prize.

From 1955 through 1968, the material that would become *Losing Battles* consumed most of the time that Welty could wrench from her family. Indeed, her need to work on the novel was so pressing that she sometimes wrote notes for her draft while driving. Yet, despite devoting almost all her creative time to her novel, Welty published three important texts about the civil rights movement during this period, texts that engage American—and southern—innocence by condemning Mississippi's repression of dissent and its violent opposition to civil rights. "Where Is the Voice Coming From?" (1963) and "The Demonstrators" (1966) are the last two short stories that Welty, a master of the form, published in her life. The third civil rights text, an essay titled "Must the Novelist Crusade?" (1965), grew out of a talk Welty gave at Jackson's Millsaps College the year before, and considers the fiction writer's responsibility of depicting the exigencies of the present in her work.[6] Given the stresses associated with caring for her family while dashing across the country to lecture and the fact that Welty tried to work on *Losing Battles* whenever she could find the peace and energy, that she produced these three texts speaks to their importance as responses to the social unrest she witnessed daily.[7] Welty claimed that "Where Is the Voice Coming From?" "pushed up through something else I was working on," and her other civil rights texts imposed themselves upon her in similar fashion, forcing her to set aside precious time to contemplate and complete them.[8] While Welty chose to avoid marches and demonstrations, these three texts collectively were her response to the problem of civil rights in Mississippi.

Welty, an incredibly private person, generally refused to detail her creative process, even denying, in the face of friends and critics who knew better, that *The Optimist's Daughter* was in any way autobiographical. Still, ten years after the publication of "Where Is the Voice Coming From?" Jonathan Yardley reported that "if there is anything in [Welty's] routine that is virtually inviolable, it is the NBC Evening News, which comes on in Jackson at 5:30PM. . . . She also listens to the radio news before going to bed, and she enjoys talking politics 'among friends.'"⁹ One wonders when Welty developed her viewing habits, for the NBC affiliate in Jackson is WLBT, the controversial station that broadcast Medgar Evers's May 20, 1963, rebuttal to Mayor Allen Thompson, a speech that led to Evers's murder weeks later on June 12. Evers's assassination compelled Welty to compose "Where Is the Voice Coming From?" and the story "begins at that crossroads of television and life where Americans had begun to live."¹⁰

The rapid expansion of television in the United States after World War II occurred everywhere except the South, in part because the FCC ceased licensing new stations from 1948 through 1952 due to a lack of infrastructure and technical problems. This freeze "left Arkansas, Mississippi and South Carolina completely without television at least until 1953" and, I suspect, similarly affected large sections of neighboring states like Alabama, Florida, Louisiana, and Georgia, despite affiliates that served population centers in New Orleans, Atlanta, Mobile, and Miami.¹¹ Television expanded rapidly throughout the South once the technical issues were resolved, with Jackson's first station, WJTV, going on air in January of 1953, and its competitor WLBT debuting in December of the same year. WLBT may have been Welty's network of choice because her father helped build the Lamar Life Insurance building, from which the station broadcast. Christian Welty joined Lamar Life soon after its incorporation, eventually rising to become vice president of the firm, and in 1923 he was tasked with commissioning the new headquarters for the rapidly growing concern. Christian "visited insurance buildings all around the country [and hired] the architects Sanguient-Staats & Hedrick of Fort Worth" to design the building, which was "thirteen stories tall and topped with a clock tower," a logical place for a television transceiver. Christian "took his family to see the building often during its construction. The five of them would climb to the top by the fire escape and look at all Jackson spread below," and it is easy to imagine Welty, with her keen sense of history and place, favoring WLBT over its slightly older rival because of this personal connection.¹²

Jackson's television stations arrived just in time to chronicle the *Brown v. Board of Education* decision and the murder of Emmett Till in 1954. For whites in Mississippi and other parts of the Deep South where television was unknown prior to 1953, the televised media's treatment of Emmett Till's wake in Chicago and the murder trial in Mississippi must have seemed intrusive, offensive, and insensitive to their mores—a definite threat to the southern way of life. The perceived hostility of the national networks caused many affiliates throughout the South to censor

broadcasts, including the evening news and important civil rights docu-
mentaries. Although nominally an NBC affiliate, WLBT refused to air the
NBC White Paper "Sit-in" episode, an investigation into the causes and
ramifications of the sit-in student movement that was spreading through
the South.[13] As a result of this decision WLBT came under dual pressures:
NBC wanted its broadcasts transmitted across the nation without alteration in order to justify the rates it billed sponsors,[14] while the Student
Nonviolent Coordinating Committee (SNCC) and National Association
for the Advancement of Colored People (NAACP) petitioned the FCC,
demanding equal time on WLBT to rebut the segregationist politicians
who purchased blocks of time at the station.[15] The progressive Mississippi
journalist Hodding Carter characterized Fred Beard, the station manager
at WLBT, as "an unofficial mouthpiece for the total resistance line of" local
politicians, and the FCC investigation that resulted from the complaints
of SNCC and the NAACP found him "the most active of all broadcasters
in the use of radio and television to promote segregation and to oppose
federal intervention."[16] With his station in danger of losing its broadcasting license, Beard permitted Evers to respond to an earlier broadcast by
Jackson Mayor Allen Thompson on May 20, 1963.

We cannot be certain if Welty actually saw Evers's seventeen-minute
speech, which interrupted the local broadcast of *The Price is Right*, and
the historical record does not suggest that the two Jackson luminaries
ever met. However, given recent events in Welty's life, she was probably
keenly interested in Evers. In the late 1950s, Welty "began to attend events
at Tougaloo Southern Christian College," a historically Black college "just
north of Jackson." These events were "sponsored by the Social Sciences
Forum . . . as part of an effort to provide a 'model of an integrated society.'"
Welty chose to attend seminars at Tougaloo even though the school was
almost certainly under surveillance by the newly formed Mississippi State
Sovereignty Commission and the local Citizens' Council. In fact, Welty
gave a lecture at the Forum at Tougaloo "five months after a 1958 furor
about the Millsaps College Religious Forum, which had dared to invite
integrationists to speak" and resulted in the resegregation of public events
at Millsaps, Jackson's leading educational institution.[17] Welty would have
been acutely aware of the Council's presence in Jackson because in 1958
they "had gone block by block through the city to recruit new members.
At the same time, [the Council] undertook to survey the 'expected conduct' of every white resident in Jackson," something that must have greatly
perturbed the independent Welty.[18]

Alarmed by the *Brown* decision and the national broadcast media's perspective towards civil rights, and determined to defeat any effort to alter the state's cherished way of life, segregationists in Mississippi created the Citizens' Councils and the Mississippi State Sovereignty Commission to beat back the threat of integration. A series of community-wide grassroots organizations committed to the maintenance of segregation, the Citizens' Councils drew their membership from the elite class in the state, a small but influential group that enabled the Councils to exact legal and extralegal reprisals against any in the local community who sought to change Mississippi's way of life.[19] The Councils, fearful of the Warren Court and the NAACP's legendary team of lawyers, successfully lobbied in 1956 for the creation of a new government agency, the Mississippi State Sovereignty Commission, "whose purpose was to redefine the struggle over Civil Rights in Mississippi. Instead of dealing with issues of segregation and civil rights, the Sovereignty Commission focused on the federal government's encroachment on the state's sovereignty."[20] "These extremists of the right" were "kept at arm's length" by traditional Mississippi politicians until the 1960 election, after which the Councils and the Commission controlled nearly all political and economic activity in the state. Having achieved hegemony, these two groups worked to create a disciplinary society where the omnipresent threat of reprisals narrowed permissible conduct for whites and Blacks by coercing anyone sympathetic to the integrationist goals of the civil rights movement into silence.[21]

Welty's participation in a forum at Tougaloo in defiance of local custom might have escaped notice in 1958, but five years later, a voting project led by SNCC and the Medgar Evers–led Mississippi chapter of the NAACP challenged segregation throughout the state. Welty was scheduled to address the Southern Literary Festival, held that year at Millsaps, on April 18, 1963, and the festival's policy welcomed all races. Millsaps, in an effort to appease the Council and the Commission, continued to segregate its public events even though most of the college's professors opposed this practice. Millsaps officials anticipated a problem if the Commission or the Council learned that seating at the festival was on a first-come, first-serve basis. Welty insisted that her lecture remain open to all, and her talk attracted an interracial audience, including Tougaloo professor and Evers associate John Salter and a group of his students, who had been turned away from another event at Millsaps two weeks earlier.[22]

In light of the sensibility Welty demonstrated by giving these lectures, and given the "widespread advance publicity" of Evers's appearance on television, she almost certainly watched his talk on May 20.[23] Evers spoke as a lifelong native of Mississippi, someone who knew intimately the place he was struggling to change, and his dignified on-air presence suggested that Mississippi was taking steps towards achieving the model of an integrated society sought by Tougaloo. Evers's speech received even greater media coverage after it aired, and Welty certainly discussed it, perhaps with her dear friend Charlotte Capers, then director of the Mississippi Department of Archives and History, who once invited Welty to review Richard Wright's *Black Boy* for the *Journal of Mississippi History*.[24] In any event, Welty certainly thought carefully about the possible consequences of Evers's televised appearance, as evidenced by "Where Is the Voice Coming From?"

After making his speech on WBLT, "Evers . . . entered a new, ultimately fatal zone of notoriety." Most people in the state knew Evers's name, but he was not as instantaneously recognizable as James Meredith, who had integrated the University of Mississippi the previous year, as indicated by the fact that of the "twenty-nine viewers who called [WLBT] to complain, only one seemed to know who Evers was; eight indignantly demanded the impertinent black man's name."[25] In the aftermath of the speech, segregationist Mississippians moved quickly to reassert their dominance, savagely beating John Salter and his Tougaloo students when they attempted a sit-in eight days after the broadcast. Unfortunately for the defenders of the Lost Cause, network television captured the attempted sit-in and the resultant beatings, as well as the utter lack of a response by Jackson police officers present on the scene, leading to an outcry that Jackson's business class found alarming.[26] Two weeks after the aborted sit-in, Medgar Evers was shot in the back while coming home from a long day at work, an act of such spectacularly poor timing that segregationist Governor Ross Barnett, segregationist Mayor Thompson, and the segregationist Jackson *Clarion-Ledger* all issued condemnations of his murder and posted cash rewards for information leading to the capture of his assassin.[27]

Welty composed "Where Is the Voice Coming From?" after learning of Evers's death, revising the story over the next few days before sending it to her agent, Diarmuid Russell, in New York. Russell sold the story to *The New Yorker*, and because Welty worked so surely and so quickly, her text arrived in New York before Jackson officers made an arrest in the case.[28] Welty would later report that she chose to tell the story as a first-person monologue because she had "lived all my life where it happened," and could create an assassin whose inner life and violent deeds exemplified the fatal logic espoused by Councils and the Commission without descending into caricature.[29] Welty adhered as closely as possible to the reported facts of the Evers case, later altering a few details over the phone, at the request of William Maxwell, fiction editor at *The New Yorker*, so as not to prejudice the trial of a recently apprehended suspect. Welty's final revision, though not of her own choosing, allowed her to add allusions to the story that further undermined southern exceptionalism.

Welty changed the name of the city where the assassination took place from Jackson to Thermopylae, the valley where Spartan forces defended the Greek city-states against an invading Persian army. Though vastly outnumbered, the Spartans, led by Leonidas, held the mountain pass at Thermopylae for days, frustrating the Persian despot Xerxes. Indeed, the Spartans were undone not by their lack of numbers but by treachery, and they regrouped a decade later and routed the Persian army. By renaming her native city Thermopylae, Welty positions Jackson as the crucial pass in the fight for civil rights, valorizing the resolve of civil rights leaders like Evers who remain at their posts though betrayed and facing the threat of death. This construction, which equates segregationist Mississippians with pagan Persians, reverses southerners' central myth of themselves as the noble descendents of an innocent and persecuted Christian people. Indeed, Evers seems the closest parallel to Leonidas, who placed fealty to the Athenian rule of law above his own desires and Spartan customs, in sharp contrast to the coerced and conscripted Persian forces who served Xerxes out of fear of death.[30]

Welty also changed Medgar Evers's name to Roland Summers, and this alteration serves to further challenge southern exceptionalism. Roland was a mythic warrior, martyred in service to King Charlemagne during Charlemagne's quest to rid Spain of the Moors who controlled that nation, and his death, like that of Leonidas, occurs because of treachery on the part of those ostensibly allied to his cause.[31] Surrounded by his enemies, Roland acquits himself with such valor that when Charlemagne learns of how nobly Roland died he renews his campaign against Spain's conquerors. Instead of dooming the movement, Roland's death merely delays the inevitable return of civilized Christian righteousness.[32] By conflating Evers with Roland, Welty suggests that just as Roland's king avenged him and achieved victory in Spain, so will Evers's ally Martin Luther King avenge Evers and ensure that the change he worked towards becomes reality.[33] The abrogation of the social contract that cost Evers his life, as with the betrayals of Roland and Leonidas, prepares the way for a more thoroughgoing triumph. These allusions demonstrate Welty's rejection of the rhetoric of the Lost Cause, yet she evokes the killer's voice so perfectly in "Where Is the Voice Coming From?" that it is easy to overlook the references that signaled her authorial intent.

Welty's speaker constantly blends the past and present tenses in the monologue, a shifting discourse that positions his audience as sympathetic companions listening to an acquaintance unburden himself about his recent deeds. The speaker's presumption of intimacy forces the reader to identify with the mix of nativist pride and anger roiling below the monologue's surface, as well as his anxiety at the relationship between the civil rights movement and television. The speaker begins by recounting how he told his wife to "reach and turn [the television] off. You don't have to set and look at a black nigger face no longer than you want to . . . It's still a free country."[34] This comment reminds both the speaker and his spouse that whites still possess the power in southern society, and he realizes that "I could find right exactly where . . . that nigger's living that's asking for equal time. And without a bit of trouble to me" (603). Notice the slippage here between the phrase equal time and the concept of equality. Roland has already achieved equal time simply by appearing on rigidly controlled southern television, time he uses to demand full equality for all Blacks, a distinction the speaker cannot bring himself to understand. Instead, the speaker resolves to trump Roland's televisual equality with an act of violence that demonstrates his superiority.

The speaker's claim that he could easily find Roland suggests familiarity with the Black community, and indicates the kind of society he wishes to preserve. He reveals, in a curious circumlocution, that although he knows how to locate the civil rights leader, "I ain't saying it might not be because that's pretty close to where I live" (603). In other words, the speaker knows how to find Roland not because the speaker lives in proximity to Black people, but because the Black section of town is "where you all go for the thing you want when you want it the most. Ain't that right?" (603) In this indirect fashion, the speaker admits that his knowledge of the Black community derives from his prurient desires, because like many segregationist white men, he heads to the Black side of town when he wants extramarital sex so badly that he is willing to pay for it, or rape for it. The speaker's rhetorical question ("Ain't that right?") demonstrates his expectation that his listeners understand, participate in, and approve of this arrangement, suggesting that the speaker murders less to protect a cherished way of life than to maintain a society where Black men lack a political voice and Black women's bodies remain available for illicit white pleasure.

While describing the route he took to Roland's neighborhood, the speaker notes appallingly "his street's been paved" (603). Based on the speaker's use of the past tense here, there are two possible reasons for his outrage: either the road wasn't paved a few years ago, and has been since demonstrations started, or the Black community chose to pave this road despite the continued indifference of the city. Either way, the paved road suggests the Black community's increased political efficacy, evoking resentment and economic insecurity from the speaker.[35] As the speaker arrives at Roland's vacant driveway, the civil rights leader is away, "out planning still some other ways to do what we tell 'em they can't" (603). In the mind of the killer, the paved driveway with its absent car symbolizes the gains made in the face of white intransigence by the Black community in their continuing efforts to defeat Jim Crow. In contrast to Roland, the speaker must borrow his transportation from a relative, linking the possession of a car and a paved drive in the speaker's mind as an indication of Roland's upward mobility, his material superiority to southern working-class whites.

Despite the late hour, the speaker "didn't come expecting not to wait" for his opportunity, and settles in behind a tree so that he won't be seen when his victim returns from his work (603). As the killer describes waiting for Roland, he insists that he does not intend to murder Roland for financial gain or to curry favor with local politicians, he "ain't ask no Governor Barnett to give me one thing" and expects no reward unless the governor "wants to give me a pat on the back for the trouble" (604).[36] Instead, the speaker contends that the assassination is for his "own pure-D satisfaction," reinforcing the link between white pleasure and the maintenance of white authority over the lives of Black people established with his earlier comments about sex. For southern whites the potential loss of this control, symbolized by Roland's appearance on television, the irregular hours he keeps, the paved drive and roadway, even the "new white car" that the civil rights leader is driving when he finally arrives, must be averted at all costs (604).

As if to foreground the maintenance of pleasure that is at the heart of the assassination, the speaker uses words more appropriate for a clandestine meeting with a lover to recall his feelings upon seeing his victim: "I knowed it [was him] when he cut off the car lights and put his foot out and I knowed him standing dark against the light. I knowed him then like I know me now. I knowed him even by his still, listening back" (604). A moment later the speaker recalls being certain that "[h]e had to be the one.

He stood right still and waited against the light. . . . He's the one" (604). The sexual undertone that tinges the speaker's apprehension of Roland highlights both his need to protect an innocent white masculine identity and his need to maintain intimate control over the Black community.

At the moment the speaker penetrates the body of his masculine counterpart, his narrative devolves into impossible assertions of innocence. The speaker now claims he has "[n]ever seen him before, never seen him since, never seen anything of his black face but his picture, never seen his face *alive*, any time at all, or anywheres, and didn't want to, need to, never hope to see that face and never will" (604, my emphasis). Embedded amid the serial contradictions of this statement is a Derridian desire on the part of the speaker to deny the power of the televisual image by privileging actual physical presence.[37] The speaker's reasoning here suggests that segregationist southerners can maintain their innocence by ignoring the moral appeals contained in the televised coverage of the civil rights movement because television presents mere images and not living men. This posture allows the speaker to ignore the moral obligation of Medgar Evers's speech, as well as the international outrage that televised images of noble Black suffering evoked outside the South. By the logic of the speaker, the televised images convey an inauthentic humanity and thus generate a false moral appeal, one that southerners are free to ignore.

Having felled his man with one shot "there on his paved driveway," the speaker explains his rationale for murder to his victim: "Roland? There was one way left, for me to be ahead of you and stay ahead of you, by Dad, and I just taken it. Now I'm alive and you ain't. We ain't never now, never going to be equals and you know why? One of us is dead. What about that, Roland? . . . Well, *you* seen to it, didn't *you* . . ."(604, my emphasis). This chilling declaration again reveals the desire to preserve a society that places the lowliest white southerners above any and all Black people as the true motivation behind massive resistance to civil rights. While disingenuous politicians might attempt to justify the maintenance of segregation through legalistic arguments about states' rights or sentimental appeals to the Lost Cause, in the end all such assertions disguise a white desire to "stay ahead." In the speaker's case, he recognizes that only white privilege grants him superiority over his victim, yet even then he seeks to maintain his innocence by displacing his capacity for violence onto Roland. "[Y]ou seen to it" suggests that Roland forced his hand by demanding equality and is thus culpable for his own murder, revealing a certain powerlessness in the very assertion of power the speaker hopes will protect his superiority.

The assassin speaks with Roland only when the civil rights leader can no longer contest his claims as he did the mayor's, a reminder that segregationist logic fails to withstand scrutiny and must continually deflect attention via serial acts of aggression defending the inalienable rights promised by an illegitimate system.

The assassin watches as Roland's wife comes to the porch to find her husband murdered. He then drops his rifle and hurries away from the scene of the crime, but not before noticing the fine condition of Roland's lawn and that his wife left several lights on to greet her husband: "That nigger wife of his, she wanted nice grass! I bet *my wife* would hate to *pay* her water bill. And for burning her electricity" (605, my emphasis). This observation indicates that the assassin's wife is the breadwinner in his household, a reversal the speaker must find galling. Later, he will complain that his wife "didn't even leave a light burning [for me] when [she] went to bed" spoiling his triumphant return by reminding him of his failure as a wage earner (605). The assassin's inability to achieve a prosperous lifestyle, one seemingly attainable for everyone born free, white, and male in the post–World War II United States, contributes to his need to preserve his standing in the racial hierarchy by bloodshed. Roland's speech interrupted the fetishized presentation of middle-class living standards on *The Price Is Right*, and the civil rights leader's attainment of this standard of living only heightens the assassin's economic insecurity.

The speaker informs his wife of his deeds the next morning, and her first question is "Didn't the skeeters bite you?" (605) The wife then begins to undermine the assassin's narrative, reminding him that the local newspaper had called for someone to "get some of these agitators out of Thermopylae. Didn't the fella keep drumming it in, what a good idea? The one that writes a column ever' day?", to which the assassin, mortified at this challenge to his accomplishment, grumbles, "[f]ind *some* way I don't get the credit" (605). She then asks, with the persistence of a wife, "Don't you ever skim the paper?" (605) This exchange, in which the speaker's wife seems not in the least bit discomforted to learn that her husband murdered a man the previous night, refutes any idealized sentiment that Welty's audience might have had about the tender sensibilities of southern belles, whose precarious psychosexual status was an oft-cited justification for segregation. The speaker corrects his wife, replying that he did not act because a columnist inspired him, or out of civic duty "to Thermopylae. Didn't do it for you. Hell, any more'n I'd do something or other for them Kennedys!" (605) By grouping his wife with the meddling Kennedy brothers, who together were responsible for James Meredith's presence at Ole Miss, the speaker equates her with other irksome know-it-alls who seek to impose their own interpretations on the thoughts and actions of white men defending southern culture. The wife's comments also remind the reader that the editorial positions of local and national media towards the civil rights movement were wildly divergent in 1963.

Southern newspapers tended to fashion a reality that reflected the values of the local community, and were far more censorious than television broadcasts, with significant exceptions such as Hodding Carter's *Delta Democrat Times*. If newspaper consumption enables a disparate society to fashion an image of itself as a nation, then southern papers during the civil rights movement helped their readers ignore the abuses committed by a segregated society by assigning blame for the violation on civil rights workers or the federal government.[38] So, while the assassin may have been genuinely ignorant about the local columnist who advocated violence against civil rights agitators, he participates in a regional narrative that will excuse, if not valorize, his action, one that is constantly at odds with the national narrative conveyed on television. His wife reminds him of this divergence by noting that Roland's funeral will "get him right back on TV" and she then chides him for not keeping up with current events. "Didn't you hear the news? The N. double A. C. P. is fixing to send somebody to Thermopylae. Why couldn't you have waited? You might could have got you somebody better" (605). The speaker, in an aside to his audience, minimizes any regrets he might have about sharing with his wife by mockingly noting, "I reckon you have to tell *somebody*" (605). Still, even as she approves of the killing, his wife's inability to validate the speaker's self-conception as a heroic individual rather than a pawn of a segregationist society necessitates an account of his deeds before a more sympathetic audience.

The speaker's recollections take a turn when he tells his wife that he left the gun near the scene of the crime. When she expresses dismay at losing their "protection," he indicts the environment for his mistake, complaining "of ever'thing in the world being just that hot to the touch! The keys to the truck, the doorknob, the bedsheet, ever'thing, it's all like a stove lid. There just ain't much going that's worth holding on to it no more" (606). This statement suggests, for the first time in the speaker's presentation of events, some level of discomfort with his action, as does his wife's exclamation that "it's so hot that even if you get to sleep you wake up feeling like you cried all night!" (606). The couple seems to be preparing for the possibility that the speaker may be apprehended for murdering Roland. In order to shift the mood, the speaker's wife tells him "one more joke before time to get up," that President Kennedy's daughter, Caroline, "can't wait to grow up big" and marry James Meredith.[39] The speaker's wife heard this joke where she works, "One rich bitch to another one, to make her cackle" (606). The assassin, ignoring his wife's attempt at levity and musing on the local newspaper's call for violence, responds, "At least I kept some dern teen-ager from North Thermopylae getting there and doing it first . . . Driving his own car" (606). The killer, who earlier attributed his deed to Roland's impertinence, now transforms the murder into an act of paternal protection meant to preserve the innocence of a younger generation.

Despite his earlier claims of selflessness, the media coverage of the assassination perturbs the speaker. The media "don't know but half of it," they "know who Roland Summers was without knowing who I am," and, as his wife predicted, his victim's face is again all over the news (606). Still, with a five-hundred-dollar reward posted for his arrest, the assassin takes morbid pleasure in knowing that he "is worth a good deal more right now than Roland is" (606). The heat remains as oppressive as it was the previous night, suggesting that the murder provides little relief for the assassin, who remains poor and unknown, who "ain't ever had [a picture] made. Not ever!" (606) When the assassin learns that the local media is speculating that the NAACP "killed Roland Summers . . . at just the right hour and minute to get the whites in trouble" he sighs, "You can't win" (606). Despite his repeated assertions that he killed Roland for his own satisfaction, the speaker's inability to take credit for his action frustrates him, necessitating his anonymous narrative.

When the killer goes into town, he finds a "thousand cops crowding ever'where you go, half of 'em too young to start shaving" (606–607). The narrator finds the presence of these peace officers worse than either the stifling heat or the lack of acclaim for his deed because these "new babyface cops" and their superiors symbolize an expansion of the local bureaucracy which has failed to benefit him. The police presence also represents a newfound inability to effectively police—which is to say terrorize and intimidate—the Black community (607). National television, with its unfortunate habit of broadcasting southern abuses across the world, has eroded southern law enforcement's efficacy. In addition to monitoring the Black community, the police now must attempt to constrain the white community from pursuing a program of extralegal violence in support of segregation. The speaker, in yet another attempt to deny culpability, suggests here that law enforcement's newfound inability to suppress the social protests of the Black community forced him to act.

By rejecting the media-enforced restraint that was changing race relations in the South, the assassin cautions those who expect southerners to adjust eventually to the new social order by asserting that "[i]t don't get you nowhere to take nothing from nobody unless you make sure it's for keeps, for good and all, for ever and amen" (607). This statement, which also serves as an exhortation to other white segregationists, functions as a corollary to the assassin's earlier claim that Roland provoked him by demanding equality, and insists white southerners be as committed to preserving segregation as Blacks are to ending it despite the specter of unfavorable press. Although civil rights workers currently hold the moral high ground due to their commitment to nonviolence, the speaker expects this to shift once Blacks reveal their true nature and "bring out them switchblade knives, like [in] Harlem and Chicago. Watch TV long enough and you'll see it all to happen on Deacon Street in Thermopylae. . . . it's *in* 'em" (607). The speaker pronounces himself "ready . . . for that funeral" an indication that he eagerly awaits an opportunity to commit more violence in defense of his society (607).

Having offered these insights on the moral imperatives of power, the speaker broadens his address, advising any members of his audience who sympathize with the Warren court, King, or Kennedy to "go careful. Ain't it about time us taxpayers starts to calling the moves? Starts to telling the teachers *and* the preachers *and* the judges of our so-called courts how far they can go? Even the President so far, he can't walk in my house without being invited, like he's my daddy, just to say whoa. Not yet!" (607) With this elaborate articulation of white male privilege, which anticipates Nixon's evocation of a silent majority, the speaker reminds the nation that change in the South can be prevented by an intransigent few prepared to protect white privilege by resisting federal authority despite unfavorable media coverage, the likelihood of "someone better" appearing to avenge Roland/Evers, and the inexorable advance of the civil rights movement since *Brown*. The speaker hopes his murder will raise the stakes, preventing the South from reaching an accord with the nation because "people are dead" (607). In light of this, the prospect of being arrested, which earlier caused him some distress, no longer bothers him, for a trial will further polarize the community and "the electric chair . . . is [just] something hotter than yesterday and today put together" (607). And, even if the speaker is wrong about any of this, even if Mississippi has changed so much that its citizens will "railroad" him at trial, they cannot negate his achievement, for "I seen him fall. I was evermore the one" (607). And in Mississippi in 1963, this knowledge can sustain him unto death.

Thanks to her work in the WPA during the Depression, Welty understood that poverty and fear of lost status made segregation palatable in the minds of many working-class southerners, and she documents the danger of this kind of thinking in her story, eloquently presenting the various class issues that are a source of the speaker's anger: his poor education and resultant lack of upward mobility, his resentment towards the nation's political elite, his jealously at the financial benefits bestowed on Mississippi's civil servants, and his anonymity in the emerging media age. In this context violence serves as a temporary balm that grants the speaker the illusion of control, even as he remains a loser in the postwar economy. "Where Is the Voice Coming From?" demonstrates just how fundamentally an important segment of the South remains essentially unchanged from its antebellum past, suggesting the need for the US government to take a more active role enforcing the rule of law in the South, but also identifying the need for a war on poverty that might provide men like the speaker a better standard of living, thereby integrating them into society.

"Where Is the Voice Coming From?" seems a daring act of composition for Welty, particularly given the repression that was then common, but despite the audaciousness of the story she minimized the odds of a reprisal from the Councils or the Commission by placing it in *The New Yorker*. In fact, when a reporter from New York asked her if "anybody burned a cross" in her yard because of her story, Welty's reply that the "people who burn crosses on lawns don't read me in *The New Yorker*. Really, don't people know the first thing about the South?" demonstrates how certain she was that this story would evade local notice.[40] Although Welty and Russell had a good relationship with William Maxwell, and *The New Yorker* generally paid better for short stories than other magazines, always a concern for Welty during this period, other venues with broader readerships would have eagerly published her story. Indeed, one can easily imagine the *New York Times Magazine*, the Atlanta *Journal-Constitution*, or Mississippi's own *Delta Democrat Times* publishing this short piece in the aftermath of the crime, but such a course of action would have alerted a broad section of the South to Welty's elaborate condemnation of Medgar Evers's assassination, and Welty was anxious to avoid such scrutiny, as much for her infirm mother's sake as for her own.[41]

Still, if Welty knew that neither the Klan, the Council, nor the Commission read *The New Yorker*, she feared for her well-being if she attempted to take a bigger role promoting interracial brotherhood in the South. Evers's assassination after appearing on local television surely played some role in her "late July, 1963 . . . deci[sion] at the last minute . . . not to be interviewed by Ralph Ellison on national television. She worried that a nationally televised appearance with [her] fellow writer . . . would create a good deal of white hostility in Mississippi, hostility that she feared would be deflected from daughter to mother . . . affect[ing] her ability to hire desperately needed care-givers for her mother."[42] Despite her progressive stance toward civil rights in her writing and lectures, Welty had to take care that she did not overstep her bounds by directly challenging the closed society, even though this television appearance might have led to increased lecturing income from colleges and universities outside the South. Indeed, by the end of that summer Welty contemplated moving to Santa Fe to escape the constant surveillance in her home state. Again, she portrayed this course of action as necessary more to protect her mother's well-being than her own; she no longer felt safe using the Yazoo City convalescent home when she was called away to lecture because that city was "reputed to be now the headquarters of the Ku Klux Klan."[43] Ultimately, Welty decided to remain in Jackson for the time being, with her brother Edward's health playing no small role in that decision.

The summer of 1964 served to make 1963 seem tame by comparison. By the time the summer was over the Klan and others would burn down more than forty Black churches in Mississippi, even as the Council continued its economic intimidation of property-owning Black and sympathetic white southerners and the Commission continued to lobby for states' rights and interposition. On June 21, 1964, Mississippi authored a civil rights tragedy that again demanded a response from Welty when three civil rights activists, white New Yorkers Michael Schwerner and Andrew Goodman and Black Mississippian James Chaney, disappeared in the small town of Philadelphia. The kidnapping and murder of the three men marked the first time since civil rights demonstrations began in 1955 that southerners defending the Lost Cause had killed prointegrationist whites, and the frantic forty-four day effort to locate their bodies allowed the national media to ruminate on the implications of the South's continued resistance to desegregation. Worse, while official Mississippians had roundly condemned the assassination of Evers and prodded the Jackson police into a credible investigation of the crime, there was considerably less understanding in Philadelphia, surrounding Neshoba County, and across the state.

The official position of local officials towards the disappearance of the men, including Mississippi's powerful Senator Eastland, was that the Council of Federated Organizations (COFO), an umbrella group funded in part by the National Council of Churches to coordinate the efforts of SNCC, the NAACP, the Congress of Racial Equality (CORE), and King's Southern Christian Leadership Conference (SCLC) in the state, had ordered them underground in order to attract attention to the Freedom Summer and raise funds while making Philadelphians and Mississippians in general look bad.[44] Ignoring this fantastic narrative, the FBI and the Department of Justice launched an intensive investigation, code-named Mississippi Burning, that unearthed a half dozen other corpses, all Black men sacrificed to preserve the southern way of life, before Schwerner, Chaney, and Goodman were finally discovered entombed at the base of an earthen dam. These other bodies provoked additional outrage, since it "was shocking . . . to anyone except black Mississippians that as soon as the authorities started dragging the rivers and swamps for the two white New Yorkers and their local colleague, they stumbled on other [Black] bodies."[45]

It was during this time, Welty reports, that she started "receiving middle-of-the-night, dead-of-night telephone calls" in which she was "harangued by strangers" from the North demanding to know why she wasn't actively promoting civil rights in Mississippi.[46] These callers, ignorant of the South, failed to appreciate the restrictions that Mississippi, with its strict disciplining of dissenting voices, increasingly placed upon progressive southerners like Welty. Consider Florence Mars, like Welty a free-thinking, college-educated, middle-aged bachelorette who had traveled to Europe and lived in metropolitan cities before returning to Mississippi.[47] *Witness in Philadelphia*, an autobiographical account of her tangential involvement in the Mississippi Burning case, describes the retribution Mars faced after providing background testimony to a federal grand jury regarding the presence of the Ku Klux Klan in Philadelphia and Neshoba County. In response to her testimony the Klan tormented her for eighteen months, organizing a boycott of the Neshoba County Stockyards, which Mars owned; forcing her from First Methodist Church, her place of worship; spreading rumors about her continued participation in "antiwhite" civil rights groups; and harassing her employees, friends, and associates.[48] Eventually tiring of the Klan's abuse, Mars sold her stake in the stockyards and her farm, but despite this was arrested for drunk driving, which, for a white woman in the South in 1965 was unprecedented.[49] Welty was well aware that, despite her fame, or because of it, she would face similar reprisals from the Klan and the local law enforcement if she took to the streets in a public display of her sentiments.

With the nation still in high dudgeon over the disappearance of the three civil rights workers, needing income and unable to make sufficient progress with her novel, Welty accepted a position as writer-in-residence at Millsaps College where she taught "a twice-a-week seminar on the art of fiction" to help pay the bills.[50] The fall semester at Millsaps began just three weeks after the FBI discovered the bodies of Schwerner, Chaney, and Goodman, and on Wednesday, December 2, 1964, near the conclusion of the semester, Welty delivered "a public lecture on 'The Southern Writer Today: An Interior Affair,'" the first draft of "Must the Novelist Crusade?" This essay serves as Welty's answer to the anonymous callers who demanded she publicly promote civil rights in the South.[51] Ironically, just two days after her talk at Millsaps, the FBI indicted nineteen people from Meridian and Philadelphia, Mississippi, in relation to the murders of Schwerner, Chaney, and Goodman, including the Neshoba County "sheriff, deputy sheriff, and [Philadelphia's] city policeman," returning Mississippi's summer of racial discontent to national attention.[52] That peace officers were implicated in the murders reinforced the national stereotype that the vast majority of southern whites were united in their efforts to maintain segregation at all costs, with a timorous minority unable or unwilling to challenge them. Welty's essay attempts to elaborate a writerly stance that avoided this Manichean view of the South by protecting individual southern innocence.[53]

Welty decided to publish her essay, placing it, with Russell's help, in the October 1965 *Atlantic Monthly*. "Must the Novelist Crusade?" demands careful explication because Welty advances a subtle argument, one that begins with a typically New Critical assertion of art's separateness from politics, but that ultimately asserts that fiction might better serve the polis than politicized writing since ethical discourse should induce a course of action that affirms the nation's democratic ideals. The essay opens with Welty chiding an unnamed critic for demanding that Faulkner be "reassessed because he was 'after all, only a white Mississippian,'" a stance that equates the Nobel Prize winner with the Klansmen who kidnapped white youths and burned Black churches.[54] Welty "feel[s] in these words and others like them the agonizing of our times. . . . They come of an honest and understandable zeal to allot every writer his chance to better the world"

(803). Welty admits that writers do have obligations *as* writers, but insists that politics are merely incidental to these goals, distinguishing the kind of symbolic action she took by lecturing at Tougaloo in 1958 and before an integrated group at Millsaps in 1963 from the act of writing itself. This is what Welty means when she identifies the writer's obligation to make "the proper use of words for the proper ends" (804), while insisting that the novelist and the editorial writer are on "opposite sides" of the writing spectrum, no matter how honest or necessary each appears (803).

The two prongs of Welty's argument seem contradictory, and perhaps if she had attained her education in the 1970s and '80s she might have possessed the tools to better balance these inconsistencies. Welty, of course, was educated in the late 1920s and '30s, when she was "wildly interested in the Fugitives . . . including Robert Penn Warren, Allen Tate, and John Crowe Ransom" and as a young writer eagerly received George Marion O'Donnell, a Southern Agrarian who would "regale [Welty and her friends] with anecdotes about all the great southern writers" he collaborated with.[55] Still, if the New Critics influenced Welty's understanding of the proper aim of writing, her own fiction, as well as Faulkner's, whom she champions in this essay, invites readings that exceed the limits of interpretation placed on fiction by the Southern Agrarians. Rather than resisting these excessive readings, Welty welcomes them, trusting that literature works a deeper and more permanent change on human sensibility than mere moralizing. Peggy Whitman Prenshaw asserts that Welty disdains conventional politics, "linked as it was in her mind with demagogic leaders and racism."[56] Rather than base her "hopes for individual rights or social justice upon a linking of the personal and the political . . . she makes a case for the supreme efficacy of the separate, personal sphere as the venue where understanding of the Other takes place . . . and where one's political beliefs may therefore take humane shape."[57] This cautious valorization of personal understanding was difficult to maintain in the face of racial violence that called for immediate action, but Welty was convinced that the tension in Mississippi would only abate when a plurality of whites attained a humane understanding of the Black Other, one that literature could help produce. This essay seems to endorse the democratic goals of the emancipationist tradition while also preserving southern innocence, an indication of the tightrope that Welty was attempting to negotiate.

Welty insists "evidence as to whether any writer, alive or dead, can be believed is always on hand in . . . any page of his work. The color of his skin would modify it just about as much as would the binding of the book."

This assertion should not be understood as a conservative attempt to viti-
ate the importance of race upon experience, but rather an assertion that
if Faulkner were Black or Richard Wright white it would not lend additional tragedy to Joe Christmas or Bigger Thomas.[58] "Integrity," she claims,
"stands outside time" (803); a classic New Critical stance that collapses
two distinct types of integrity, the literary and the social. Welty elevates
literary integrity over social integrity because integration into one's society means joining the crowd, and "nothing was ever learned in a crowd,
from a crowd, or by addressing or trying to please a crowd." This does not
apply to common utterances, but to political speech, for "the voice that
seeks to do other than communicate when it makes a noise has something
brutal about it . . . no longer using words as words but as something to
brandish . . . threaten, brag or condemn" (809). For Welty, a writer overly
concerned with persuasion compromises his "working vision," the "living
principle on which [a plot] hangs together and gradually earns its shape"
(807) to appeal instead to the pieties of the day, writing to please his audience rather than explore the contours of a situation.

Welty rejects these self-conscious attempts at instructing an audience, which is the raison d'être of a crusading writer, for "to cater is not
to love and not to serve well either" (812). A novelist who shapes a text to
convert his audience attempts to achieve a "personal vision [that] can be
made to order, [but] then we should lose, writer and reader alike, our own
gift for perceiving, seeing through the fabric of everyday to what to each
pair of eyes on earth is a unique thing" (807). Persuasive speech, for Welty,
must cater to the crowd's preconceptions in order to be effective, and thus
ill-serves its constituents. I do not think that Welty intends to denigrate
the measured tones of Medgar Evers or Martin Luther King, who took
pains to ground their speech in love and redemption, but to the political
voice employed by demagogic leaders in Mississippi and elsewhere, who
exhorted their supports to act immorally. Welty claims that most political speech, good intentioned or ill, needs to silence or invalidate differing
perspectives, but that the novel escapes this temptation because it strives
to create "the possibility of a shared act of the imagination between its
writer and reader" (804). Welty does not mean to suggest that fictions
must therefore be apolitical and unethical, for "morality as shown through
human relationships is the whole heart of fiction" and the consumption
of this morality broadens one's ethical universe, offering a reader new
perspectives and insights into contemporary problems without necessarily addressing those problems directly (804). Welty transforms the New

Critical assumption about the estrangement of the artist from the values of society into the means for achieving genuine communal understanding.

Pandering to an audience with political speech based upon a cynical evaluation of what's permissible, Welty continues, also leaves little room for growth by speaker or crowd. The developing novelist best serves his audience not by crusading, but by "assum[ing] at the start an enlightenment in his reader equal to his own, for they are hopefully on the point of taking off together from that base into the rather different world of the imagination" (808). The assumption of enlightenment, the expectation of common ground, permits the writer to embrace ambiguity, which "allow[s] his reader to see and hear something for himself" (805) by forcing the reader to rethink his assumptions in order to fully participate in the life of the novel. When, struggling with the internal logic of the text, "a novel of power reveals" to a reader "what we are" it makes a genuinely new perspective possible (808). Only a sincere literary effort can accomplish this revelation, a literary text that "is very seldom neat, is given to sprawling and escaping from bounds, is capable of contradicting itself, and is not impervious to humor" (806), thereby letting "truth . . . in all its great weight and angelic lightness [be] accepted as home truth" by a reader (808). Appeals to the shared act of the imagination, Welty asserts, do not retreat from the unpleasantness of the present but permit the possibility of transcending it through a recognition of each member of a community's enduring humanity.

Welty would not have produced "Where Is the Voice Coming From?" or "The Demonstrators" if she disapproved of topical stories, but she reminds those who demand crusading texts that "[i]f human beings are to be comprehended as real, then they have to be treated as real, with minds, hearts, memories, habits, hopes, with passions and capacities like ours" even if they are racist assassins (807). Welty rejects writing that flattens, that, in its rush to judgment, fails to "show us how to face our feeling and face our actions and have new inkling about what they mean" (810). Invective in the place of insight seems useless to Welty, for "[t]o deplore a thing as hideous as the murder of the three civil rights workers demands the quiet in which to absorb it. Enormities can be lessened, cheapened, just as good and delicate things can be. We can and will cheapen all feeling by... parading in it" (809). While Welty appreciated the commitment of the three civil rights workers to the democratic ideals of the nation, she would not sacrifice a full understanding of southern whites in an attempt to valorize them. Only through an understanding of the full humanity brought to

bear in a confrontation between southern Blacks, white civil rights workers, and southern whites is it possible to create a society that might transcend the violence and hatred of the present.

While this is true, it also permits the maintenance of southern innocence. Welty acknowledges that "[w]e in the South are a hated people
these days; we were hated first for actual and particular reasons, and now
we may be hated still more in some vast unparticularized way. . . . Our
people hate back" (811). Still, if southern writers devoted themselves to
repudiating all the outrages committed in the South since 1954, let alone
1800, there would scarcely be any time for anything else, and despite their
intentions these texts would fail to transform those capable of committing
such deeds, while permitting others a false sense of moral superiority. For
Welty the only way out of this double bind was to write with love, as her
exemplar Faulkner had done, for "to enter into the minds and hearts of
our own people, *all of them*, to comprehend them (us) and then to make
characters and plots in stories that in honesty and with honesty reveal
them (ourselves) to us, in whatever situation we live through in our own
times: this is the continuing job [of the novelist]. To write honestly and
with all our powers is the least we can do, and the most" (813, emphasis
added). This sensibility, this need to comprehend even violent racists and
apologists, allowed Welty to produce "Where Is the Voice Coming From?"
and "The Demonstrators," stories that allude to contemporary events
without propagandizing. Welty believed that fiction, if properly received,
might operate obliquely on the heart and soul of its reader, and is therefore
more likely than direct political appeals to produce an understanding that
makes a genuine change in sensibility possible.

Contemporary critics, of course, understand that readers often resist
texts, engaging in misreadings that can come to shape the reception of a
text or even an individual. This resistance to the shared act of the imagination—particularly a shared act that challenges one's self-conception—was
common in the South. Welty would acknowledge in 1981 that when she
appealed to communal acts of the imagination twenty-five years earlier
she was "thinking of the people whose hearts were in the right place, but
that wasn't enough. It took more learning. I think we've been through an
experience which was more profound than we'd guessed; both black and
white. . . . Now, seeing how much more there was to communication than
the wish, and the desire, and the heart, I feel I have more to learn now
than I had to learn then."[59] Welty came to realize that her earlier claim that
the "novel itself always affirms. . . . and it would waste its time if it told us

what we ought to be like, since we already know that, don't we?" granted intractable southerners far too much credit (808). Unlike Welty's ideal readers, many people in the South neither questioned nor cared about the subjugated status of Black people, and would have been perfectly happy had the changes that occurred in the South during the 1960s been delayed a century in the interest of keeping the peace, and their status.

Contemporary scholars might disagree with many of the claims that Welty makes in "Must the Novelist Crusade?"[60] It remains unclear, for example, why fiction cannot both "beat the drum" for social change, and depict "the private place" where "life is lived," something that *Huckleberry Finn* seems to accomplish (809). Welty objects to bad writing, which she collapses into politically engaged writing by assuming that crusader-novelists cannot create characters with fully formed interior lives, but if this is so it is the fault of the writer and not the topic. Also, given that Black literary culture since Frederick Douglass has attempted to demonstrate both Black people's humanity and their ability to achieve in the field of culture, skin color plays an important role in whether an author might be believed if the author is Black. To claim otherwise is extremely naïve, especially after Mississippi whites asserted their collective innocence, in the face of global disbelief, by claiming that the three missing civil rights workers were in hiding. Further, questions that strike at a writer's attempts to remain faithful to the values of his community while composing fiction often produce a better understanding of that society's political values, as revisionist scholarship of Faulkner and Conrad (among others) has demonstrated. And, as Welty archly remarked in the *Times Literary Supplement* in 1954, "[I]t is also true that nobody is buying books in [small-town Mississippi] or generally in the South," a fact that suggests that fiction has little, if any, role in producing shifts in political consciousness in that region of the country.[61] Ironically, Welty is correct in maintaining that great literary texts remain integral to an understanding of ourselves as political and social beings, but fails to comprehend how these texts retain this integrity as cultural and critical perspectives change. Still, as Welty noted when describing a forthcoming collection of short stories about Mississippi in the 1960s which she was unable to finish before her death, "[T]ime is an important ingredient in understanding a situation."[62]

Welty again found herself speaking at the Southern Literary Festival in April of 1965, a tribute to Faulkner held in his hometown of Oxford at Ole Miss. Despite there having been an integrated audience in Jackson two years prior, in Oxford "a mob . . . harassed the Tougaloo College delegation

that had hoped to participate in the festival," an indication that even literary events were vulnerable to pressures from segregationists.[63] As a result
of the harassment, only whites attended that year's festival, but Welty and
other distinguished guests like Robert Penn Warren decided to remain
at the festival to promote the interracial perspective of Faulkner's fiction
rather than leaving in solidarity.[64] Meanwhile, the Mississippi Burning
trial was proceeding in fits and starts, with local officials dismissing the
indictments against the men involved on December 10, 1964, and again on
February 24, 1965. Welty began work on "The Demonstrators" in the summer of 1965, while the eyes of the nation focused on the civil rights drama
unfolding in Selma, Alabama. At this time the men involved in the deaths
of Schwerner, Chaney, and Goodman had not seen trial and were being
feted throughout the state. Despite the cessation of the summer project
that brought white students into the South in 1964, SNCC, SCLC, CORE,
and the newly formed Mississippi Freedom Democratic Party continued
to challenge segregation vigorously throughout the state in 1965, with pre-
dictable results.

     Welty drafted "The Demonstrators," the last short story she published
in her life, over the summer and fall of 1965; it got to "Russell in November
1965 and it was taken by *The New Yorker* within a few weeks" although it
"was published . . . almost a year later" in October 1966.[65] The story is set
in the fictional town of Holden, in the western section of the state near the
Mississippi Delta, an area long targeted by civil rights workers due to its
large Black population. Despite the title of the story and its contemporary
setting in a region singled out by SNCC and other groups, Welty adheres
to the strictures she detailed in "Must the Novelist Crusade?" and focuses
her tale around a white male protagonist, in this case a disaffected country
doctor named Dr. Richard Strickland. Like "Where Is the Voice Coming
From?" this story traces its main character through important events in
his life, with Welty collapsing his personal history by presenting many of
the details of his life via flashback. Welty employs a third-person limited
narrator, which grants her readers a thorough understanding of her protagonist, Dr. Richard Strickland, and his society by granting some access
to his thoughts.[66]

     "The Demonstrators" depicts Dr. Strickland, the only physician in the
town of Holden, as he calls upon his patients one fall evening. Strickland,
we learn, followed in his father's footsteps by becoming the town doctor,
and, like his father, sees fit to practice on Blacks and whites alike. Strickland's wife, Irene, left him that summer, months after their paraplegic

daughter, Sylvia, the couple's only child, "died at age thirteen [having] never sat up or spoken" (616). Sylvia's "death from pneumonia last Christmas" causes Irene to reevaluate her life, and she recognizes that she can no longer abide the hypocrisies that Holden demands of her husband, a realization that she articulates as the couple entertain a white civil rights worker named Philip. Strickland scolds Philip for his organization's exaggeration of an episode "in the next county. . . . in June" (617). Despite Philip's justification that "they won't know the difference [in the North] where the paper is read," Strickland refuses to accept "putting a false front on things . . . even for a good cause." After Strickland makes this statement, his wife reminds him that he "won't tell Herman Fairbrothers [the mayor of Holden] what's the matter with him" before "jump[ing] up from the table," confronting Strickland with his complicity in the town's self-deception (617). Irene's readiness to reveal an untold truth in the presence of a stranger indicates her unwillingness to perpetuate the town's fictions.

Irene's disavowal exposes Strickland's complicity with the town's narrative by invalidating his claims to impartial truthfulness, and the community offers a censure of its own. Someone scatters "broken glass . . . the length and width of [Strickland's] driveway" a warning that indicates the community's awareness that he hosted a civil rights worker in his home, an act that punctures Strickland's sense of well-being as well as his tires. Despite years of reprisals in Mississippi against any and all who interacted in the most innocuous fashion with civil rights workers, Strickland imagined that his family's status in the town would permit a visit with Philip. Because of this, he "hadn't seen in time what it wouldn't have occurred to him to look for." Irene "suddenly brok[e] into laughter" at this turn of events, another indication of her disinclination to overlook the injustices in the town (617). If Irene's laughter indicates her hostility toward her husband and his social position, then the broken glass reminds Strickland that everyone must conform to the xenophobic restrictions demanded by southern reactionaries, especially country doctors who indiscriminately practice medicine in the Delta.

Welty subverts Irene's moral authority by suggesting that her new-found inability to abide Strickland and Holden signals a retreat into childhood following the loss of her daughter. Strickland understood intellectually that his daughter's paralysis would probably not improve and he had "mourned her all her life" while she was living, but "Irene had done more; she had dedicated her life to Sylvia, sparing herself nothing, tending her, lifting her, feeding her, everything (616–617). Irene invested emotionally in a lost cause, failing to admit to herself that eventually, in spite of her devotion, her child would weaken and die, which links her to southerners just as unwilling to abandon the society that has become their Lost Cause. Without Sylvia as a locus for her energies, Irene gives her "devotion to something else that could not be helped . . . shun[ning] all the terrible reminders, and turn[ing] not to a human being but to an idea." Welty never specifies what this idea is, but given her comment about Strickland's prevarication to Mayor Fairbrothers and how much her self-deception about Sylvia's condition cost her, one might surmise that Irene has found a newfound appreciation for the unvarnished truth.

Strickland seems paralyzed by Irene's disapproval and the town's reprisal against his seemingly innocuous dinner with Philip. In an effort to acknowledge his wife's grief, Strickland offers to leave town, but Irene caustically reminds him that he "wouldn't leave Holden without its Dr. Strickland. . . . to save [his] soul," a statement he is unable or unwilling to challenge (617). Irene recognizes that carrying on the family tradition ties Strickland to Holden, even as he becomes increasingly dissatisfied with his hometown. In any case, Strickland eventually "agreed that she . . . withdraw herself for as long as she liked," an abandonment that only intensifies Strickland's sense of loss and bewilderment without impelling him to any decisive action. Irene retreats back to her childhood home, where people from her earlier life "were all giving parties for her," but Irene's devotion to the truth does not produce understanding or change; her celebrations fail to address the racial problems in the town or Strickland's passive equanimity that fails to address Holden's racial problems (617). Strickland's interracial practice dissatisfies his wife and his community while leaving him with little recourse.

Strickland remains estranged from his community after he separates from his wife. He returns to his office at "eleven o'clock that Saturday night," after attending to an elderly patient he inherited from his father (608). Miss Marcia Pope, Strickland's patient, is a retired educator who has recurring seizures and yet refuses to take the medicine that might alleviate her condition. Strickland recalls that, despite her poor health, Miss Pope "could amuse herself by giving out great wads of Shakespeare and 'Arma virumque cano' or the like" (608). This fondness for classical literature is unremarkable, given that Pope once taught "Latin, civics, and English" to "three generations of Holden, Mississippi" at the local high school (608), but "Welty's reference here to the opening line of Virgil's *Aeneid* invites multiple interpretations." The quote, which can be translated "'I sing of warfare and a man at war' might refer to the pervasive racism in the Jim Crow era, to the civil rights movement's war against segregation and racial injustice, [and] to the white South's feelings of being embattled by the movement."[67] Welty's allusion to the literature of antiquity here also recalls her evocation of Thermopylae in "Where Is the Voice Coming From?" though the reference here suggests the dual wars raging in Holden, Strickland's inner turmoil over his life and the nonviolent war against the segregated South. Leaving his office for home after making his rounds, Strickland encounters a young Black child who cryptically informs him he is needed, and will only volunteer directions on where she wishes him to go.

While following the girl's instructions driving towards the Black section of Holden, Strickland "met the marshal's car as both bounced over the railroad track" going in the opposite direction. As the cars pass each other Strickland observes "no passenger . . . with the marshal that he could see" (609). The narrator does not tell the reader what prompted Strickland's examination of the marshal's car, but the presence of a marshal in Holden suggests recent criminal activity by whites, since Mississippi law enforcement consisted of the town police officer(s), the county sheriff and his deputies, and the intrastate Mississippi Highway Patrol. A marshal in a small community was almost always an indication of an ongoing investigation at the behest of the Justice Department or the FBI into crimes against civil rights workers or the local Black community. As the town's only doctor, Strickland has undoubtedly been called upon to tend to the victims of segregationist abuse in the past, and his scrutiny of the marshal's car suggests an attempt to discern if racial violence necessitates his presence in the Black community.

While the presence of a marshal in Holden foregrounds state law enforcement's unreliable commitment to the rule of law in small-town Mississippi, a lesson that hardly needed belaboring after Philadelphia, Welty might be alluding to something more specific by locating Holden's Black community beyond railroad tracks. There had been a recent bombing campaign in the town of McComb, a center of civil rights activity since Robert Moses, SNCC leader and one of the architects of the Freedom Summer project, began working there in 1961. The perpetrators focused on the homes of known civil rights leaders in the area, as well as Black churches. This outrage prompted the FBI to send a task force to the town, though because it was staffed with agents sympathetic to segregation it proved ineffective in apprehending the culprits. In addition to being a front of civil rights agitation, McComb was one of several towns through which the Illinois Central Railroad line ran. It was then common for Black neighborhoods to be literally on the "wrong side of the tracks" throughout Mississippi, and in McComb the "Illinois Central . . . tracks neatly separated McComb's 9,000 whites from its 4,000 black residents" much as in Holden. The situation in McComb was of some note in Mississippi at the time, though it escaped the notice of the national press, who were chronicling King's efforts in Alabama.[68]

After passing the marshal while crossing the railroad tracks, Strickland arrives at his destination, encountering an environment that challenges the faculties of his perception. The power has gone out in Holden during his trip, and initially Strickland can only make out the impossible sight of white chickens roosting in the silhouette of a tree and "the reds of cigarettes" from a group of Black men milling about in front of a domicile (609). The lack of illumination makes it difficult for Strickland to recognize anything as he stumbles through the house into the bedroom where his prospective patient lies. The repetition of white and red emerging out of blackness continues when Strickland gains his patient's bedside and observes a "young, very black-skinned woman . . . in a white dress with her shoes on. A maid? Then he saw . . . the white was not . . . a uniform but shiny, clinging stuff," offset by a crumpled red banner. That Strickland can confuse what is obviously festive attire with a maid's uniform indicates his difficulty diagnosing this situation, an example of his increasing inability to adjust to the shifting narratives of the society around him. In addition to the red sash there were "splashes of blood on the dress, now almost dry" an indication that her wound occurred some time ago, and Strickland wonders aloud why he was not summoned sooner (609).

As a doctor who practices on both races, Strickland depends upon the indulgence of whites to stay in business. The behavior of Strickland's patient, and the women who attend to her, suggests that they, like Strickland's wife, have begun resisting the static social arrangement in an attempt to assert control over their life stories, rejecting the town narrative that Strickland reluctantly represents. The child who summoned Strickland refuses to inform him as to the nature of the emergency, and when Strickland enters the room where his patient lies, the women present greet him with silence or derision, fail to answer his initial questions, volunteer his patient's name, or reveal how she came to be wounded. Their failure to acquiesce disorients Strickland, and it is several moments before he recognizes that it is Ruby Gaddy, a cleaning lady who works in his office building, lying wounded before him. Strickland tries to assert his familiarity with her by asking, "What have you been up to?" only to be rebuffed by the women in the room who respond *"Nothin'!"* (611) Even the mortally wounded Gaddy refuses to cooperate with Strickland's examination, clawing at his hands as he tries to inspect her injury, holding her breath when he listens to her chest, and covering her puncture wound with her hand when her son's crying distracts the doctor. Frustrated at this response, Strickland asks if he is "supposed to just know" what is wrong with Ruby, an admission of dependence and exasperation that loosens the tongues of some in the room.

After surmising that Dove Collins stabbed Gaddy with an ice pick—an inference reluctantly confirmed by the women in the room—Strickland attempts to reassure them about his loyalty to the Black community. He reminds them that he's "sew[n Collins] up enough times on Sunday morning, you know that. I know Ruby, I know Dove, and if the lights would come back on I can tell you the names of the rest of you, and you know it" (612). Strickland's claim of familiarity only increases the women's hostility, which suggests that they hesitated in summoning him precisely because they didn't want knowledge of this event to cross the tracks since it reflects badly upon Gaddy and Collins, and by extension upon the Black community. Strickland fails to understand the women's desire to control the dissemination of this event, blithely wondering if "the marshal is out looking for" Collins, an indication of his outsider status despite his earlier claims of intimacy. Even Gaddy, nearing death, has eyes "filled with the unresponding gaze of ownership," eyes that empower her while discomforting the good doctor (613). Confronted with the hostility of the women, Strickland realizes that individual acts of transracial good will no longer grant him immunity from the hostility of their silence.

Up to this point, the women have been steadfast in their reluctance to identify themselves to Strickland. Yet, when one of the women is unhappy with his care for Gaddy, she compels an explanation from Strickland by revealing her intimate connections to him. "Remember Lucille?" asks one of the women, thrusting a hot kerosene lamp into Strickland's face. "I'm Lucille. I was washing for your mother when you was born. Let me see you do something . . . . You sure ain't your daddy!" (613) Stung by Lucille's challenge to his legacy, Strickland informs her that Gaddy is mortally wounded, which mollifies Lucille. Having established some control over the room by informing them of Gaddy's impending death, Strickland requests "'a drink of water'. . . in the same tone" and prepares to leave (614). As he exits he recognizes another woman from his past who "used to be the sole factotum at the Holden depot . . . she called the stations [with] just the power of her lungs. . . . [s]eiz[ed] all the bags, two by two, in her own hands . . . [and] saw to it that [passengers] left" the depot on time. With her powerful voice and efficiency, Strickland once thought of this woman as a "tyrant," but, his voice still full of authority, he orders her to watch over Gaddy after he departs (614). As Strickland quits the house, "he heard it become as noisy as the yard had been, and the men in the yard went quiet to let him through," a further reminder of his outsider status in the community he serves (615).

The moon has risen since Strickland entered the house, enabling him to notice "his mother's gardening dress, his sister Annie's golf dress, his wife's favorite duster . . . and more dresses, less substantial" hanging from a line that runs to the porch (615). As he drives back toward the other side of town, he notices "a grass fire" which is, he tells himself, "not to be confused with a burning church," another allusion to the strife in McComb (616). While waiting at an intersection for a train to pass, Strickland begins to meditate on the past, carried along by the "slow creaking" of the train's cars combined with his own car's gentle rocking as it sits awaiting passage. In his reverie Strickland notes that "[h]e had been carried a cup tonight that might have been his own mother's china or his wife's mother's . . . a thin porcelain cup his lips and fingers had recognized. In that house of murder, comfort had been brought to him at his request. After drinking from it he had all but reeled into a flock of [his family's] dresses stretched wide-sleeved across the porch of that house like a child's drawing of angels" (616).

The doctor's temporary ability to command the women in the room as his father might have done gives him a "feeling of well-being. . . . [which] increased, until he had come to the point of tears" (616). In a changing world, where even Strickland is unsure of his place in the social order, this momentary return to "the way they used to seem" reassures him because he "had felt as though someone . . . had offered to carry his load for a while . . . some old, trusted, half forgotten family friend" (617–618). Still, as the glow from Strickland's assertion in the face of Lucille's challenge fades, certain facts remain: "his father and mother were dead, his sister had married and moved away . . . his child had died. He and his wife had separated, by her wish" (616). The past can act as a salve, but the contemporary problems inherent to any time of great transition remain.

The fleeting protections of the past remind the doctor that he wearies of playing his father's role, "practicing in his father's office [with] all the older patients, like Miss Marcia Pope—and like Lucille and Oree—[remembering] his father" (616). The unrest brought about by civil rights demonstrations has unearthed all the conflicts suppressed by southern gentility and tradition and Strickland "was so incredibly tired, so sick and even bored with the bitterness, intractability that divided everybody and everything" that he yearns for "the sensation, now returning, that there was still allowed to everybody on earth a *self*—savage, death-defying, private" (617, 618). The doctor finds the appeal of this private self irresistible, the "pounding of his heart was like the assault of hope, throwing itself against him without a stop, merciless." (618). Yet, as the train leaves and these "feelings gradually eb[b] away, like nausea put down," Strickland realizes that he cannot regain the innocence of the past in a Mississippi where nameless citizens monitor whom he has dinner with to determine if he remains committed to segregation despite his egalitarian practice. Strickland tires of the repressive society Holden has become and drives through town rather than return to the family home next door to the Fairbrothers' house, or the tradition-bound country club, which "he'd only [joined] to please his sister" (618).

While driving around the town square the doctor notices "the shutdown movie house with all the lights removed from [its] sign," still another reminder of the racial conflict that has engulfed the South (618).[69] Turning towards his office, Strickland comes across Dove Collins, who looks up at him and asks to be hidden before he expires. Having discovered Collins's whereabouts, the doctor returns to his blacked-out home to ready a report. Mayor Fairbrothers's wife, Eva Duckett Fairbrothers, calls him at daybreak, complaining that her husband, whom Strickland has apparently informed of his condition, feels depressed. Strickland proves unable to offer a tactful response, "shout[ing] at her, 'If I had what Herman has I'd go down in the back yard and shoot myself!'" (619) This exchange demonstrates the danger of being the bearer of truth, because Strickland, who presumably kept Mayor Fairbrothers's affliction from him in order to preserve his dignity, finds it impossible to dissemble now that the mayor understands the enormity of the situation.

Strickland finds an official report of the intrigue between Gaddy and Collins in the weekly edition of the Holden *Sentinel*, the local paper "owned and edited by Horatio Duckett" (619). While Welty told the first part of the story from Strickland's perspective, the newspaper article represents the views of Holden's elite towards integration and change, and takes every opportunity to denigrate the Black community. The article's headline reports that Collins's and Gaddy's deaths contained "no racial content," a declaration that implies that other crimes in Holden featured "racial content" as their motivation (619). The article later quotes Rev. Alonzo Duckett, either the editor's father or brother, who opines that Blacks cannot "expect to be seated in our [white] churches" if they continue to behave in this fashion (621). "County Sheriff Vince Lasseter," who has taken no part in investigating the incident, declares "they can't pin the blame on us for [the double murder]. That's how they treat their own kind. Please take note our conscience is clear" (621). The sheriff's statement not only establishes the innocence of the white community in these murders, but also seeks to absolve him from prior misdeeds committed to keep Blacks in their place. The article also notes that the murder weapon was recovered at the "new $100,000 Negro school," a reminder of Holden's commitment to keeping the races segregated despite the *Brown* decision and the 1964 Civil Rights Act that made separate public facilities illegal.

If the article reveals the racial attitudes of Holden, it also calls attention to the stratified nature of the town, since Dove Collins worked at "the Fairbrothers Cotton Seed Oil Mill," owned and operated by the mayor's family. The article also reveals that Eva Duckett Fairbrothers, the mayor's wife, is related to the Rev. Alonzo Duckett and Horatio Duckett, the paper's publisher. This extended family dominates the economic political and social activity in Holden and is an example of how, in Welty's words, "small town society in the South is often in the control or the grip, whether benevolent or malevolent, of the solid powerful family. It makes it all the harder for any change to penetrate a town like that."[70] Thus, it is no surprise that the paper describes Mayor Fairbrothers's terminal illness as "an ailment" in an attempt to minimize public discussion of the powerful family's problems (620).

Dr. Strickland is the only town authority outside the solid family, and he is the only one that declines to transform the deaths of Gaddy and Collins into a demonstration of the inherent inferiority of Black people. Indeed, Strickland "offered no statement" when asked about possible reasons for Collins's death, denying Horatio Duckett the opportunity to speculate about why Dove Collins's last words were "Hide me" (620, 619). Still, despite his noble intentions, the Gaddy-Collins episode shows him just as capable of taking comfort from his family's traditional status and his father's authority as a doctor. Yet for Strickland these feelings are transitory and he does not seek to preserve the conditions that permit these feelings of comfort. Still, even as Strickland reads this account of the previous weekend's events, he fails to notice his servant refilling his cup, just as he failed to initially recognize Gaddy despite the fact that she worked as his cleaning lady.

As Strickland reads the official version of events on his back porch, he recalls how his daughter used to take sun in the garden. Looking out into his garden, which has become overgrown since Irene left, he sees a pair of woodpeckers picking through the brush. As Strickland idly observes the birds, "the cock spread one wing, showy as a zebra's hide, and with a turn of his head showed his red seal" (622). This blend of black and white followed by red brings Strickland back to the family business, and he imagines that he is the one person who understands the blood ties that link black and white in Holden, ties exemplified by his family's dresses on the wrong side of the tracks and the strong family's desire to control the labor in the town through the maintenance of white supremacy. Strickland cannot quit Holden now, for only he has the standing to see "Herman and Eva Fairbrothers through" the changes to come (622).

Although not as sensational as "Where Is the Voice Coming From?," "The Demonstrators" was quite well received, winning the O. Henry award for short fiction in 1967. Again, Welty correctly trusted that the story's placement in *The New Yorker* would enable it to escape notice of those who might be compelled to spread glass across her driveway, but the story is so dense that she needn't have worried. Indeed, given Welty's indirect treatment of racism in her story, the text seems written to demonstrate the points she made about crusading fiction in "Must the Novelist Crusade?" Having produced these texts from the front line as it were, Welty moved on to her long-delayed novel *Losing Battles*. She hoped one day to issue a collection of short stories that would reflect upon the powerful changes that the civil rights movement had wrought on the character of the South. Her final two short stories were to be part of this collection, which would "reflect the way we were deeply troubled in that society and within ourselves at what was going on in the sixties. [These stories] reflect the effect of change sweeping all over the South—of course, over the rest of the country too, but I was writing about where I was living."[71] Though Welty did not publish any of the other civil rights stories she was said to have been working on up until her death, "Where Is the Voice Coming From?" and "The Demonstrators," along with "Must the Novelist Crusade?," represent Welty's sincere effort to document the loss of innocence demanded by the civil rights movement without becoming a polemicist or an apologist.

Chapter Four

"NEGROES, AND BLOOD, AND HORROR"

William Styron, Existential Freedom,
and *The Confessions of Nat Turner*

For those who lived through it, 1968 must have seemed like an apocalyptic year, a year that perhaps portended the end of the American experiment. On Thursday, April 3, 1968, just four days after Lyndon Johnson announced that he would not seek reelection, Martin Luther King was murdered. Towards the conclusion of that same April, as urban centers throughout the nation struggled to assess the damage from the riots that followed King's assassination, Students for a Democratic Society began what would become the takeover of Columbia University. Then, on June 5, as the nation and the media were attempting to grasp the implications of a suddenly militant student movement, Robert Kennedy was gunned down while campaigning in California. A summer of unrest and uncertainty followed the King and Kennedy assassinations, and in August the Democratic National Convention degenerated into what Norman Mailer aptly described as the siege of Chicago. That same August, Beacon Press published *William Styron's Nat Turner: Ten Black Writers Respond*, a collection of essays edited by distinguished historian John Henrik Clark.

The publication of a collection of essays critiquing a literary work seems to pale in comparison to the other events listed above. Yet the controversy that resulted from this response to William Styron's Pulitzer Prize–winning novel, the conflict between supporters of *The Confessions of Nat Turner* and those who endorsed the reply from the Ten Black Writers, neatly parallels the other problems afflicting the nation. To liberal thinkers and academics, the Ten Black Writers represented the logical end of the more militant strains of the civil rights movement that had infected the student movement: an ideological thought police that restricted artistic and academic freedom by demanding a revisionist history that suited their contemporary needs. For those sympathetic to the Ten Black Writers, Styron's book criminally denied the historical Nat Turner revolutionary agency, diminished the impact of slavery, overlooked the importance of religious thought in Black life, and cherry-picked historical evidence in order to reinforce notions central to white supremacy. For the Ten Black Writers and their supporters any celebration of the novel was a celebration of these themes. Styron's guise as a transplanted liberal southerner who, by virtue of his upbringing, could sympathize with Black Americans, made his novel's failure even more reprehensible in the eyes of his critics. The overwhelmingly positive reception of the book, which culminated in the Pulitzer, only confirmed the worst fears of the "militant" scholars who were deeply offended by the novel.

The controversy surrounding Styron's *Confessions of Nat Turner* has been amply considered, and I do not seek to rehash the old arguments but rather to trace the role that white racial innocence plays in the construction and reception of this text. Many have written in the aftermath of these two texts, a work of fiction that sought to transform America's perception of race and the work of criticism that was in some ways more effective in altering racial perceptions than the novel it sought to refute. Yet, with the exception of Albert Stone's fine *The Return of Nat Turner*, the texts that have followed these two books have been decidedly unbalanced, despite the passage of time. You are either for William Styron and support the rhetorical strategies he daringly employs in *The Confessions of Nat Turner*, or you find him a vastly overrated talent, notable only for the deliberately controversial novels he produced.

Rather than take up either of these positions, I contend that Styron's fourth novel is deeply flawed because Styron contradicts himself, depicting Nat Turner in a fashion that works against the critique of American exceptionalism he offers earlier in his career. *The Confessions of Nat Turner*, despite the disproportionate praise heaped upon it, seems in this regard a bad-faith effort by Styron. The body of work that Styron produced in the 1950s and '60s, from *The Long March* to *The Confessions of Nat Turner*, reveals a writer interested in connecting narratives of race and democracy to the existential ideas that came to preoccupy his writing. Styron is not a reformed apologist for the southern way of life, like Robert Penn Warren, nor is he ambivalent about the writer's role in the struggle to reform the South, like Eudora Welty. Unlike his friend and rival Mailer, Styron endorsed the mainstream liberal ideals which helped produce the age of consensus during the postwar period, even as the various protest movements of the 1960s attempted to discredit these values. As he matured as a writer, Styron, like Lionel Trilling, saw the importance of offering a "defense of the imagination against the encroachments of political thinking, whether Marxist, populist or liberal."[1] Still, Styron's defense of the imagination, joined with an ethical stance based in part on Camus's writing, amounts to a political stance in itself, and it was his steadfast refusal to acknowledge this that provided fuel for his detractors, but may also grant some insight into why his writing failed to achieve his lofty intentions.

While the emergence of the Cold War and McCarthyism bedeviled Mailer, most postwar liberals did not believe in an approaching apocalypse, and Styron is typical in this regard. Influential postwar thinkers like Trilling and Hannah Arendt perceived ideology, Marxist ideology specifically, as far more insidious than the rise of the military-industrial complex that accompanied the Cold War. This fear of totalitarian ideology contributed to the American exceptionalism that produced the so-called age of consensus, a period when, according to Godfrey Hodgson, most people held that "American capitalism was a revolutionary force for social change, that economic growth was supremely good because it obviated the need for redistribution [of wealth] and social conflict, [and] that class had no place in American politics."[2] Cold War liberals like Trilling and the New York intellectuals that orbited him at Columbia were, in a sense, the final inheritors of the pragmatic tradition that grew out of the detritus of the Civil War in that they mistrusted teleological thinking, yet refused to use this as an excuse to excise the political from their considerations of art and culture.[3] While the New York intellectuals were far more ambivalent about late market capitalism than Hodgson's quote suggests, they certainly felt antipathy towards social narratives that produced any conflict that threatened to disrupt consensus.

This tendency to reject assertions that challenged consensus often put liberal intellectuals at odds with the means, if not the goals, of the civil rights movement.[4] For the participants in that movement, issues of inequality were best solved via social protest and lawsuits, practices that revealed the complicity with injustice that was often necessary to produce consensus. Unfortunately, the sit-ins, marches, and voter registration drives conducted by civil rights organizations increasingly led to retaliations that produced bloodshed and death. Thus, as in Arendt's "Reflections on Little Rock," antitotalitarian intellectuals could simultaneously admit that segregation was morally indefensible, yet still condemn those seeking to end it by demonstration and litigation.[5] This is a bad faith argument, with thinkers like Arendt demanding a change in tactics because a sanguinary backlash to civil rights protest must be avoided at all costs. Styron, although much younger than the New York intellectuals, came to share their views about the dangers of provoking confrontations that might end in bloodshed. Styron's second major work, the novella *The Long March*, demonstrates his antipathy to strategies of confrontation, and this reluctance develops as a theme throughout his subsequent novels. Styron's aversion to even the threat of violence derives from his rather benign experience in the marines during World War II and the Korean War and his exposure to existentialism, particularly the thoughts of Albert Camus.

Styron's distaste for bloodshed, his sense of the fundamentally tragic nature of violence, grew out of his experiences in the military. Styron joined the marines in October of 1944 at the age of nineteen, and during boot camp staff sergeants who had seen combat would regale their charges with grisly stories that shocked the sensitive Styron. Hearing that Japanese soldiers "sizzle like a bunch of roaches," and seeing a marine in possession of mummified Japanese testicles that he fondled "like worry beads," disabused Styron of the adolescent notion of war as a glorious affair.[6] After completing boot camp on Parris Island in South Carolina, Styron was sent first to Camp Lejeune in North Carolina and then to Platoon Commander School in Quantico outside of Washington, D.C. At Quantico, Styron's officers warned his class that "four out of five of you will get your assess shot off" in the war, and he felt certain that he would be one of those who would die. After all, "the class ahead of me in college was virtually wiped out . . . Beautiful fellows who had won basketball championships and Phi Beta Kappa keys died like ants in the Normandy invasion. Others . . . stormed ashore at Tarawa and Iwo Jima and met ugly and horrible deaths on the hot coral and sands."[7] The atomic bomb spared Styron combat in the Pacific Theatre; he would not get his ass shot off after all. Still, Styron's sense of the futility of combat, his identification with the fallen soldiers, both Japanese and American, contributed to his perspective that all violence must be tragic. Given his perspective, it is unsurprising that Styron is possibly the only member of what a prominent newsreader has declared "the Greatest Generation" to refer to World War II as an ignoble conflict.[8]

While World War II taught Styron to abhor violence, it was at the onset of the Korean War that he acquired his detestation of ideology. Styron was a military reservist, and in May of 1951 the marines called him back into active duty to serve in Korea. This dismayed Styron, in part because his first novel, *Lie Down in Darkness*, was in galleys. The recall forced Styron to mark the corrections to his novel on a bunk at Camp Lejeune, not the best conditions for a fledgling writer to polish his prose. Worse, Styron was slated to fight in a war that he found "futile and pernicious, with no clear moral issues."[9] To Styron, beautiful fellows were again being sent to die, and not to avenge Pearl Harbor or stop Hitler's inexorable march across Europe, but because "the lunatic fringe of both the Republican and Democratic parties" feared the spread of an ideology that challenged American exceptionalism.[10] Like the New York intellectuals during the Depression, Styron learned during his second stint in the marines that ideology was not an abstract thing, that once let loose in society it could destroy the very people it purported to protect.[11]

While completing his second tour of Camp Lejeune, Styron witnessed an accident during a training exercise thirty-three miles from the base. A group of marines were targeting mortars when a leftover World War II shell veered off course and landed amidst another group of soldiers. Nine men died in the incident, and twenty-three were wounded. The commander of Styron's regiment decided to march the surviving soldiers back to camp rather than have them take transport. This choice struck Styron as nothing less than sadistic (the idea that soldiers might have to march after witnessing far worse in combat apparently escaped him). The commanding officer, hoping to inure the reservists to the emotional toll of experiencing death, marched most of the way next to his troops. Styron also completed the march, and his own acquiescence to what he felt was a pointless and cruel rationale worried him. The commander of his unit, Styron realized, was a man who unquestioningly believed in the mission and means of the military, to the point where he could transform a fatal accident into an object lesson for his men. Styron, nominally an officer, brooded over his reluctance to confront the commander, because by keeping silent he participated in behavior he abhorred. Styron fictionalized his experiences that day in *The Long March*, developing his ideas about the ethics of coercion in the name of national defense.

Interestingly, the effects of the Lejeune march seem to have shaped Styron's literary style as well as his sensibility. His debut, *Lie Down in Darkness*, is modernist in subject and narration, as the novel shifts from the direct address of the introductory chapter to a kind of flitting, omniscient narrator similar to the "Hades" chapter of *Ulysses*. Styron's first novel is also, despite its heavy psychological overtone, a family tragedy similar to Faulkner's *As I Lay Dying* with the suicidal Peyton Loftis's narrative resembling the Septimus sections of Woolf's *Mrs. Dalloway*. The novel concludes, like Faulkner's *The Sound and the Fury*, with the patriarch emotionally shattered, the matriarch deranged and Peyton and her sibling deceased. As in Faulkner's novel, there is nothing explicitly political about *Lie Down in Darkness*, unless you count the passing references to the Byrd political machine in Virginia that add local color to the narrative. *Lie Down in Darkness* contains, in lieu of political commentary, a strong rejection of religion. In the novel the venal Carey Carr seems more interested in demonstrating his ability to heal through the judicious use of Christian Science than in actually attempting to understand what troubles his supplicants, while the traveling Black revival preacher Daddy Faith exerts a powerful and mysterious hold on his childlike followers, who seem unable to perceive him as an exploitative charlatan.

The Long March, which the usually laborious Styron completed in just six weeks while visiting Paris in 1952, breaks in almost every way from his debut. Rather than the shifts in tone and perspective that marked *Lie Down in Darkness*, Styron "filtered all action through the mind of a peripheral character, a Jamesian vessel of consciousness," Lt. Tom Culver.[12] Lt. Culver marks the first appearance of Styron's "silent first person narrator," the passive witness who seems slightly out of synch with the society he lives in and the company he keeps.[13] All of the novels that follow *The Long March* feature a similar character—from Peter Leverett in *Set This House on Fire* to Thomas Gray in *The Confessions of Nat Turner* to Stingo in *Sophie's Choice*—an indifferent yet implicated Virginian, a participant-observer who bears witness to the violence and self-destruction that afflicts the protagonist.[14] All of Styron's Virginian narrators resemble him in some fashion, yet also recall the noncommittal midwesterner Nick Carraway from *The Great Gatsby* because, like Nick, Styron's participant-observers become embroiled in conflicts only tangentially related to them, conflicts that reveal the shape of the society in which they live. Interestingly (with the possible exception of Stingo), despite every novel but his first containing a narrator that resembles him, Styron often filters his personal views through the actions of the protagonists of his tales, and examining these characters reveals the evolution of Styron's ideas about violence.[15]

In *The Long March*, Styron constructs the military as an alternate society, parallel to the civilian world abandoned by Culver and the other reservists. Abruptly thrust back into military life, Lt. Culver conforms to the mores of military society rather than challenging rules that he now recognizes as perverse. Culver is prepared to endure whatever the military demands of him in order to return to the real world, but this resignation seems at odds with his civilian profession. Culver is a lawyer, a calling that presupposes a willingness to place different interpretations of the law into conflict in order to force a resolution. Culver, like Styron's other lawyer-narrators, seems uneasy with the crusading aspect of the law, as emblematized by Thurgood Marshall. The practice of the law, as Styron depicts it, serves as a means to enable its practitioner to live a comfortable life. Indeed, Culver's vague description of himself as "one of the brightest juniors in a good New York law firm" suggests a prosperous young man more worried about banking billable hours from corporate clients than the pursuit of justice.[16] Styron's portrayal of Culver suggests that lawyers serve as mediators who skillfully negotiate the competing claims of commerce, producing minor adjustments in the way business is run but exerting little influence on the society as a whole.

Colonel Templeton, the unit's commanding officer, appalls Culver when he orders his troops to march back to base following the botched training exercise. Captain Al Mannix, the protagonist of the novella, is equally upset, and registers his displeasure immediately. The dispassionate Culver is drawn to the earthy Mannix, whom Culver reports is "a dark heavy-set Jew from Brooklyn," because he "seemed to bring a spark of relief . . . to Culver's feelings of futility and isolation" (17). Mannix despises the marines, but in this he is a typical reservist. What distinguishes Mannix from his compatriots is his willingness to protest openly, a daring posture that kept Culver "in a constant state of mild suspense—half amusement, half horror" (19). While Culver maintains his sardonic detachment throughout the text, Mannix is willing to challenge the value system of military society. As with the lawyer/narrator represented here by Culver, the noble ethnic outsider will also reappear in Styron's later fiction, and it is important to view the failed rebellion in *The Long March* in light of the other failed rebellions that Styron would later construct.

While Mannix is willing to challenge Templeton's order to march, he functions in the story as a reforming rather than a revolutionary figure. Mannix never attempts to shatter the logic of the military; he instead appeals to Templeton to delay the march until the reservists have had adequate time to adjust to the marines. Yet even as Mannix engages the colonel, Culver remains committed to silently following orders. "Born into a generation of conformists," Culver rationalizes that "even Mannix was aware that his gestures were not symbolic, but individual, therefore hopeless, maybe even absurd, and that he was trapped like all of them in a predicament which one personal insurrection could, if anything, only make worse" (55). Culver becomes, in this passage, a stand-in for a conformist yet innocent society, and his defeatist assertion that Mannix can never transform the culture of the military condemns Mannix to attempt reform alone. Culver fatalistically recognizes that, although this march might be put off if he and others join in protest, the colonel would eventually have his way. Given this reality, Culver submits, despite his lack of sleep and lingering after-effects from the morning's traumatic accident. In such an environment, Mannix's gestures of protest indeed appear hopeless.

Futile and absurd persistence seems to be a dominant theme of the novella. Mannix completes the march despite having a nail lodged in his boot, but only spites himself with his perverse display of heroism. Culver marches stoically alongside Mannix in solidarity, but this solidarity rings false given Culver's refusal to actively support him. Culver completes the march with his dignity intact, but the preservation of dignity seems meaningless when contrasted with the injustice of the march. The story ends with the revelation that Mannix will be reprimanded for his insubordination during and after the march, and then sent to the front in Korea. Culver notes that Mannix appears "sullen and beaten" at the prospect of being sent into combat, yet Culver has taken no action to prevent this from happening (112). Gavin Cologne-Brookes perceives in Styron's fiction an attempt "to harmonize various voices into an apparently unitary whole," yet, at the conclusion of *The Long March*, Styron's attempt at establishing a unifying harmony fails.[17] Authority, represented by Colonel Templeton, successfully banishes the dissenting voice of Captain Mannix, while the other soldiers remain, coerced into silence by their sense of futility and isolation.

Mannix is the Christ figure of the story: the heroic Jew with a nail through his foot who suffers, not just for his own sins but also for the sins of his companions who refuse to acknowledge his truth. Sacrificed to militaristic expectations of quietude and loyalty, Mannix leaves behind followers hesitant to make protests of their own. Unfortunately, Mannix's impending death promises no salvation or redemption. Indeed, as resisting subjects like Mannix are banished from military society, people like

Templeton assume a higher degree of control over those left behind. With Mannix gone there is no one who will say "*Fuck* you" to Colonel Templeton and the logic he represents (112), no one inside the military who will fondly recall his futile but noble protest, including his friend Culver.[18] Styron, writing from Paris, seems to fear the rising tide of conformity he perceives across the Atlantic.

In *The Long March*, Mannix's ethnic identity informs his sense of social justice—he is the Jewish working-class hero willing to act to correct an inequality. None of Mannix's fellows share his need for reform because they have been thoroughly normalized by military society. In fact, Culver calls the officers who uncritically accept Templeton's order "regulars" (16 and elsewhere), a generic military term given new meaning here. Indeed, the only character that sympathizes with Mannix's act of protest is an unnamed Black maid who confronts Mannix and Culver at the end of the novella. The maid surprises Mannix as he painfully limps toward the bathroom clad in nothing but a towel. Startled, Mannix drops his towel and is unable to bend to pick it up due to his injury. Instead of being taken aback by Mannix's nudity, the nameless maid sympathizes with him immediately, looking at his bloody and swollen foot and asking him, "Do it hurt?" before answering her own question: "Deed it does" (119). Styron's introduction of the Black maid suggests that, in the postwar United States, only another minority can appreciate Mannix's gesture. Exhausted and broken, yet redeemed by his communion with the maid, Mannix repeats her statement in a curious affirmation of her perception: "Deed it does" (120). Mannix, the subjugated minority within the military, communes with another subjugated minority, a figure who, despite her subservient position to Mannix, instantly understands him.

With this conclusion Styron tries to establish equivalence between Mannix and the maid, but there is a profound difference between *Captain* Mannix, who has status and rank in both military and civilian society, and a Black maid, who cleans toilets on a military base in North Carolina in 1952. To suggest otherwise, as Styron does with his denouement, trivializes Mannix's oppression. As Norman Kelvin observes, Styron wants Mannix "to declare kinship with those who must resist [racial subjugation,] an uncontained, objective social evil." Styron can only accomplish this sentimental declaration by adopting "an analytic view of the spectrum of pain. All manifestations and experiences of pain are as a result seen as equal, and whatever depth there is beneath any one of them is never fully explored."[19] Styron's inability to distinguish between Mannix and the maid suggests a facile understanding of repression in American society.[20] Soon, Styron would draw from existentialism to support his refusal to categorize evil, but the ending of *The Long March* rings hollow due to this lack.

Styron's ending attempts to indict Culver for his passive conformity by contrasting his reluctance with the maid's instantaneous identification with Mannix. Unfortunately for Styron, Culver's position seems only rational for an innocent participant of his social standing. Military conscription was a temporary inconvenience for the men selected, one that could be endured or evaded, and Styron only calls attention to the transitory nature of military servility by introducing the Black maid, whose social condition is static. This contrast disrupts Styron's attempt to link Jews and Blacks as exemplary noble sufferers. The endurance of Mannix and the maid in the face of injustice, his bounded and particular, hers endemic and routine, simultaneously inspires Culver, the liberal witness, while remaining ultimately unthreatening to the power structure that subjects each of them to abuse.

After completing *The Long March*, Styron spent the year in Rome as winner of the Prix de Rome of the American Academy of Arts and Letters. Styron first read the French existentialists during this fellowship, and he must have marveled at how their notions of absurdity conformed with his recent experience in the military and his childhood distaste of evangelical religion. During his immersion into contemporary French thought, Styron's biographer reports, "Camus spoke with special urgency to him; he never forgot the experience of reading *The Plague, The Rebel* and *The Myth of Sisyphus* that fall and winter."[21] Camus's notion of an existential man in despair, seeking justification for his action in the absence of any external value system, exerted a powerful influence on Styron.[22] These ideas helped him understand the submerged themes of Mannix's absurdity and Culver's despair contained in *The Long March*. Camus's contention, expressed in *The Rebel*, that the rebel slave must create for himself an ideology that endows him with a "confused conviction of an absolute right" would shape Styron's depictions of his protagonists in his next two novels, *Set This House on Fire* and *The Confessions of Nat Turner*.[23]

Set This House on Fire is a sprawling mess of a book, difficult to summarize, yet vital to understanding the choices that Styron makes in *The Confessions of Nat Turner*. Peter Leverett, the narrator of the novel, is a lawyer working in Rome with a United States relief agency. While Lt. Culver used the law chiefly as a means to achieve a middle-class lifestyle, Peter holds the law in slightly higher esteem. Although Peter practices in a "drab province"

of the law, "where only torts, wills, and contracts are at stake" (5), he prefers it to composing music, his first calling. "In America," Peter claims,
"no one listens to composers, while the law, in a way that is at once subtle
and majestic and fascinating, still works its own music upon the minds of
men" (5). This seems an oblique reference to the litigation of the NAACP;
by 1960, when the novel was published, the lawsuits filed by the civil rights
group had begun to transform US society. Indeed, Peter's father, Alfred,
condemns the decision of the Warren court to enforce school desegregation, claiming that the South will "suffer and suffer because of it," but rue-
fully admits that southerners "don't realize that the nigro has *got* to get his
just payment, for all those years of bondage" (14). Alfred recognizes that
the law has successfully countermanded the white supremacist rhetoric
of the South but not the violence that springs from it. Civil law, the law of
Peter Leverett and Thurgood Marshall, demands adjustment rather than
confrontation in order to perfect society, but Alfred fears that southerners
will prove unwilling to adjust.

Styron set his third novel in Sambuco, a fictionalized version of the
resort town Ravello, in a postwar Italy struggling to come to terms with
its embrace of fascism. Despite the setting of this novel, *Set This House
on Fire* is as concerned with contemporary American ideals as Mailer's
"The White Negro." Indeed, parts of *Set This House on Fire* refute notions
advanced by Mailer three years earlier, with Styron attempting to articulate an alternative to finding meaning in postwar America through an
embrace of hipster nihilism. While the protagonist of the novel, Cass Kinsolving, is not quite an ethnic other like Mannix, the antagonist, Mason
Flagg, like Colonel Templeton before him, qualifies as a cruel "regular"
in the world of show business, perhaps the only subculture of the United
States as rule bound and hierarchical as the military during the 1950s. Like
Templeton, Mason treats the people around him as means, and not ends
in themselves. Mason and Cass represent two important vectors in contemporary life in the United States: the amoral northern hipster-hedonist
and the conflicted southern idealist, and *Set This House on Fire* forces the
neutral Peter to choose between their antithetical values.

Mason Flagg, the epitome of the wealthy, puerile hedonist-hipster,
functions in part as a stand-in for Norman Mailer, allowing Styron some
measure of revenge for the criticisms Mailer leveled against him in *Advertisements for Myself*.[24] Mason is something of a straw man for Styron, sim-
plistic to the point of parody: "a wealthy, egocentric . . . sexual pervert who
lives in an elegant Italian villa and goes through the motions of being a

patron of the arts."[25] The dilettante Mason is narcissistic, oedipal, manipulative, "a hipster. A juvenile delinquent. A potty-mouthed little boy" (116). Styron presents hipsterism as another method of coercion men like Peter and Cass must ultimately reject. Still, even though Peter was "alienated from Mason and all that he stands for," (5) Mason is a childhood friend, and Peter seems reluctant to turn his back on his boyhood companion. Yet, when Peter learns that Cass has murdered Mason, Peter quickly reassures Cass, telling him he "could have done away with five hundred Masons for what he did" (246). Mason's actions in the novel support Peter's assertions: Mason, who is fascinated with sex and pornography, physically and mentally abuses his lovers, rapes a servant girl for having the temerity to resist his advances, and psychologically torments the alcoholic Cass when he realizes he is not an accomplished painter.

Cass, a World War II veteran from the working classes of North Carolina, struggles in Europe to achieve his vision as an artist, taking his wife, Poppy, and their four children along for the journey. Cass's search for an artistic method frustrates him because he is inauthentic: he seeks the means to play the role of artist rather than letting art become the thing that defines his life. Cass is discouraged by his inability to achieve anything meaningful as an artist and terrified at the thought of returning to the United States when he encounters Mason. Mason seems to aid Cass by paying his rent, thus extending Cass's stay in Europe; commissioning (pornographic) artwork from him; and supplying him with an endless supply of spirits to salve Cass's dissatisfaction at his artistic failure. Cass, in Italy in part because he rejects the mercenary capitalism of the United States, allows Mason to support him as long as this forestalls his return to the US. Cass introduces Mason to Francesca, an Italian peasant girl in desperate need of gainful employment. When Mason rapes Francesca, an assault that leads directly to her death, Cass murders Mason.[26] For Cass, the assault on Francesca represents "an intrusion that is considered intolerable," an intrusion that—Styron would have you believe—transforms him into Camus's "rebel slave."[27]

The novel suggests that Cass must murder Mason in order to free himself from his blandishments and avenge Francesca, yet after he commits the murder, Cass confesses to Peter that "[t]hese limbs are plumb wore out. Look at them. . . . What was they made for, I ast you. . . . To make monuments? . . . Nossir! They was made to destroy and now they are plumb wore out, and my head aches, and I yearn for a long spell of darkness" (238). Cass struggles to retain his identity after the murder; the violence has so traumatized him that he contemplates suicide. Cass ultimately resists the urge to take his own life, but Peter reports that "in the space of a day, [he] had aged a dozen years" (241). Cass recognizes that he has acted in bad faith, that, although Mason was a monster, killing him was self-indulgent and self-justifying. He struggles to live with the knowledge of what he has done.

Peter visits Cass in South Carolina the following summer, hoping to piece together the events in Italy that compelled Cass to murder Mason. Once he arrives, Peter discovers that Cass has transcended the self-destructive urges that bedeviled him in the aftermath of Mason's death and "is alive and flourishing." Cass has discovered humility, order, and meaning, symbolized in the novel by his contentment with his job teaching art classes, his embrace of patriarchal domesticity, and his happily pregnant wife. Cass's transcendence explains why Peter considers Cass "a hero . . . I suppose" (4). Cass has murdered Mason, but despite committing that horrific act he has wrested meaning from the world by learning to cherish small triumphs instead of retreating into a meaningless quest for artistic transcendence that will only lead back to the bottle. As Peter interrogates Cass, hoping to understand how Cass has arrived at such a felicitous ending, Cass reveals that his pattern of violence predates Mason Flagg, and something more than artistic frustration brought about his descent into alcoholism.

Even before he met Mason and Peter, Cass imagined himself "a way out liberal, for a southerner anyway," in part because he has lived in the North and married a northerner (369). In order to maintain this self-image, Cass must repress memories that contradict it. When Cass arrives in Europe with his family, his self-deception starts to crumble. Cass's first awareness of the discrepancy in his identity comes from the dreams he is having, first in Paris and then in Sambuco. In these dreams there are "[j]igaboos everywhere! Ever since I'd been in Europe about half of whatever nightmares I'd had—the ones I remembered anyway—had been tied up with Negroes . . . replete with Negroes, and blood, and horror" (369). Though resistant to psychoanalysis, Cass admits that "[i]t really doesn't take any supreme genius to know that these various horrors and sweats you have when you are asleep add up to something, even if these horrors are masked and these sweats are symbols" (369). Cass dreams about gassing himself in a gas chamber aboard a flying airplane, followed by two Black men asking him, "Man, why did you kill him . . . Man, why did you let him die?" (368), and he awakens with the recollection of "something wretched and horrible that I had done when I was about fifteen years old—something really dreadful and wicked that I must have kept way in the back of my mind all these years" (370). This dream, a collision of the dehumanizing ideologies of white supremacy and Nazi fascism, reminds Cass of his complicity in a racially charged episode in Virginia.

Cass, a native Carolinian, lived with a relative in Colfax, Virginia, during the summer of his fifteenth year, and worked part-time at a Western Auto store with a young man named Lonnie. Lonnie, Cass reports, "was somewhat unlettered, a Baptist, and only half a cut removed from trash" but remains, despite these handicaps, "the fairest flower of southern manhood" (371). Lonnie brings Cass with him to collect the debt of a Black sharecropper named Crawfoot because he was late on his monthly payment for a radio. Cass's inclusion implicates him for the first time in the maintenance of white supremacy. At the time, Cass never questioned the logic of Lonnie requiring the assistance of a fifteen-year-old boy to complete this errand, and as they drive towards Crawfoot's home, Lonnie attempts to educate young Cass, informing him that while he could entrust some Blacks "with every nickel you got," Crawfoot is "a crook, criminal type . . . uppity" with "a son lives up in Philadelphia, Pennsylvania" (374). It is unclear whether Lonnie is more threatened by Crawfoot's reluctance to pay his installments in a timely fashion or his son's presence in the North where he might escape the dehumanizing effects of southern racism, but he responds by striking out against Crawfoot.

After breaking into Crawfoot's empty shanty, Cass and Lonnie search for the radio, which they find hidden under a floorboard. Infuriated, ostensibly at finding the plastic casing of the radio cracked, Lonnie begins demolishing Crawfoot's cottage, including a picture of Crawfoot's family that struck Cass as a "sweetly gentle, calm-visaged mood of solidarity and pride and love" (376).[28] This picture demonstrates to Cass the falsity of Lonnie's earlier claims about Crawfoot's perfidy, and Cass's first instinct is to stop Lonnie, to preserve the photograph as well as the other artifacts in the room that suggest community and hope. Repulsed by Lonnie's senseless violence, yet unwilling, in part because of his age, to challenge him, Cass instead tries to leave, but Lonnie coerces him into participating in the destruction of Crawfoot's home. Cass's refusal remains "unspoken at the back of his throat" and his failure to resist Lonnie's coercion produces feelings of guilt derived from "his ponderous share of the blame" (377).

Despite the guilt he now feels about this incident, Cass remains in awe of "[w]hat we did!" (375) Cass recalls that, despite his initial reluctance, as he began to help Lonnie demolish Crawfoot's home, a feeling came over him,

> almost a feeling of anger, too, as if I'd picked up some of this young lout of a maniac's fury and was set on teaching the niggers, too. By God, this feeling, you know, I remember it—it was in my loins, hot flowing, sexual. I knew it was wrong, I knew it, I knew it—bestial, horrible, abominable. I knew all this, understand, but it was as if once I'd lost my courage anyway, once I'd given in—like some virgin, you see, who's finally stopped struggling and said to hell with it—then I could actually do what I was doing even with a sense of righteousness. All the clichés and shibboleths I'd been brought up with came rolling back—a nigger wasn't much more than an animal anyway, specially field niggers, crooked niggers like this Crawfoot—so I heaved and pushed there with Lonnie. . . . " (377–378)

Cass compares himself to a rape victim here in an attempt to protect himself from blame, ignoring the impulse to stop Lonnie from his terroristic act. This capitulation is tied to Cass's emerging sexuality, linking violence both to the maintenance of white supremacist discourse and patriarchy. The rhetoric of white supremacy forces Cass to conform, just as the ideology of the military coerced Culver, but in the youthful Cass this coercion leads to despair.

Cass carries these conflicted memories, these feelings of guilt and sexual power and racial violence, repressed inside of him until he arrives in Europe. As Cass and Peter try to make sense of what happened, Cass admits that his feelings over this episode with Lonnie "figured in with what happened to me in" Italy (370). After Cass recalls this event, even though he recognizes that "there are no amends or atonements for a thing like that," he tries to expiate his sin because if Cass were "shown one more dirty face, one more foul and unclean image of [him]self, [he] would not be able to support it" (379). Until he encounters the peasant Michele and his daughter Francesca, Cass flounders in his guilt, wasting his life by getting into meaningless philosophical debates with an Italian policeman named Luigi and becoming Mason's drunken sycophant.

Michele is afflicted—in typical Styronic understatement—with tuberculosis and a shattered leg, and his penniless daughter is powerless to help him. As he sits in their cottage, Cass makes an uncomfortable connection to his past: "Lord God I know [the smell inside the peasant hut] as well as my own name . . . it is niggers. The same thing, by God. It is the smell of a black sharecropper's cabin in Sussex County, Virginia. It is the bleeding stink of wretchedness" (416). Standing again in an impoverished shanty, Cass becomes filled with a sense of purpose, the "need to do something [overcame him] like a panic" (417). Unable to create art that is meaningful or fulfill his role as patriarch due to his participation in a sadistic and ritualistic act of violence, Cass believes helping Francesca will assuage the feelings of guilt and emancipate him. This hope would prove futile, for Styron portrays Cass's impulse as nothing but a noble form of being-for-others, with Cass hoping to emerge from his charitable mission with his innocence restored.[29]

Cass convinces Mason to hire the beauteous Francesca as his maid, and encourages her to steal money and food from Mason in order to help her father. Meanwhile, Cass has Mason purchase various medicines that can heal Francesca's father, exploiting his position as "house-boy" to acquire the means for Michele's salvation. While Cass helps Francesca and Michele, he slowly pulls his life together, drinking less and plotting to escape Mason's psychological domination.

> Because for more time than I care to think about I had allowed him to own me—out of spinelessness at first, out of whiskey-freed and desolation of the spirit, but at last out of necessity. And the paradox is that this slavish contact with Mason that I had to preserve in order to save Michele freed me to come into that knowledge of selflessness I had thirsted for like a dying man, and into a state where such a thing as dependence on the likes of Mason would be unheard-of, an impossibility. (443)

Existentially speaking, the knowledge that Cass attains through his self-less devotion to Francesca, a devotion that forces him to further neglect his wife and children, is not authentic, for Cass aids her in part to realize his own freedom. Indeed, on the night that Cass kills Mason, he was willing to "repudiate this new independence of mine" in order to pilfer Mason's medicine chest and take pills to Michele (444). Because Cass has not yet grasped his existential freedom, his attempt to aid the Italian peasants in order to somehow negate his earlier abuse of a Black peasant ends in a repetition of the violence that he seeks to redeem.

In the end, it is an act of willful acceptance that rescues Cass. Cass's violence makes his self-rationalizations impossible, and deprived of innocence he faces despair. Luigi provides him with an alibi for the murder and declares the case closed. Cass, freed from his master yet longing for the companionship of his fellow servants, faces the abyss and there is no transcendence there: "I suppose I should tell you that through some sort of suffering I had reached grace . . . but this would not be true" (500). "To choose between" being and nothingness, Cass continues, is "simply to choose being, not for the sake of being, or even the love of being . . . but in hope of being what I could be for a time" (500–501). By killing Mason, Cass thought that he would avenge Francesca, symbolically exorcise Lonnie, and emancipate himself from feelings of doubt and guilt. Instead, Cass can only achieve that freedom by "simply choos[ing] being," an epiphany that grounds him and allows him to return to his family and to the South. Cass may still be at odds with the values of his society, but he now possesses a self-contained, self-justifying system that will sustain him in America.

Set This House on Fire tries to avoid the problems with proportion that bedeviled *The Long March*'s use of racial oppression as a moment of epiphanic discovery. It is in fact easier to accept the comparison between a Black sharecropper in the American South and a landless peasant in postwar Italy than between Mannix and the Black maid. Cass's rejection of Lonnie's white supremacist narrative is appropriately traumatic and the nightmares that afflict him reveal the need for him to find another narrative to support his sense of self. Indeed Cass's comment that, if the federal government tries to enforce the *Brown* decision, "guys [like Lonnie are] going to make the blood flow in the streets" (378) demonstrates that he is no longer bound by this rhetoric even if he has not yet accepted emancipationist discourse. Cass's eventual acceptance of his role in Mason's murder makes sense because it remains a solitary incident, unlike the violence perpetrated by white southerners against Blacks that reinforces narratives of violent domination.

Styron's depiction of Cass Kinsolving's violence provides an interesting point of comparison with *The Confessions of Nat Turner*. Cass, like Mannix before him, represents a particular kind of existential man, and there is no reason why Styron could not have extended this theme by transforming Nat Turner into an existential hero. Indeed, Cass and Nat Turner resemble each other in many ways. Both reject the southern logic that subjugates Blacks, both endeavor to rescue landless serfs from their downtrodden condition, both embrace violence as a solution to their problems, both have delusions of grandeur, and both are guided by visions.[30] Styron could have transformed the "heroic" Cass into Nat Turner with little effort, demonstrating, a la Richard Wright, the true "universal quality" of existentialism, but he would make different choices for his next novel. Indeed, while existentialism ultimately preserves Cass, it serves to undo the fictionalized Nat Turner.

I will not attempt to elaborate all of the deviations from the historical record—incomplete as that may be—or defend the virtues of *The Confessions of Nat Turner*; I would only be retracing the steps of dozens of scholars before me. Instead, I assert that Styron's reluctance to endorse emancipatory violence in some way is the fatal flaw of the book,[31] the flaw that prevents him from creating a Nat Turner palatable to the Black intelligentsia of the 1960s or to contemporary critics attempting to reassess his work. Styron's reluctance to treat the fictionalized Nat Turner as he does the fictional Cass does not represent overt racism on his part. Indeed, with *Confessions* Styron attempts to foreground the emancipationist discourse that had always been present in his work. As the black maid from *The Long March* and Crawfoot from *Set This House on Fire* demonstrate, Styron long sought to use Black characters to "ignite critical moments of discovery or change or emphasis" in his white protagonists.[32] These moments of discovery force Styron's protagonists to reject static notions of American innocence by calling attention to the coercive nature of American society. Yet, Styron proved unwilling to follow this literary practice to its logical end when confronted with a Black protagonist, reverting instead to shallow psychology.

With *The Confessions of Nat Turner*, Styron has the opportunity to reverse the binary at work in his previous texts. This novel promises to focus on a primogenitor of Crawfoot and the nameless maid, and counteract the logic of Lonnie's narrative by presenting an existential Black hero determined to wrest meaning from his absurd enslavement. Most felicitously, Thomas Gray, a Virginia lawyer, recorded the original *Confessions of Nat Turner* so Styron could rely on a lawyer/narrator in *Confessions of Nat Turner* as he had in *The Long March* and *Set This House on Fire*. Using Gray as narrator presented Styron with a challenge, because while the lawyers in *The Long March* and *Set This House on Fire* ultimately approve of the actions of their protagonists, Gray's location in southern society in 1831 would prevent Styron from using him in a similar fashion. So, while both *Set This House on Fire* and *The Confessions of Nat Turner* tell their stories through a series of flashbacks, Gray cannot occupy the same place in *Confessions* as Lt. Culver or Peter Leverett.

Styron chose to open his novel with Gray arriving to interview Nat Turner in jail following his capture after a month-long manhunt. This choice allowed him to introduce Mr. Gray, who took down the original confessions, and to have a kind of ironic counterpoint between these confessions—which had a lot of white man's hokum in them—and Nat's own story. The major reason, however, was that I wanted to get Nat after the insurrection, when he was questioning the entire relationship he had with God, with the God who had been his guide and mentor and light throughout his life as a preacher. I wanted to discover what was going on in his mind, now that he had instigated and committed murder, and now that he is bereft of God. ("Interview," 71–72)[33]

Styron assumes that Nat Turner's attitude towards violence would resemble his own, and so structures his response to the failed rebellion accordingly. For Styron, anyone who commits an act of violence must face the existential angst that arises with that act. Styron cannot imagine a mind that is perfectly certain about the morality of his action, and would later be flabbergasted at his Black contemporaries who insist on this interpretation, despite his youthful interaction with self-satisfied marines at Camp Lejeune.[34]

Styron's protagonists typically evince his views, and since the spiritual Turner was the secular Styron's protagonist, we should expect something similar here, no matter how jarring this may be to historical accuracy, and yet this does not seem to occur. Nat Turner's religiosity presented Styron with problems, since he rejected teleological thinking from his earliest writing. Despite the incredible restraint displayed by King's faith-based protesters in Montgomery and beyond, despite their passivity and faith in the face of inhumane violence, Styron could not assign such qualities to a man who murders, no matter what the justification.[35] Rejecting these possible contemporary models, Styron chose to portray Turner in the throes of a profound doubt.

Turner's existential angst is evident from the beginning of the novel. Incarcerated, sitting chained in a damp jail six weeks after the insurrection, Turner admits that he "had never known it possible to feel so far removed from God—a separation that had nothing to do with faith or desire . . . but with a forsaken solitary apartness so beyond hope that I could not have felt more sundered from the divine spirit had I been cast alive . . . beneath the largest rock on earth" (10). Like Cass, once Nat has committed an act of violence, he finds no succor from the beliefs that had once sustained him. It is possible, of course, that Turner might have lost his faith during the time he hid in the countryside after his rebellion was defeated, for white reprisals against the enslaved and free Blacks of

Virginia were severe. Styron, however, presents Turner as shrinking from violence from the very beginning of the insurrection, musing, after witnessing the revolt's first deaths, "Ah, my God . . . Hast thou truly called me to this?" (391) The Old Testament fervor that the historical Turner—and contemporary civil rights leaders—so ably stoked in his followers seems entirely absent here, as is any sense of a "confused conviction of absolute right." Turner's faith has abandoned him, and he sinks into a despair that would only subside when he was facing the gallows.

Later, while making his confession to Thomas Gray, Turner silently muses that enslaved Blacks do not commit mass suicide to escape bondage because their intense religious faith has sapped their willpower. Previously, Turner believed that "a Negro's Christian faith, his understanding of a kind of righteousness at the heart of suffering . . . swerved him away from the idea of self-destruction" (27). This statement suggests that enslaved Blacks have taken a Kierkegaardian leap of faith, that religion helps them to cope with the absurdity of their situation.[36] Yet if this is Turner's initial understanding of "Negro forbearance," upon further reflection he concludes that "black shit-eating people were surely like flies . . . lacking even that will to destroy by their own hand their unending anguish" (27). For a writer committed to existentialism to claim that a group of people lack will suggests that those people are subhuman, which changes Turner's bleak assertion into something suspiciously like a proslavery position. Turner's comment also undermines the ending of *The Long March.* Presumably it was the maid's own "righteousness at the heart of suffering" that enabled her to recognize Mannix's heroic gesture. Yet if religion serves to rob Black people of their will, as Turner asserts here, then the maid's sympathy with Mannix's suffering is meaningless since she lacks the will to transform her own situation.

While Turner sits in prison awaiting trial, the Lord's absence torments him. He attempts to calm his nerves by reciting a psalm, but "the same feeling of apartness from God which I had felt early that morning . . . washed over me in a chill desolate gush of anguish" (78). Turner's feelings of isolation evolve into more than simply a lack; instead they now convey "a sense of repudiation . . . of denial, as if He had turned His back on me once and for all" (78). The crusading Turner now doubts that the Lord ordained his rebellion, and suspects that God repudiates such violence. Turner's faith, and thus his sense of self, has been so shaken that, while he was willing to risk death in pursuit of his freedom, he now possesses "a sudden fear of death" caused by "my own failure in praying to Him" (79).

This is a revealing passage, for we learn, almost by accident, that Turner's sense of abandonment is not in fact caused by God's rejection of him but by Turner's subconscious refusal to connect with his Divinity. In other words, Turner seems to be in denial about something.

Despite his psychological apostasy, Turner continues to present himself to the world as a devout believer. When Gray confronts Turner's faith with some recent discoveries of modern science, Turner quietly responds that "by the Lord's grace all things can be believed" (111). This assertion, which replaces the phrase "are possible" with the more ambiguous "can be believed," deprives Turner's Christianity of its teleological inflection, transforming Turner's apocalyptic religiosity into a self-delusion. Yet this is not enough for Gray, who, after Turner's rote response exclaims: "Hogwash! . . . Christianity is finished and done with. . . . Don't you realize further that it was the message contained in Holy Scripture that was the cause, the *prime mover*, of this entire miserable catastrophe? Don't you see the plain ordinary *evil* of your dad-burned Bible?" (111) Turner finds himself unable to answer this attack, and Gray continues his tirade by observing that Turner's brand of "Christianity accomplished the mob. The *mob*" (113). Gray's vituperation leaves Turner badly shaken, but it is uncertain which mob Gray refers to, Turner's slaves who killed for their freedom or the mob of whites who extracted retribution for weeks after. Left alone in his cell, Turner experiences a Nietzschean doubt, wondering if "God is dead . . . otherwise why should God not heed me" (115). Christianity, the text asserts here, replaces man's individual ethical choice with a false sense of certitude derived from an uncritical belief in a nonexistent savior.

Styron's interpretation of the Southampton Rebellion allows Margaret Whitehead, the only person Turner kills, to serve the same role as Francesca did for Cass. It is Whitehead's death that sends Turner into despair, and not until he admits to himself on his way to the gallows that he would have "done it all again. I would have destroyed them all. Yet I would have spared [Margaret Whitehead]" that he hears the commingled voices of God and Whitehead welcoming him to heaven (428). This admission is troubling, for earlier the text revels that Turner's sexual desire for Whitehead plays a decisive role in fomenting the rebellion. Given this, Turner's decision to spare her may destroy his motivation to plan the revolt. Worse, in a novel that seeks to portray the futility of violence, Turner's ascension to heaven suggests that violence born of sexual desire is somehow permissible.[37] Turner's desire for Whitehead cheapens the rebellion, reducing it to a crime of passion that leaves the logics of white supremacy untouched and unquestioned.

The Confessions of Nat Turner reveals Styron's embrace of existentialism as incomplete. For Camus, the only foundation for humane values is an embrace of freedom in the face of the absurd. Yet, in the case of Nat Turner, Styron refuses to see the denial of freedom as a justification for violence and confrontation. Indeed, Styron never presents the "intrusion" that Turner finds "intolerable"; the reader never experiences the epiphany that transforms Nat Turner into a rebel. In *The Confessions of Nat Turner* violence disrupts, even when it is intended to redress a systemic wrong, the narrative of white supremacy that Styron claims to find abominable. By comparison, Cass is permitted the luxury of transcendence, coming to terms with his violent nature—including a murder!—to achieve peace and tranquility. This portrayal is even more problematic if one recalls that Cass murders to escape a metaphorical enslavement, while Turner murders in an attempt to free an entire community of enslaved people.

Styron has doggedly defended himself from claims that *The Confessions of Nat Turner* is in any way prejudiced, issuing many defenses of his approach in crafting this novel, one of the most recent appended to the twenty-fifth anniversary edition of the text. In it Styron claims that "when I began writing the book the Civil Rights movement still had the quality of conciliation . . . [and] was dreamed in a spirit of amity, concord, and the hope of a mutual understanding."[38] According to Styron this spirit of conciliation shaped his production of *Nat Turner*, but given the amount of backpedaling by Styron and his surrogates after the publication of *Ten Black Writers Respond*, of which "Nat Turner Revisited" is merely the latest, the reviews and essays he published and interviews he granted *before* the publication of *Ten Black Writers Respond* offer an opportunity to divine Styron's unvarnished ideas for the text. Despite the many ex post facto rationalizations for the choices he made, a careful examination of these reports reveals that the logic Styron employed crafting *The Confessions of Nat Turner*, a logic that demanded he temper his presentation of existentialism, was not as benign as he imagined.

One should take what I call Styron's nonfictional *Nat Turner* writings with a grain of salt. In *Advertisements for Myself* Mailer complained that— while laboring over *Set This House on Fire*—Styron "spent years oiling every literary lever and power which could help him on his way, and there are more medals waiting for him in the mass-media" (464). While Mailer disparaged this behavior he understood the impulse behind it, for "it is not easy to work many years on a novel which has something hard and new to say without trying to shape the reception of it" (465). If, as Mailer contended, Styron was in the habit of trying to shape the reception of his forthcoming novels, a careful perusal of these sources should reveal what conclusions Styron wished his audience to draw. There is a self-serving quality to these pieces, but they are more revealing than anything Styron issued after the controversy over *The Confessions of Nat Turner* erupted.

Styron's earliest public mention of Nat Turner comes in an exchange with James Jones in the July 1963 *Esquire*. The two authors discuss their current projects, and Styron asserts that Nat Turner's rebellion "*was* one of the practical causes of the Civil War which very few people know." Despite the circumstances of his life, Styron finds Turner "an extraordinary man. . . . a man of *heroic* proportions."[39] This bodes well for Nat Turner, but the character we finally see is, for most of the novel, most unheroic. Styron follows this interview with "This Quiet Dust," an essay published by Willie Morris in April of 1965 in a special issue of *Harper's Magazine* focused on the South. This essay, which was reprinted later that year in the collection *The South Today: 100 Years After Appomattox*, has become Styron's most important piece of nonfiction writing.[40]

Commissioned by Morris in November of 1963 and composed in three parts, "This Quiet Dust" treats Styron's childhood fascination with Nat Turner, his scholarly research into the revolt, and finally his search for some trace of Nat Turner's rebellion in contemporary Southampton, Virginia.[41] In this essay Styron testifies that segregation during his Virginia childhood was so effective that it "tended almost totally to preclude any contact between black and white" (12). Given the prescribed social distance between whites and Blacks, Styron contends that "the entire sexual myth needs to be re-examined," for he suspects that "theories involving sexual tension have been badly inflated" (12). Styron notes here that Faulkner was unwilling to portray Dilsey, the black maid in *The Sound and the Fury*, "from that intensely 'inner' vantage point, the interior monologue" (13). This, he reports, he will attempt to do in his forthcoming novel.

Styron provides a list of the sources he has consulted to assist him in constructing his narrative, including Thomas Gray's original *Confessions* and Erik Erikson's psychoanalytic *Young Man Luther*, which Styron praises as "a brilliant study of the development of the revolutionary impulse in a young man, and the relationship of this impulse to the father figure" (16). Incredibly, Styron claims that, in the course of his research, "the evidence does not appear to be that Nat was ill-treated" (17), but later concedes, without seeming to notice the contradiction, that Turner's "bold and desperate bid for liberty" (21) was "so wild and daring that it could only have been the product of the most wretched desperation and frustrate [*sic*] misery of soul" (19). Styron acknowledges that Turner's "gifts for preaching, for prophecy, and his own magnetism seem to have been so extraordinary that he grew into a rather celebrated figure among the Negroes of the county" (18). Styron reports here that during the insurrection Turner spared poor whites, visiting destruction only on those families that participated in the slave system. Styron reveals that, in the aftermath of the revolt, "it has never been determined . . . how many black people, not connected with the rebellion, were slain at the hands of rampaging bands of white men who swarmed all over Southampton in the week following the uprising. . . . A contemporary report . . . put the number at close to two hundred Negroes, many of them free" (20). Although Turner "brought cold, paralyzing fear to the South, a fear that never departed. . . . He went to his death with great dignity and courage" (21). Turner, as Styron describes him here, seems a man of heroic proportions, ethical in his own fashion, who spares the lives of innocents and refuses to permit his men to rape or torture.

In the last section of "This Quiet Dust," Styron engages in speculation about Nat Turner's motivations for revolt as he drives through the Virginia countryside searching for a surviving sign of him. Styron wonders why during the course of the rebellion Turner killed only one person, Margaret Whitehead, and why after committing this act Nat seemed "dispirited, listless, as if all life and juice had been drained from him" (29). Styron speculates that Turner's sole murder forced him to face what he was doing: "Did he discover his humanity here, or did he lose it?" (29). This is an existential question in keeping with those that plagued Cass, a question the readers of "This Quiet Dust" familiar with *Set This House on Fire* must have assumed Styron would confront in his novel. The final pages of "This Quiet Dust" move from reportage to lyric, with Styron at last finding the remains of a house that Turner visited during his insurrection. Styron finds himself transported back to 1831, "that day and this day seem[ing] to meet and melt together, becoming almost one" (30). Styron presents himself as uniquely qualified to travel back to antebellum Virginia and tell Nat Turner's story, and I suspect this article had quite an influence on the reviews of *The Confessions of Nat Turner* that were published two years later.

Styron next mentions his current project during a January 14, 1965, conversation with a literary magazine at the University of Pennsylvania.[42] Here, Styron admits that "I don't think you can really define what evil is.

[The] use of the word 'misunderstanding' is interesting, because somehow the idea of misunderstanding is at the center of all human relationships which go awry." Styron then discloses that he "tend[s] to regard evil in a totally abstract way, simply because I believe that every human being is capable of it."[43] The diminution of evil to mere misunderstanding confirms Kelvin's complaint that Styron sees "[a]ll manifestations and experiences of pain...as equal, and whatever depth there is beneath any one of them is never fully explored."[44] Styron seems to forget the themes he invested into *The Long March*, refusing to acknowledge that broad historical traumas, like the Holocaust (which he would later be accused of not treating with enough sensitivity in *Sophie's Choice*), chattel slavery, and racial segregation derive from far more than just simple misunderstanding, and rely on more than continual misunderstanding to perpetuate themselves.

The reverent tone that Styron uses to describe Nat Turner in "This Quiet Dust" is totally missing from an expansive interview he granted in September of 1965 to Robert Canzoneri and Page Stegner.[45] Styron summarizes his novel here, which he had just completed, and it is perhaps the most inflammatory of his nonfictional *Nat Turner* writings. In this interview Styron reveals that he has honed in on "the relationship with God" as "the central thing in my own conception of the man."[46] Styron later describes Turner's only victim, Margaret Whitehead, as "an eighteen-year-old nubile, *religious nut* very similar to" Nat.[47] Somehow, during the composition of the novel, Styron shifted his consideration of the questions that surround Nat Turner from the existential to the religious and psychological. Turner is described repeatedly here as demented and delusional, as is his young victim. Styron also downplays the centrality of Turner's rebellion to the story he is composing, since his book is "not just a story about a revolt. I hope that it deals . . . responsibly with the problem of responsibility itself, or moral choice, [or the] use of violence."[48] *The Confessions of Nat Turner*, Styron suggests here, will present as equivalent the violence of slavery and the violence of resistance.

Styron's earlier supposition that the young Nat Turner was not ill treated by the Turners has grown here into the speculation that the Turners "were enlightened masters like so many Virginia planters of the time, opposed to slavery but trying to find a way out." Styron draws this conclusion "because it seemed to me that there could be only one way to justify the fact that Nat *had* been educated, *could* read the Bible and knew it by heart" and that was through the beneficence of the Turner family.[49] Although Nat Turner, who was born in 1800, would have, by the time he was twenty-five, heard talk of sexual abuse, seen captured runaways flogged, and witnessed entire plantation communities uprooted and sold to Carolina, Georgia, Mississippi, and Alabama to pay debts, Styron insists he experienced "a kind of slave life in which—as a child, as a boy, as a young man and so on—he once was happy by anybody's standards."[50] According to Styron, it is only when the Turner family, forced to adjust to the depressed economy that pertained in Virginia throughout the 1820s, sold Nat Turner rather than freeing him that Turner experienced the desire to rebel. Styron now finds Turner's longing to lead his people out of bondage unexceptional, not a proper moment for existential rebellion, for anyone might have acted as Nat did, "if you had a measure of *madness* in your head, anyway" (74, emphasis added). Styron also contends that people don't revolt when they are oppressed because once "you oppress people, you've got them under your heel. It's when you've given them the smell of something grand" that they are apt to rebel (74). Thus, Nat Turner's rebellion was set in motion not by the intolerable conditions of slavery, but by "kindly, educated people influenced by the University of Virginia and Thomas Jefferson" who allowed Nat Turner to envision a better life before snatching it away (74–75).

In this interview, Styron begins to explicate Nat Turner's relationship with Margaret Whitehead. Turner, Styron admits, is exceptional, "an educated slave, and a man even of some refinement in a curious way. A man of that sort I think in a deep part of his heart would scorn the average, illiterate, pathetic colored woman—slave woman" (76). Even if we grant Styron this assertion, he seems to conveniently forget that, as he mentioned in "This Quiet Dust," there was a sizable population of free Blacks in Southampton from which Turner might have taken a lover or a wife. Styron dismisses this out of hand, as he does the idea that Turner might choose celibacy because of his religious calling. Instead Styron assumes that Turner desires the virginal Whitehead, but the social barrier between them seems "impermeable" and Turner could only destroy this obstruction by attacking it "in the most apocalyptic way that is possible for a human being. You break through it by killing" (76).[51] These, then, are the twin motivations for Turner's rebellion: his outrage at the insufficient kindness paid to him by his master, who taught him to read and write and gave him the liberty to preach the Gospel, but would not free him; and his lust for a teenaged "religious fanatic" (76). Styron submits this as an explanation as to why Turner would lead a rebellion but kill only once, and why his one victim was "the only nubile girl, so far as I can find out, killed" during the entire insurrection (76). So much for Styron's reexamination of the sexual myth of the Black man.[52]

The final interview that will be considered here is a transcript of a conversation that took place between Styron, C. Vann Woodward, and R. W. B. Lewis on November 5, 1967, about three months after the novel's release, on "Yale Reports, a weekly broadcast review program presented by Yale University and WTIC" (Yale, 83).[53] Styron was a colleague of Woodward's and Lewis's at Yale, teaching informally in the English department there, so it comes as no surprise when, early in their conversation, Woodward pronounces *The Confessions of Nat Turner* "a very valid and authentic use of history for the purposes of fiction" (85), and soon after declares the novel "above criticism" (86). Although *Confessions* had received overwhelmingly positive notice, there were two prominent negative reviews, Wilfrid Sheed's, which appeared on the front cover of *The New York Times Book Review*, and Martin Duberman's, in *The Village Voice*. Woodward's comment here seemed designed to reassure Styron that he is among friends who properly venerate his efforts.

Moving into a discussion of the novel itself, Styron again links the existential angst that Turner experiences in the novel to "his failure to have achieved anything in the rebellion [which] is more or less connected to his failure to make contact with God, who ordered his life and with whom he carried on a very close relationship" (Yale, 87). Styron consistently attributes a loss of faith to Turner, but fails to attribute this to an existential confrontation with his being, but rather a kind of psychological depression. Again he claims that "given decency on the part of a solicitous master, and given an intelligent and impressionable young Negro like Nat, life was and could have been, as I portrayed it, tolerable. Even more than tolerable. Yet [the] insecurity that one lived with during slave times was such that I think Nat snapped into a kind of obsessive fanaticism" (90–91).

In this interview, as in the novel, Styron depicts Turner as a fanatic bent on destroying as many whites as possible. This is at odds with what Styron reports in "This Quiet Dust," yet he must create a psychological justification for Turner and his company's ability to murder whites. He concludes that Turner and his men must have held all whites in contempt in order to exterminate them.[54] Styron discusses Turner and his rebellion here, as in the novel, in almost exclusively psychological terms. By placing such a strong emphasis on Turner's supposed tolerable circumstances, Styron supports the same individualistic ethos he took such pains to denounce in *Set This House on Fire*. It seems not to occur to Styron that, as a preacher, to say nothing of a member of an enslaved community, Turner may have considered selfish individualism to have been anathema.[55]

Styron claims that "it is impossible to live in America these days without giving the racial problem a great deal of thought," and indeed *The Confessions of Nat Turner* represents the culmination of years of thought about race by Styron (Yale, 81). It is, however, telling that as Styron thought about Nat Turner, he shifted away from presenting him as an existentialist and instead chose to portray him as a seething collection of psychological and sexual urges. Styron claims that "the efforts I made to recreate Nat Turner, to bring him back to life, represented at least partially the accomplishment of an imperious moral duty: to get to know the blacks" (Yale, 81). Unfortunately, try as he might, Styron is unable to truly reproduce an emancipationist narrative that would suggest he knew "the blacks" as well as he thought. Indeed, in the hands of Styron, "General" Nat Turner remains an unknown, but Styron's predilections become all too clear.

Epilogue

PERFECTING INNOCENCE

One way to understand the interplay between the shifting rhetorical referents of American exceptionalism and American innocence is to turn our gaze to an event which may be understood as a culmination of the civil rights movement, tangible proof that the African American community's pursuit of full equality in America has reached a high-water mark: the election of Barack Obama to the presidency of the United States of America.[1] But, in order to fully comprehend how Obama's ceaseless invocations of American exceptionalism throughout his election campaign served to support—indeed to reinvigorate—the premise of American innocence, we must turn to the pivotal moment in that campaign. While Obama's improbable rise to the presidency faced many challenges, it is important to remember that he became the front-runner after he emerged victorious in the Iowa caucus (where polls predicted he would finish second) and followed that with a narrow loss in New Hampshire and then a resounding win in the South Carolina primary. After South Carolina, the field winnowed to two candidates, Obama and Hillary Clinton, and the senator from Illinois inexorably built an insurmountable lead in pledged delegates. He would surely claim the nomination of the Democratic Party and then win the White House. And then came Rev. Wright.

Rev. Jeremiah Wright was pastor of Chicago's Trinity United Church of Christ, the church Obama attended for more than a decade. Rev. Wright married Barack and Michelle Obama, baptized their children, and served as one of Obama's closest advisors when he was an Illinois state senator moonlighting as a lecturer at the University of Chicago Law School. So, when video emerged of Rev. Wright profanely condemning American foreign policy in the aftermath of 9-11, it threatened to inject a potentially fatal strain of racial resentment into a campaign that, until that point, been carefully calibrated to render questions of race inert.[2] Rev. Wright's comments, played incessantly on the nightly news and across the web, seemed poised to destroy in a number of days the months of groundwork laid by Obama and his campaign team by sowing doubt about Obama's narrative and thus his viability in the general election. As the media furor grew, and calls for him to step aside and cede the Democratic Party nomination to Sen. Clinton increased, Obama needed to neutralize Wright's toxic words, to stop voters from associating Wright's statements with his candidacy.[3] To accomplish this, he prepared a speech that celebrated American exceptionalism and sanctified the premise of American innocence even as it attempted to place America's racial history in a context that would allow Obama's campaign to survive.

"A More Perfect Union" is an incredible rhetorical performance, masterfully separating Obama from the views of his erstwhile mentor, as was its design. It served to reassure a significant plurality of American voters that Obama possessed the proper temperament to be president. And it did so by invoking the particularly American narrative of exceptionalism, progress, and innocence, one that Obama had referenced before and one that often attaches itself to matters of race and reform.[4] Deriding the "racial stalemate we've been stuck in for years," Obama asserted that, in order "to continue the long march of those who came before us, a march for a more just, more equal, more free, more caring and more prosperous America," the nation should take this moment of political crisis as an opportunity to reflect on the history of racial progress in the United States. "The fact is," Obama stated, "that the comments that have been made [by Rev. Wright and others] . . . over the last few weeks reflect the complexities of race in this country that we've never really worked through—a part of our union that we have yet to perfect." It is, Obama continued, only by coming to terms with these historical complexities that the United States can begin to tackle the "two wars, a terrorist threat, a falling economy, a chronic health care crisis and potentially devastating climate change" that presently challenge the nation.

This is an amazing bit of sleight of hand. Obama connects the political crisis bedeviling his campaign (Rev. Wright's toxic rhetoric) with the United States' history of ambivalence to emancipationist discourse. He then asserts that only by properly understanding how this reluctance to accept the claims of emancipationist discourse continues to affect our social and political narratives can Americans address the other challenges facing the nation. Thus, it is only by confronting the history behind both the venom of Rev. Wright's statements and the outsized reaction to

it—which in Obama's framing is merely a reflection of the nation's continuing difficulty in fully weaving Black Americans into the fabric of the
nation—that we can begin to finally live in the here and now: to embrace
our emancipationist past is the first step in beginning to rescue our present. A refusal by the American people, Black and white alike, to confront
the morass of racial resentment dredged up by Rev. Wright's comments
represents in this framing a shirking of patriotic duty, a turning away from
the ceaseless quest to correct the flawed circumstances of the past to produce a brighter, more hopeful future. All of these claims rest on a premise
that Obama invokes with the very title of his speech but does not explicitly dwell on: that our nation is exceptional even as it remains a work in
progress. But, even as he calls for an engagement with the nation's racial
past, Obama ultimately evades a full consideration of emancipationist discourse in his speech.

Obama evokes this suppressed history when he notes that the nation
"requires a reminder of how we arrived at this point" of racial stalemate.
Although he decides against "[r]ecit[ing] here the history of racial injustice in this country" Obama does see the need "to remind ourselves that
so many of the disparities that exist in the African-American community
today can be directly traced to inequalities passed on from an earlier generation that suffered under the brutal legacy of slavery and Jim Crow."
Obama invokes William Faulkner to drive home the need for a reflection
that might enable an emancipationist catharsis, citing the bard of Oxford's
insight that "[t]he past isn't dead and buried. In fact, it isn't even past" to
justify his foreshortened presentation of Black historical trauma.[5] This is a
curious stance since it seems to acknowledge the substance if not the spe-
cifics of Rev. Wright's central claim: that Black Americans have every right
to be skeptical of the claims made by the government of the United States
about their treatment of people of color abroad based on the nation's past
treatment of people of color who sought to assert their constitutionally
guaranteed rights as Americans. This sentiment also works against the
tenets of American exceptionalism and innocence by asking its audience
to accept the deliberately effaced history that implicates white Americans
as beneficiaries of an unjust racial regime.

Having engaged this narrative, Obama then neutralizes it by contrasting the historical legacy of racial stratification with the attitudes of
"[m]ost working- and middle-class white Americans [who] don't feel that
they have been particularly privileged by their race. Their experience is
the immigrant experience—as far as they're concerned, no one's handed

them anything, they've built it from scratch." This is the central moment in the speech, the place when Obama turns away from reanimating the emancipationist discourse that has withered in the post–civil rights era and instead endorses a continued forgetfulness by extending the premise of innocence to any "working- and middle-class white Americans" inclined to see their status as unconnected to and unaffected by race. Adam Mansbach criticizes Obama for "let[ting] white people off the hook. Though I grasped the political necessity of the move, my expectations of [Obama] were sufficiently high that it was disheartening to hear him fudge the difference between institutional racism and white bitterness."[6] Mansbach, I fear, misunderstands the intent of "A More Perfect Union." Obama, no longer an academic, did not want to initiate a conversation on race centered around a reconsideration of our nation's history; he wanted to restore himself as an exemplar of American exceptionalism capable of rescuing an American innocence imperiled by the depredations of the Bush presidency in the eyes of potential voters. And in this regard the speech worked masterfully.

Obama understood that he could not hope to displace the American innocence that supports American exceptionalism and hope to win the presidency. Instead he embraced it. While Mansbach complains that "to characterize ire at affirmative action and at *the thought that others might think them prejudiced* as 'similar' to the frustration felt by the victims of entrenched structural racism [is] disingenuous and even irresponsible," Obama wished to be elected president, and thus gave a speech that would enable him to achieve this seemingly impossible goal (74–75, emphasis in original). Perhaps Obama assumed that simply granting emancipationist discourse equal status with narratives of white innocence might serve to neutralize the white racial resentment that stems from feelings of being unfairly burdened, and thus make it easier for the nation to admit to matters of social inequality.[7] While Mansbach correctly notes that a national conversation on race cannot be held until all sides (which is to say whites) acknowledge "that structural racism is a cancer metastasizing through every aspect of American life," Obama understood that the "essence of white privilege is not knowing you have it" and thus backed away from this point (75). By calling attention to structural racism and then retreating into a familiar narrative of American exceptionalism, Obama sought to have it both ways, balancing these competing narratives to show that he was capable of governing constituents from both Americas.[8]

"A More Perfect Union" succeeded in part because Obama had already established the narrative of his campaign, one that positioned him as a break from the sordid recent past of the Bush-Cheney years and the overly politicized climate of the Clinton presidency. This is why during the campaign he resisted calls to investigate potential misuse of power by the Bush administration even as he worked to cast Hillary as an establishment figure. Indeed, Obama framed his election as an event capable of producing a miraculous rebirth, the return of a forward-looking and optimistic American spirit. He recognized that past elections had served the national narrative of innocence and exceptionalism in precisely this fashion. Obama compared himself to Ronald Reagan during the campaign not because he necessarily admired Reagan's policies, but because he understood how the 1980 presidential election allowed the nation to forget the criminality of Nixon, the malaise of Carter, and the increasing fractiousness of the 1970s that presaged the culture wars of the '80s and '90s.[9] Pundits compared Obama to JFK for a similar reason, since Camelot offered a respite from the stifling conformity of the 1950s that was the by-product of the fears of the Cold War and the accusations of McCarthyism. Kennedy's rhetoric, like Obama's, acknowledged the competing discourses contained in a pluralistic America but ultimately evaded a full endorsement of emancipationist narratives in order to preserve American innocence. Obama's speech, like the writing of Robert Penn Warren, Eudora Welty, Norman Mailer, and William Styron, is engaged in a similar project.

Notes

INTRODUCTION

1. To call any of these writers liberal is problematic, particularly in the cases of Robert Penn Warren and Norman Mailer. But that each of these writers supported the goals of the civil rights movement—an opinion that is crucial to the goals of this study— allows me to make this claim, which is dubious in other ways.

2. In *Black Is a Country*, Nikhil Pal Singh identifies this as "the short civil rights era" and contrasts this truncated understanding of the struggle for civil rights with a longer movement that emerges in the 1920s. For another perspective on the long civil rights movement, see Jacquelyn Dowd Hall, "The Long Civil Rights Movement and the Political Uses of the Past," *Journal of American History* 91 (4) (2005): 1233–1263.

3. Welty certainly used black characters in her fiction, but there is a marked difference in her use of these characters during the civil rights movement.

4. Lionel Trilling, *The Liberal Imagination: Essays on Literature and Society* (New York: Harcourt Brace Jovanovich, 1979), x.

5. A comparison, for example, of Lillian Smith's writing during the period to Eudora Welty's makes this difference clear.

6. David Blight, *Race and Reunion: The Civil War in American Memory*, 5.

7. In *After Appomattox: How the South Won the War*, Stetson Kennedy notes how the South was able to "wrest . . . ideological and political victory out of military defeat" (2). For a more balanced account of how the gains of the Civil War were reversed, see Eric Foner's *Reconstruction: America's Unfinished Revolution, 1863–1877*.

8. Robert Penn Warren, *The Legacy of the Civil War*, 15.

9. Blight, 5.

10. William Spanos, *American Exceptionalism in the Age of Globalization*, ix.

11. It astonishes me that politicians and Lost Cause partisans continue to insist that slavery had nothing to do with the Civil War, that it was a war about states' rights versus federalism.

12. The Tulsa race riots of 1921 exemplify this kind of forgetting. See James R. Hirsh, *Riot and Remembrance: The Tulsa Race War and Its Legacy*.

13. John R. Gillis, *Commemorations: The Politics of National Identity*, 5–6.

14. I do not mean a literal forgetting—most Americans understand that slavery had something to do with the Civil War. I mean an ideological forgetting, whereby

participating in that conflict—or living in a society that limits individual achievement based on a person's race—fails to require any restitution. See Ronald J. Fiscus, *The Constitutional Logic of Affirmative Action.*

15. In *The Constitutional Logic of Affirmative Action* Ronald J. Fiscus observes that "[t]he charge [against affirmative action] is that such programs are always unfair to the individual (white or male) against whom the preferential treatment is directed, unless those individuals themselves participated in the discrimination against now-preferred minorities. If they have not personally participated in the particular discrimination in question, then they are considered innocent, and the imposition of . . . affirmative action . . . is . . . unfair."

16. See Amy Kaplan's "'Left Alone with America': The Absence of Empire in the Study of American Culture" for a comprehensive look at how American studies naturalized the hegemonic discourse of Cold War America.

17. Donald Pease, *The New American Exceptionalism*, 8, 9. The process of forgetting is already at work here, since the Civil War, and later the excesses of the Vietnam War, must be elided in order to maintain this fictional status of American exception.

18. Floating signifier.

19. http://www.ushistory.org/paine/commonsense/sense4.htm; accessed June 11, 2011.

20. Thus state fantasies enable violence, which must also be seen as exceptional and thus disavowed. As Lopa Basu notes, Art Spiegelman's *In the Shadow of No Towers* is in part a rejection of Bush's cynical use of American exceptionalism after 9-11.

21. For the purposes of this project, one of the most interesting things about Michael Dennent's *The Cultural Front* is how the events of the 1930s, which he painstakingly details, must be forgotten to accommodate the Cold War consensus that emerges after World War II.

22. Spanos, *American Exceptionalism in the Age of Globalization*, 22.

23. Malcolm X's use of the rhetoric of American exceptionalism is one of the reasons that whites in the 1960s found his speeches so troubling. Malcolm often compared himself to Patrick Henry, reversing the colonial myth by casting Black Americans as exceptional and oppressed.

24. Phillip Barrish, *White Liberal Identity, Literary Pedagogy, and Classic American Realism*, 95.

25. Although I don't consider it in this chapter, Warren's *Democracy and Poetry* represents an interesting postscript to his racial evolution.

26. Styron returns to these themes in *Sophie's Choice.*

CHAPTER ONE

1. For an extended discussion of Agrarianism's eclectic nature, see Marc Jancovich's *The Cultural Politics of the New Criticism.*

2. The racial stratification that makes leisure and contemplation possible for some goes completely unmentioned.

3. There are dozens of books on the failure of Reconstruction, from C. Vann Woodward's *The Strange Career of Jim Crow* (1955) to Jerrold Packer's *American Nightmare: The History of Jim Crow* (2005).

4. Warren's embrace of historical teleology here aligns him more closely with Marxist thought than perhaps he realized. Several of the other Agrarians were put off by Warren's stance on this issue, to the point where Donald Davidson, the organizing force behind the volume, considered dropping Warren's contribution from *I'll Take My Stand*, before Allen Tate and John Crowe Ransom (of all people) convinced Davidson to allow it. As Anthony Szczesiul noted in *Racial Politics and Robert Penn Warren's Poetry*, many Warren scholars seize upon this dispute as proof that this essay was progressive for its time and circumstance, a claim that does not hold up when one considers larger historical and cultural events from the period.

5. Full text of this speech is available at http://historymatters.gmu.edu/d/39/. For a bound copy, see Louis R. Harlan, ed., *The Booker T. Washington Papers*, Vol. 3, 583–587.

6. The controversial poem "Pondy Woods" treats as its subject a "Black buck" named Big Jim Todd who shares an instinctive connection with nature. In *All the King's Men* Warren establishes his trope about the simultaneity of modernity and the past by contrasting the new highway that snakes through Louisiana with a Black peasant who works the land by the side of the road.

7. Ironically, this view is shared by Black Nationalist groups including Marcus Garvey's UNIA in the 1930s and the Nation of Islam in the 1950s and '60s.

8. Forrest Robinson, "A Combat with the Past: Robert Penn Warren on Race and Slavery," 513.

9. I do not mean to suggest that Warren was not seriously interrogating race in his fiction and poetry. Race plays a crucial role in the development of both. For an in-depth consideration of the role race played in the development of Warren's poetry, see Szczesiul's *Racial Politics and Robert Penn Warren's Poetry*.

10. Warren's essays grounded his fiction and vice versa. As he began crafting novels Warren became less interested in writing polemical defenses of the South and more interested in discovering the nature of the society in which he lived. This search, however, is not necessarily distinct from the values of Agrarianism. As M. Thomas Inge notes in "The Fugitives and the Agrarians: A Clarification," for Agrarian writers "there are profound and significant connections between them [art and politics]. . . . [T]he Agrarian movement was not a desertion of art and poetry for politics and social change. In both contexts, they saw themselves preeminently as men of letters" (492).

11. "Warren on the Art of Fiction," *Talking with Robert Penn Warren*, ed. Floyd C. Watkins, John T. Hiers, Mary Louise Weaks, 33.

12. Ibid.

13. Joseph Blotner, *Robert Penn Warren: A Biography*, 202.

14. Randolph's stratagems were probably not what Warren anticipated when he called for whites to permit Blacks to organize their labor. See James Neyland's *A. Philip Randolph* for more on Randolph's role in these decisions.

15. Blotner, 302.

16. See James A. Perkins, "Robert Penn Warren and James Farmer: Notes on the Creation of New Journalism," *rWp: An Annual of Robert Penn Warren Studies*, 1:1 (2001), for a discussion of Warren's journalistic tendencies. Frustratingly, Perkins focuses his study on 1965's *Who Speaks for the Negro?* instead of the earlier *Segregation.*

17. John Hollowell claims, in *Fact and Fiction: The New Journalism and the Nonfiction Novel*, that the new journalist is often a novelist "placed in the role of witness to the moral dilemmas of our time" in a literary form that incorporates "aspects of the novel, the confession, the autobiography, and the journalistic report" written with a sense of crisis (15–16). If this is so, both *Segregation* and *Who Speaks for the Negro?* qualify as specimens of the genre.

18. "Warren on the Art of Fiction," 33.

19. While his mention of the shacks recalls "The Briar Patch," Warren's description in *Segregation* of traveling on "Highway 61 striking south from Memphis, straight as a knife edge through the sad and baleful beauty of the Delta country, south towards Vicksburg and the Federal cemeteries, toward the fantasia of Natchez" is remarkably like his famous beginning of *All the King's Men* a decade earlier. The novel opens with a depiction of "Highway 58 . . . straight for miles, coming at you [with] the heat dazzl[ing] up from the white slab," but while Jack Burden could comfortably regard the sharecroppers' "white washed shacks, all just alike" as he drove along Willie Stark's new highway, Warren must grapple with the reality that these supposedly immutable objects, now abandoned or improved, represent an unnerving indication of shifting social conditions in the South (3).

20. Autherine Lucy entered the University of Alabama during the spring semester in 1956, the first Black student in its history. She attended her first class on Friday, February 3, and students protested her presence by rioting that Saturday while the university president was away. The following Monday hundreds of Alabama students, augmented by an equal number of "local B. F. Goodrich rubber workers" who were, ironically, also card carrying members of A. Philip Randolph's AFL-CIO, rampaged across campus and drove Lucy from the school. See Diane McWhorter, *Carry Me Home: Birmingham, Alabama, the Climactic Battle of the Civil Rights Revolution*, 99, 103

21. This is an interesting assertion considering that the stories from the South in the national consciousness at the time included the conflict at the University of Alabama; the Montgomery bus boycott, which had begun late the previous year and would continue until December; the ramifications of the *Brown* case; and, looming over all of this like a half-forgotten dream, the murder of Emmett Till.

22. This is the earliest reference that I could find of the term. Dabney, who was a prolific and felicitous writer, might have coined it himself.

23. Wallace Hettle, "The Minister, the Martyr, and the Maxim: Robert Lewis Dabney and Stonewall Jackson Biography," 357.

24. Ibid., 366.

25. Blotner, 84.

26. Civil War historian Wallace Hettle credits Dabney with being the first to equate fallen Confederate soldiers with Christian martyrs and describes him as "the Lost Cause defender of slavery and social hierarchy." Hettle, 363–365, 366.

27. Ibid., 356, my emphasis.

28. Blotner, 304.

29. Ibid., 343.

30. If Warren's argument here seems familiar, it is because he anticipates Louis Menand's *Metaphysical Club*. While *Legacy of the Civil War* addresses the psychological ramifications of the war as such, Warren doesn't dwell on the depths and development of Holmes's and James's thought, while Menand traces this exhaustively in his text.

31. As Kenneth Warren observes, this rejection of extremism also allowed the South to construct the plantation narratives that justified the establishment of Jim Crow during what historians termed the period of reconciliation. See *Black and White Strangers*, 13, 35, and as follows.

32. Stetson Kennedy makes a similar point in *After Appomattox: How the South Won the War* (1995).

33. Dudziak, 115–118.

34. Ibid., 128. The 101st is an army division, so Eisenhower actually sent in the army.

35. Oliver Wendell Holmes, quoted in *Legacy*, 19.

36. Blotner, 344, my emphasis.

37. Warren published two novels after *Legacy—Wilderness: A Tale of the Civil War* (1961) and *Flood: A Romance of Our Time* (1964). These works were critical failures, earning scathing reviews for a variety of reasons. Given that the two texts together run to almost eight hundred pages, there is no easy way for me to deal with them within the context of this chapter. Still, it is worth noting that each text occurs in past historical eras, with *Wilderness* set during the Civil War and *Flood* opening in 1935 during the Depression as it follows the fortunes of a Kentucky town for a generation. Warren seems reluctant, at least with his fiction, to assess the political ramifications of the contemporary moment as he had once done masterfully in *All the King's Men*. This is not to suggest that Warren ignored the reality of the 1960s in these novels, particularly in *Wilderness*, but that the frames through which he chose to explore issues of racial justice and democracy seemed increasingly irrelevant to those reviewing the texts.

38. Blotner, 359.

39. Ibid., 360. In less than four years, from 1961 to May of 1965, Warren produced a 110-page intellectual history of the Civil War, 770 pages of fiction, and 445 pages of text composed of interviews, critical assessments of current scholarship on the Negro problem, and personal evaluations of nearly every person of interest in the text. He also made a number of appearances throughout the country and taught classes at Yale. Warren's productivity seems impossible.

40. Taylor Branch, *Pillar of Fire*, 417–420.

41. Michael Szalay, "*All the King's Men*; or, the Primal Crime," 34.

42. James Perkins details how tightly Warren edited the interviews, but I trust that he represents his subjects and their positions faithfully. "Robert Penn Warren and James Farmer: Notes on the Creation of New Journalism," 164–166.

43. Clarke's study, *Dark Ghetto*, was published in 1965 a month after Warren's text. Warren was certainly aware of Clarke's work, he cites Clarke's claim that practicing nonviolence in the face of violence might psychically harm Blacks throughout the text. Warren asked several of those he interviewed, including King, about Clarke's idea.

44. Szalay claims that Warren disliked the northern liberal identification with, and in some cases hero worship of, Black civil rights workers, even though he approved of the cause. Assuming this is true, it might explain Warren's obsession with Brown rather than Nat Turner or Denmarck Vescey.

45. In this sense, "Conversation Piece" resembles nothing as much as *The Fire Next Time*.

46. According to Warren, the northern liberal "has to find out if he really wants a Negro family next door. If he really wants to take orders from a Negro department head. If he really wants to be arrested by a Negro cop. If he really wants to have his children bused into a school in a Negro neighborhood. If he really wants a tax boost for a crash program for the 'disadvantaged'—i.e., Negroes. If he really wants his daughter on mixed dates" (430).

47. See Jerry Gafio Watts's *Ralph Ellison: Heroism and the Black Intellectual* for a discussion of Ellison's views on various government policies designed to help Black people.

CHAPTER TWO

1. *Advertisements for Myself*, 92.

2. Truman Capote's refusal to collaborate any further with his cousin may have had something to do with Lee's retirement.

3. *Advertisements for Myself*, 27. Further references are cited in the text. If "The White Negro" is, in Mailer's estimation, his most important work, *Advertisements for Myself* is as pivotal to a scholar seeking to understand the development of Mailer's career. Mailer is delightfully self-critical throughout this collection, offering up rationalizations for each of his developmental missteps while playing down the importance of *The Naked and the Dead*. Throughout this investigation of Mailer, I try to resist blindly accepting his claims at face value, and instead unpack his statements and evasions to better make sense of the choices he made en route to developing his distinctive literary style. Many of the more innocuous statements in *Advertisements* prove to be most revealing, and so, even as I consider *Barbary Shore*, *The Deer Park*, and "The White Negro," I will deploy Mailer's own claims about these works in *Advertisements for Myself* to support many of my contentions.

4. Manso, 179.

5. The hostility of *The Naked and the Dead*'s Sergeant Croft—a native of the American Southwest—to the urbane Captain Hearn demonstrates this point clearly.

6. Although critical respect is itself a form of currency, so perhaps it might be more accurate to state that Mailer desired more than mere monetary compensation.

7. Louis Menand, "Norman Mailer in His Time," *American Studies*, 147.

8. See Mary Dearborn's *Mailer: A Biography*, 54–76 for an account of his time during this period.

9. *The God That Failed* would exemplify the crisis of faith Marxist writers went through as Hitler rose to power and the left stood by impotently. Louis Menand makes this point about Richard Wright in "Richard Wright: The Hammer and the Nail" in *American Studies*. Some writers in the 1950s were compelled by McCarthyism to rethink their political commitments, but many became dissatisfied with Communism during the war.

10. Godfrey Hodgson, *America in Our Time*, 72–73.

11. By Richard Poirier's estimation, despite its many flaws, "*Barbary Shore* is nonetheless marked by passages of lurid, startling brilliance" (Manso, 65).

12. Apparently, while in Paris, Mailer missed the news that Sartre had declared *Native Son* the first existentialist novel in America.

13. "The White Negro," 339.

14. I certainly do not mean to suggest that modernist or social realist texts were or are moribund, simply that Mailer's willingness to abandon the more contemporary idiom he created for *The Naked and the Dead* for these forms in *Barbary Shore* demonstrates his search for a literary style all his own.

15. It is important to note here that by describing himself as a libertarian socialist Mailer indicated his disdain for both the USSR and the USA.

16. Louis Menand, "Norman Mailer in His Time," 146.

17. One wonders what the young Mailer would have made of Foucault's *Discipline and Punish* and *The History of Sexuality*.

18. Dearborn, 92.

19. For example, in *Must You Conform*, Lindner claims that "there exists *nothing* [in contemporary society] which does not require the young to conform, to adjust, to submit, to become regimented. Examine religion, education, psychology, social work, philosophy, recreation, pediatrics . . . each is infused with the rot-producing idea that the salvation of individual and of society depends upon conformity and adjustment" (27–28).

20. Mailer's critique of American society predates Marcuse's study, of course. As a result, I would add Marcuse to Sean McCann's list of thinkers that Mailer anticipates (McCann, 295).

21. Seemingly every conversation in the novel involves a misunderstanding, and characters declare their love for one another at inopportune times, either too early or too late. Eitel ultimately fails because he cannot declare his love for Elena, while Sergius realizes his love for Lulu after forces conspire to break them apart.

22. Marion Faye is based on Mickey Jelke, a New York pimp who happened to be the scion of rich socialites from the Upper East Side (Dearborn, 101).

23. A sense of exactly how much help Mailer offered, aside from an initial cash stake, depends on your source. In Mailer's eyes he was essential.

24. King would give the *Voice* an interview in 1965, an indication of how quickly the paper grew to prominence.

25. I distinguish King's program of direct action and confrontation from the juridical efforts of the NAACP and the rhetorical efforts of forebearers of the modern civil rights movement. King's program, while nonviolent, appealed to Mailer even as it dismayed other liberals.

26. Mailer includes an excerpt from "The Hip and the Square" in *Advertisements*.

27. Mailer, *The Time of Our Time*, 15. The title of this collection recalls his short story "The Time of Her Time," included in *Advertisements*, where Mailer first attempts the new literary style that writing "The White Negro" allowed him to achieve.

28. Manso, 258.

29. Poirier asserts that "many of [Mailer's] arguments about historical or social change are really arguments about changes in the language, changes in verbal fashion" (65).

30. I am almost certain Mailer invented his illiterate "Negro friend," much as he did the thief and madam in his letter to Faulkner.

31. Mailer states parenthetically some pages later that "it is the ultimate human right of the Negro to mate with the white" (356).

32. The modern reader is of course likely to find this example wholly ridiculous, in that there is nothing particularly subversive or novel about a man at a party not actually listening to what the woman he is in conversation with is saying but rather what her subtext reveals about the prospect that the two of them will have sex. And while interracial relationships have indeed served as a catalyst for change at a social level, if only because of the contested legal status of the progeny of such affairs, the kind of coupling that Mailer describes here would seemingly only resonate on a personal level.

33. One might perceive Till's alleged wolf whistle as an example of hip language: a risky communication designed to explore the possibilities of a context others perceived as fixed.

34. According to Rhoda Wolf, wife of Dan Wolf, one of Mailer's partners in *The Village Voice*, "When he'd been planning *The Deer Park* he'd started picking people's brains for their insights into the unconscious. He was doing it with Lindner, the psychiatrist, and also with Dan, trying to get information about psychoanalysis. I was in Reichian therapy, and he was asking me all sorts of questions, maybe because he was turned on by Reich. This was back in '53 and '54" (Manso, *Mailer: His Life and Times*, 231).

35. As his biographer Mary Dearborn notes, "However ridiculous Mailer's extrapolation of issues about masculinity from a musical movement might seem, his exploration of the jazz world shows his creative process at work. He found, in this culture,

themes that obsessed him personally: in this case, an apprehension approaching paranoia about black male sexuality and his own ability to measure up . . ."(Dearborn, 117).

36. Interestingly, perhaps the best literary example of such a man is not *An American Dream*'s Stephen Rojack, who, after all, flees a stable upper-middle-class life, but Ken Kesey's McMurphy from his *One Flew Over the Cuckoo's Nest* (1963), a character truly at the mercy of the dehumanizing system that Mailer hopes to escape.

CHAPTER THREE

1. Welty addresses race throughout her career: her first short story collection, *A Curtain of Green and Other Stories* (1941), contains "Keela, the Outcast Indian Maiden" and "Powerhouse," both evocative and effective set pieces that center around a the creative and communicative potential of a Black man in the midst of performance, as well as "A Worn Path," a touching story about memory and loss. Her last collection, *The Bride of the Innisfallen and Other Stories*, contains "The Burning," a story about Union soldiers carrying out Sherman's occupation of the South told from the point of view of a Black servant still caring for her white mistresses. Still, all of these works were completed before *Brown* changed the political and social climate so dramatically and thus fall outside the purview of this study.

2. Michael Kreyling, *Author and Agent*, 202.

3. Ann Waldron, *Eudora: A Writer's Life*, 253–255, 261–264.

4. Ibid., 263.

5. Ibid., 282.

6. Suzanne Marrs, "'The Huge Fateful Stage of the Outside World': Eudora Welty's Life in Politics," 82.

7. Waldron, 281.

8. *Conversations with Eudora Welty*, ed. Peggy Whitman Prenshaw, 83.

9. *More Conversations with Eudora Welty*, ed. Peggy Whitman Prenshaw, 10–11.

10. Carol Polsgrove, *Divided Minds: Intellectuals and the Civil Rights Movement*, 187.

11. Sasha Torres, *Black, White and in Color: Television and Black Civil Rights*, 20.

12. Waldron, 20.

13. Torres, 22. *NBC White Paper* was a forerunner of shows like NBC's *Dateline* and CBS's *60 Minutes*.

14. Ibid., 6.

15. Kay Mills, *Changing Channels: The Civil Rights Case That Transformed Television*, 39.

16. Ibid., 20, 46. WLBT remained so intransigent throughout the period that local Blacks were eventually granted the station's broadcasting license by the FCC.

17. Marrs, 75.

18. Adam Nossiter, *Of Long Memory: Mississippi and the Murder of Medgar Evers*, 94.

19. Ibid., 90. The Citizens' Councils exist today as the Council of Conservative Citizens, www.cofcc.com, which was organized in the mid-1990s in part by Robert Patterson, the founder of the original Citizens' Council.

20. Ibid., 96; Maryanne Vollers, *Ghosts of Mississippi: The Murder of Medgar Evers, the Trials of Byron De La Beckwith, and the Haunting of the New South*, 52.

21. James Silver, *Mississippi: The Closed Society*, 35. Foucault has much to say about the disciplinary power of social expectations on individual behavior. See his *Discipline and Punish*, especially 170–194. Interestingly, with their loyalty oaths, litmus tests, and consensus forged from intimidation, the Council and the Commission functioned similarly to today's GOP.

22. Marrs, 77, 79; John Salter, *Jackson, Mississippi: An American Chronicle of Struggle and Schism*, 102.

23. Myrlie Evers, with William Peters, *For Us, the Living*, 267.

24. Waldron, 160. Welty declined the invitation.

25. Nossiter, 30.

26. Salter, 57.

27. Nossiter, 6.

28. Kreyling, 202.

29. *Conversations*, 83.

30. For an insightful discussion of the concept of law and political leadership as it pertained to Leonides and the Spartans and Xerxes and the Persians, see James Romm, *Herodotus*, 179–189.

31. I do not mean to suggest that the Muslim Moors who ruled Spain, without which many of the texts rediscovered during the Enlightenment would have been lost, were godless pagans, merely that Charlemange and Roland viewed them as such.

32. For a brilliant examination of the myth of Roland and its parallels in the twentieth century, see Peter Haidu's *The Subject of Violence: The Song of Roland and the Birth of the State.*

33. In the aftermath of the assassination, Mississippi's leaders were terrified that King would come to Jackson to continue Evers's program. Of course, Evers's NAACP and King's SCLC, though nominally allies, often found themselves at cross purposes, a division most liberal and conservative whites were completely unaware of.

34. Eudora Welty, *The Collected Stories of Eudora Welty*, 603. All subsequent references in text.

35. There is also the possibility that federal highway money has trickled into the Black parts of Jackson, but this fails to occur to the assassin.

36. This is prescient on Welty's part, for the actual assassin, Byron De La Beckwith, would find himself shaking hands and exchanging pleasantries with Governor Ross Barnett in court during his trial in a shameless effort by Barnett to influence the jury. See Nossiter, 108–109.

37. In *Of Grammatology*, Derrida famously asserts that Western philosophy attempts to privilege the spoken utterance over its written representation in much the same fashion that the speaker denies the visual over the actual.

38. As Benedict Anderson claims in *Imagined Communities*, 5.

39. Meredith and Evers were friends, with Evers defending the eccentric Meredith to the national NAACP, who were doubtful that he was the proper student to desegregate Ole Miss. When Meredith registered for his second semester at the school, Evers was among the party that accompanied him.

40. The Citizens' Council kept detailed notes on anyone even remotely associated with the civil rights movement, so it would be interesting to peruse the Council files (which are supposedly sealed despite the stream of citations from them in recent books about Mississippi) to see if Welty had a file, and if so, what was in it.

41. *Conversations with Eudora Welty*, 31. The *Times*, I suspect, would have happily matched *The New Yorker*'s price for the privilege of publishing her story in their Sunday magazine.

42. Marrs, 80.

43. Ibid., 81.

44. Florence Mars, *Witness in Philadelphia*, 84–87.

45. Vollers, 220.

46. *Conversations*, 182.

47. Mars, 41. Mars, who was forty-one when Schwerner, Chaney, and Goodman disappeared (Welty was fifty-four), lived for a time in New Orleans and Atlanta, just as Welty had lived in New York and San Francisco.

48. The presence of the Citizens' Councils had limited the growth of the Klan in Mississippi for ten years following the *Brown* decision. After the 1963 March on Washington, the Klan experienced a resurgence in Mississippi as it became clear that the rest of the nation admired the civil rights marchers, which called into question the Councils' ability to coerce Blacks without resorting to violence.

49. Mars, 184, 191. According to Mars, southern custom dictated that a sheriff drive an intoxicated woman home in his cruiser after having her park her car where she could later retrieve it.

50. Waldron, 275.

51. Ibid. I have not seen a draft of this essay, though I suspect that it is in her archives at Ole Miss.

52. Mars, 143; Seth Cagin and Phillip Dray, *We Are Not Afraid*, 436.

53. Outrage against the South was such that Styron, working on *The Confessions of Nat Turner* at the time, recalls a woman in a Manhattan salon suggesting that the federal government drop napalm on white southerners rather than on the North Vietnamese. James L. W. West III, *William Styron, A Life*, 335.

54. "Must the Novelist Crusade?" in *Eudora Welty: Stories, Essays, & Memoir*, 1998. All following citations in text.

55. Waldron, 59–60.

56. Peggy Prenshaw, "Welty's Transformation of the Public, the Private and the Political," 20.

57. Ibid., 21.

58. She is wrong in this, of course, for Faulkner's Blackness would have eliminated many things, and it is possible that Welty might never have come to read him. Certainly the New Critics would not have embraced him as the paragon of American writing.

59. *Conversations*, 337.

60. Some of Welty's assertions could readily serve as straw men for various schools of criticism. Her valorization of E. M. Forster, for example, or her claim that the novelist "will do anything at all with his material: shape it, strain it to the breaking point, double it up, or use it backward; he will balk at nothing–see *The Sound and the Fury*–to reach that heart and core," which falls apart when modern readers realize that Faulkner in fact balked at narrating the final fourth of *The Sound and the Fury* from Dilsey's point of view (807). Making such anachronistic arguments fails to address how Welty's writing at the time was shaped by the local events of the civil rights movement, which is the point of this chapter.

61. "Place and Time: The Southern Writer's Inheritance," *The Mississippi Quarterly* (1997), 545. Originally published in 17 September 1954 *Times Literary Supplement*.

62. *Conversations*, 261.

63. Marrs, 85.

64. Ibid. See Robert Hamblin's "Robert Penn Warren at the 1965 Southern Literary Festival: A Personal Recollection," *Southern Literary Journal*, UNC–Chapel Hill, 22.2 (Spring 1990).

65. Kreyling, 204.

66. See Howard Zinn's *The New Abolitionists*, 63 and passim, for a history of Moses' activities in the Mississippi Delta region.

67. Suzan Harrison, "'Racial Content Espied': Modernist Politics, Textuality, and Race in Eudora Welty's 'The Demonstrators,'" 95.

68. John Dittmer, *Local People*, 100.

69. After Johnson signed the Civil Rights Act passed in 1964, several movie theatres, hotels, and restaurants closed so they wouldn't have to comply with the law and accept Black patrons, including the Robert E. Lee Hotel in Jackson. See Shirley Tucker, *Mississippi from Within*, 17.

70. *Conversations*, 260.

71. Ibid., 259.

CHAPTER FOUR

1. *Gates of Eden*, 264.

2. Godfrey Hodgson, *America in Our Time*, 89–90.

3. See Louis Menand's *Metaphysical Club* for a detailed analysis of pragmatism's influence on Columbia and New York City intellectual life.

4. I make this distinction to distinguish King's program of direct action and confrontation from the juridical efforts of the NAACP and the rhetorical efforts of forebearers of the modern civil rights movement.

5. See "Reflections on Little Rock," *The Portable Arendt Reader*, 231–246.

6. West, 119.

7. Ibid., 120.

8. "The Red Badge of Literature," *This Quiet Dust*, 203.

9. West, 189, 195.

10. Ibid., 195.

11. Contemporary scholars understand that ideology is far more complex than Styron seems to credit, but I will be using ideology as he understood it for the sake of clarity.

12. West, 225.

13. Kelvin, "The Divided Self: William Styron's Fiction from *Lie Down in Darkness* to *The Confessions of Nat Turner*," 212.

14. Although I will not discuss *Sophie's Choice* here, I think Styron makes an attempt to critique the logic of early feminism there that is consistent with his hesitancy about the confrontational nature of the civil rights movement.

15. Again, with the exception of Stingo, Styron's narrators often seem to perform as his imagined or ideal reader.

16. *The Long March*, 7. All subsequent references will be made in the body of the text.

17. *The Novels of William Styron*, 10.

18. Despite the suffering Culver and Mannix endure, Culver finds himself "unable to hate" the colonel. Instead Culver pities "Old Al . . . with the back unbreakable" (117). By refusing to take sides, Culver protects himself from a loss of standing. He claims, after the march, that "he had hardly ever known a time in his life when he was not . . . sick with loneliness or afraid" (117), despite his earlier report that Mannix was one of the few people able to break through his isolation. Culver's construction of a false memory demonstrates the dangers conformity poses even to our inner lives.

19. Kelvin, 215, 209.

20. Styron faced this criticism with *Sophie's Choice* as well as *The Confessions of Nat Turner*. See, for example, Morris Dickstein, "The World in a Mirror: Problems of Distance in Recent American Fiction," *Sewanee Review*, 1981.

21. West, 253.

22. Camus expresses these ideas most fully in *The Rebel* (1951) and *The Myth of Sisyphus* (1942).

23. Camus, *The Rebel*, 13.

24. "Evaluations: Quick and Expensive Comments on the Talent in the Room" in *Advertisements for Myself*.

25. Finkelstein, *Existentialism and Alienation in American Literature*, 218.

26. When Cass murders Mason, he is under the false impression that Mason has not only raped Francesca but also beaten her to death. Eventually, Styron reveals that a mentally handicapped field hand killed Francesca as she fled from Mason in a panic, making him culpable in her death. For the sake of simplicity, I refer solely to Mason's rape rather than spelling out the chain of events that results in her death.

27. Camus, 13.

28. Lonnie's reference to plastic here seems anachronistic.

29. For a thorough discussion of existential states of being, one could examine part one of Martin Heidegger's *Being and Time*, though I don't recommend it.

30. The dreams that Cass has, in addition to confronting him with his suppressed racist behavior, compelled him to leave Paris: "I can't help but believe that something *forced* me to go to Sambuco. These nightmares I had" (248).

31. That Styron is unable to do so is unsurprising; Sartre broke with Camus over the same issue.

32. Morrison, *Playing in the Dark*, iv.

33. It is interesting that in various interviews Styron refers to Thomas Gray by his last name and to Nat Turner as "Nat."

34. See Louis Menand's *Metaphysical Club* for a discussion of how the civil rights movement and the Cold War revived attitudes of certitude that existed prior to the Civil War.

35. Nor could Styron portray Turner as an antebellum Malcolm X, since his aversion to violence no doubt prevented him from recognizing the obvious similarities between their two characters.

36. See *Either/Or* for an elaboration of Kierkegaard's Christian philosophy.

37. Styron would recapitulate this logic in *Sophie's Choice*.

38. "Nat Turner Revisited," 434. This is a revealing turn of phrase, since, according to David Blight, reconciliationist narratives enable a kind of forgetting after the Civil War that leads to Jim Crow.

39. "Two Writers," 44, 45.

40. The title of the essay is drawn from an Emily Dickinson poem. When Styron published a collection of essays and other nonfiction in 1982, he entitled it *This Quiet Dust and Other Writings*.

41. The essay bears more than a passing resemblance to Alice Walker's recounting of her search for Zora Neale Hurston.

42. Although this interview predates the publication of "This Quiet Dust," the essay was likely finished before Styron granted the interview.

43. "Conversation," 60, 61.

44. Mailer noted this tendency in 1957, years before *Lie Down in Darkness* or *The Confessions of Nat Turner* demonstrated it to the world. See his "Evaluations: Quick and Expensive Comments on the Talent in the Room" in *Advertisements for Myself*.

45. This interview was not published until the summer of 1966 in *Per/Se*, a short-lived quarterly that ceased publication in 1969.

46. "An Interview with William Styron," 72.

47. Ibid., 75, emphasis added.

48. Ibid., 69.

49. Ibid., 72.

50. Ibid., 73.

51. In a later interview Styron claims that Turner "desired her; he wanted her
. . . I believe this must have been true. I cannot prove it. I think that if there is any
psychological truth in these insights, it partially lies in the fact that one often wishes to
destroy what one most earnestly desires" (Yale, 90).

52. Styron's statements here suggest that he made an authorial choice to depict
Turner in this fashion, if only because this seems the only sensible way for him to
present Turner. After the controversy erupted, when pressured to explain why Nat
Turner lacked a wife when at least one contemporary newspaper mentions her presence,
Styron asserts that the historical record did not decisively indicate that she had existed.

53. This interview is entitled "The Confessions of William Styron" in *Conversations
with William Styron*. In order to avoid the confusion of referring to yet another set of
confessions, I refer to this interview as the Yale interview.

54. One wonders if the rise of H. Rap Brown and Stokely Carmichael influenced
Styron's shift in attitude.

55. Styron's novel also omits an episode from Gray's *Confessions* where Turner
reports that he had escaped for several months but returned to the community and thus
back into servitude in order to lead everyone to freedom, perhaps because this account
would make depictions of Turner's isolation and individualism unbelievable.

EPILOGUE

1. Interestingly, Donald Pease connects a different geneology of American
exceptionalism to the election of Barack Obama in *The New American Exceptionalism*.

2. Black patriotism is often suspect.

3. To be clear, the media's imputation of Wright's ideas to Obama was entirely fair,
given that in his autobiography, *Dreams from My Father*, Obama identifies Wright's
church as offering "a spiritual harbor and the chance to see one's gifts appreciated . . . in
a way that a paycheck never can" (285). Moreover, Obama's second book, *The Audacity
of Hope*, takes its title from one of Wright's less controversial sermons.

4. Obama's keynote speech at the 2004 DNC rests on a similar assertion
of American exceptionalism. See http://www.americanrhetoric.com/speeches/
convention2004/barackobama2004dnc.htm for the full text of that speech. There are
interesting—and troubling—parallels between this speech and both Martin Luther
King's address on the mall and Booker T. Washington's Atlanta address in that each
was more a narrative of (African) American exceptionalism and eventual progress
unattached from any policy proposals. The point of each speech was to win the hearts
and minds of its auditors, not reshape legal practices.

5. Obama actually misquotes Faulkner. The proper line, from *Requiem for a Nun*, is
"The past is never dead. It's not even past."

6. Adam Mansbach, "The Audacity of Post-Racism" in *The Speech: Race and Barack
Obama's "A More Perfect Union,"* 69–84.

7. Obama certainly understood the burden that presumptions of innocence place on calls for redress from his days of teaching critical race theory at the University of Chicago Law School. He was not going to throw away his chance at the presidency to present this case to a skeptical audience.

8. This is why he took pains to proclaim that Rev. Wright's statements not only "denigrate both the greatness and the goodness of our nation; [they] rightly offend white and black alike." This was a brilliant rhetorical move, for it collapsed into one the very different American narratives that exist inside the Black and white communities.

9. Both Pease and Spanos note attempts by G. H. W. Bush, Bill Clinton, and G. W. Bush to invoke the same kind of triumphalist innocence, but these attempts largely fail, in part because the fallenness of the USA was not in question during their elections the way it was during the presidential elections of 1960, 1980, and 2008. I am fully aware that Jimmy Carter never mentions the word "malaise" in his 1979 address, but that continues to be the way that his speech is remembered. A Google search for "Jimmy Carter malaise" returns about five hundred thousand hits. A search for "Jimmy Carter peanut farmer" returns two hundred fifty thousand. This should indicate persistently that this misnomer continues to attach itself to our public understanding of his presidency. For more, see Kenneth Morris's *Jimmy Carter, American Moralist.*

Works Cited

Anderson, Benedict. *Imagined Communities: Reflections on the Origin and Spread of Nationalism*. New York: Verso, 1991.

Arendt, Hannah. "Reflections on Little Rock." *The Portable Hannah Arendt*. Peter Baehr, ed. New York: Penguin Books, 2003. 231–246.

Baldwin, James. *The Fire Next Time*. New York: Vintage International, 1993.

Barrish, Phillip. *White Liberal Identity, Literary Pedagogy, and Classic American Realism*. Columbus, OH: Ohio State University Press, 2005.

Blight, David. *Race and Reunion: The Civil War in American Memory*. Cambridge, MA: The Belknap Press, 2001.

Blotner, Joseph. *Robert Penn Warren: A Biography*. New York: Random House, 1997.

Branch, Taylor. *Pillar of Fire: America in the King Years, 1963–65*. New York: Simon and Schuster, 1998.

Cagin, Seth, and Phillip Dray. *We Are Not Afraid: The Story of Goodman, Schwerner, and Chaney and the Civil Rights Campaign for Mississippi*. New York: Macmillan, 1988.

Camus, Albert. *The Rebel: An Essay on Man in Revolt*. Anthony Bower, trans. New York: Knopf, 1967.

Carson, Clayborne, et al. *Reporting Civil Rights: Part One, American Journalism 1941–1963*. New York: The Library of America, 2003.

———. *Reporting Civil Rights: Part Two, American Journalism 1963–1973*. New York: The Library of America, 2003.

Clarke, John Henrik, ed. *William Styron's* The Confessions of Nat Turner: *Ten Black Writers Respond*. Boston: Beacon Press, 1968.

Cologne-Brookes, Gavin. *The Novels of William Styron: From Harmony to History*. Baton Rouge: Louisiana State University Press, 1995.

Crossman, Richard H. S. *The God that Failed*. New York: Columbia University Press, 2001.

Dabney, Robert Lewis. *A Defense of Virginia: (and through her, of the South) in Recent and Pending Contests Against the Sectional Party*. New York: E. J. Hale, 1867.

Dearborn, Mary. *Mailer: A Biography*. Boston: Houghton Mifflin, 1999.

Denning, Michael. *The Cultural Front: The Laboring of American Culture in the Twentieth Century*. New York: Verso, 1996.

Dickstein, Morris. *Gates of Eden: American Culture in the Sixties*. New York: Basic Books, 1977.

———. "The World in a Mirror: Problems of Distance in Recent American Fiction." *Sewanee Review* 89:3 (1981): 386–400.

Dittmer, John. *Local People: The Struggle for Civil Rights in Mississippi*. Urbana: University of Illinois Press, 1994.

Dudziak, Mary L. *Cold War Civil Rights: Race and the Image of American Democracy*. Princeton: Princeton University Press, 2002.

Ellison, Ralph. *Shadow and Act*. New York: Random House, 1972.

Evers, Myrlie, with William Peters. *For Us, the Living*. Jackson: University Press of Mississippi, 1996.

Faulkner, William. "American Segregation and the World Crisis." *Three Views of the Segregation Decision*. Atlanta: Southern Regional Council, 1956.

———. *Requiem for a Nun*. New York: Random House, 1951.

Fiscus, Ronald J. *The Constitutional Logic of Affirmative Action*. Durham, NC: Duke University Press, 1992.

Foner, Eric. *Reconstruction: America's Unfinished Revolution, 1863–1877*. New York: Perennial Classics, 2002.

Gates, Henry Louis. *Figures in Black: Words, Signs and the Racial Self*. New York: Oxford University Press, 1986.

Gillis, John R. "Memory and Identity: The History of a Relationship." *Commemorations: The Politics of National Identity*. John R. Gillis, ed. Princeton: Princeton Univeristy Press, 1994.

Haidu, Peter. *The Subject of Violence: The Song of Roland and the Birth of the State*. Bloomington: Indiana University Press, 1993.

Hall, Jacquelyn Dowd. "The Long Civil Rights Movement and the Political Uses of the Past." *Journal of American History* 91(4) (2005): 1233–1263.

Hamblin, Robert. "Robert Penn Warren at the 1965 Southern Literary Festival: A Personal Recollection." *Southern Literary Journal* 22.2 (Spring 1990): 53–62.

Harrison, Suzan. "'Racial Content Espied': Modernist Politics, Textuality, and Race in Eudora Welty's 'The Demonstrators.'" Nancy Pollack and Suzanne Marrs, eds., 89–108.

Hettle, Wallace. "The Minister, the Martyr, and the Maxim: Robert Lewis Dabney and Stonewall Jackson Biography." *Civil War History* 49:4 (2003): 353–369.

Hirsh, James R. *Riot and Remembrance: The Tulsa Race War and Its Legacy*. Boston: Houghton Mifflin, 2002.

Hodgson, Godfrey. *America in Our Time*. Garden City, NY: Doubleday, 1976.

Hollowell, John. *Fact & Fiction: The New Journalism and the Nonfiction Novel*. Chapel Hill: University of North Carolina Press, 1977.

Inge, M. Thomas. "The Fugitives and the Agrarians: A Clarification." *American Literature* 62:3 (September 1990): 486–493.

Jancovich, Mark. *The Cultural Politics of the New Criticism*. New York: Cambridge University Press, 1993.

Johnson, James Weldon. *The Book of American Negro Poetry*. New York: Harcourt, Brace and World, 1983.

Kaplan, Amy. "'Left Alone with America': The Absence of Empire in the Study of American Culture." *Cultures of United States Imperialism*. Amy Kaplan and Donald Pease, eds. Durham: Duke University Press, 1993.

Kelvin, Norman. "The Divided Self: William Styron's Fiction from *Lie Down in Darkness* to *The Confessions of Nat Turner*." *The Achievement of William Styron*. Robert K. Morris and Irving Malin, eds. Athens: University of Georgia Press, 1975. 208–226.

Kennedy, Stetson. *After Appomattox: How the South Won the Civil War*. Gainesville: University of Florida Press, 1995.

King, Martin Luther, Jr. *Why We Can't Wait*. New York: Harper & Row, 1964.

Kreyling, Michael. *Author and Agent: Eudora Welty and Diarmuid Russell*. New York: Farrar, Straus, Giroux, 1991.

Lindner, Robert. *Must You Conform?* New York: Rinehart & Company, 1956.

Mailer, Norman. *Advertisements for Myself*. Cambridge: Harvard University Press, 1992.

——. *An American Dream*. New York: Dial Press, 1965.

——. *Barbary Shore*. New York: Rinehart, 1951.

——. *The Naked and the Dead*. New York: Rinehart, 1948.

——. *The Time of Our Time*. New York: Random House, 1998.

——. *The Deer Park*. New York: Putnam, 1955.

Mansbach, Adam. "The Audacity of Post-Racism." *The Speech: Race and Barack Obama's "A More Perfect Union."* T. Denean Sharpley-Whiting, ed. New York: Bloomsbury, 2009. 69–84.

Manso, Peter, ed. *Mailer, His Life and Times*. New York: Simon and Schuster, 1985.

Marcuse, Herbert. *One-Dimensional Man: Studies in the Ideology of Advanced Industrial Society*. Boston: Beacon Press, 1964.

Marrs, Suzanne. "'The Huge Fateful Stage of the Outside World': Eudora Welty's Life in Politics." Nancy Pollack and Suzanne Marrs, eds. 69–87.

Mars, Florence, and Lynn Eden. *Witness in Philadelphia*. Baton Rouge: Louisiana State University Press, 1977.

McCann, Sean. "The Imperiled Republic: Norman Mailer and the Poetics of Anti-Liberalism." *ELH* 67(2000): 291–334.

McWhorter, Diane. *Carry Me Home: Birmingham, Alabama, The Climactic Battle of the Civil Rights Revolution*. New York: Simon & Schuster, 2001.

Menand, Louis. *American Studies*. New York: Farrar, Straus, and Giroux, 2002.

——. *The Metaphysical Club*. New York: Farrar, Straus, and Giroux, 2001.

Mills, Hillary. *Norman Mailer: A Biography*. New York: Empire Books, 1982.

Mills, Kay. *Changing Channels: The Civil Rights Case That Transformed Television*. Jackson: University Press of Mississippi, 2004.

Morris, Kenneth. *Jimmy Carter, American Moralist*. Athens, GA: University of Georgia Press, 1996.

Morrison, Toni. *Playing in the Dark: Whiteness and the Literary Imagination*. Cambridge, MA: Harvard University Press, 1993.

Neyland, James A. *A. Philip Randolph*. Los Angeles: Melrose Square Publishing Company, 1994.

Nossiter, Adam. *Of Long Memory: Mississippi and the Murder of Medgar Evers*. Reading, MA: Addison Wesley, 1994.

Obama, Barack. *The Audacity of Hope: Thoughts on Reclaiming the American Dream*. New York: Crown, 2006.

———. *Dreams from My Father: A Story of Race and Inheritence*. New York: Crown, 2004.

Packer, Jerrold. *American Nightmare: The History of Jim Crow*. New York: St. Martin's Press, 2005.

Pease, Donald. *The New American Exceptionalism*. Minneapolis: University of Minnesota Press, 2009.

Perkins, James A. "Robert Penn Warren and James Farmer: Notes on the Creation of New Journalism." *rWp: An Annual of Robert Penn Warren Studies* 1:1 (2001): 163–175.

Pollack, Nancy, and Suzanne Marrs, eds. *Eudora Welty and Politics: Did the Writer Crusade?* Baton Rouge: Louisiana State University Press, 2001.

Polsgrove, Carol. *Divided Minds: Intellectuals and the Civil Rights Movement*. New York: W.W. Norton, 2001.

Prenshaw, Peggy Whitman. "Welty's Transformation of the Public, the Private, and the Politcal." Nancy Pollack and Suzanne Marrs, eds. 19–46.

Robinson, Forrest. "A Combat with the Past: Robert Penn Warren on Race and Slavery." *American Literature* 67:3 (September 1995): 511–530.

Romm, James. *Herodotus*. New Haven: Yale University Press, 1998.

Ruppersburg, Hugh. "Robert Penn Warren and the 'Burden of Our Time': Segregation and *Who Speaks for the Negro?*" *Mississippi Quarterly: The Journal of Southern Culture* 42:2 (Spring 1989): 115–128.

Rushdy, Ashraf. *Neo-slave Narratives: Studies in the Social Life of a Literary Form*. New York: Oxford University Press, 1999.

Salter, John. *Jackson, Mississippi: An American Chronicle of Struggle and Schism*. Malabar, FL: RE Krieger Publishing Company, 1987.

Schrecker, Ellen. *Many Are the Crimes: McCarthyism in America*. Boston: Little, Brown, 1998.

Silver, James. *Mississippi: The Closed Society*. New York: Harcourt, Brace & World, 1966.

Singh, Nikhil Pal. *Black Is a Country: Race and the Unfinished Struggle for Democracy*. Cambridge, MA: Harvard University Press, 2004.

Sharpley-Whiting, T. Denean, ed. *The Speech: Race and Barack Obama's "A More Perfect Union."* New York: Bloomsbury, 2009.

Spanos, William. *American Exceptionalism in the Age of Globalization: The Specter of Vietnam*. Albany, NY: State University of New York Press, 2008.

Stone, Albert. *The Return of Nat Turner*. Athens: University of Georgia Press, 1992.

Styron, William. "Acceptance Speech for the Howells Medal." *Critical Essays on William Styron*. Arthur D. Casciato and James L. W. West III, eds. Boston: GK Hall, 1982.

——. *The Confessions of Nat Turner.* New York: Bantam Books, 1982.

——. *Conversations with William Styron.* James L. W. West III, ed. Jackson: University Press of Mississippi, 1985.

——. *Lie Down in Darkness.* New York: Random House, 1971.

——. *Set This House on Fire.* New York: Random House, 1960.

——. *Sophie's Choice.* New York: Random House, 1971.

——. *The Long March.* New York: Random House, 1960.

——. *This Quiet Dust and Other Writings.* New York: Random House, 1982.

Szalay, Michael. "*All the King's Men,* or, The Primal Crime." *Yale Journal of Criticism* 15.2 (2000): 345–370.

Szczesiul, Anthony. *Racial Politics and Robert Penn Warren's Poetry.* Gainesville: University of Florida Press, 2002.

Torres, Sasha. *Black, White, and in Color: Television and Black Civil Rights.* Princeton, NJ: Princeton University Press, 2003.

Tucker, Shirley. *Mississippi from Within.* New York: Arco Publishing Company, 1965.

Vollers, Maryanne. *Ghosts of Mississippi: The Murder of Medgar Evers, the Trails of Bryon De La Beckwith, and the Haunting of the New South.* Boston: Little, Brown, 1995.

Waldron, Ann. *Eudora: A Writer's Life.* New York: Doubleday, 1998.

——. *Hodding Carter: The Reconstruction of a Racist.* Chapel Hill: Algonquin Books of Chapel Hill, 1993.

Warren, Kenneth. *Black and White Strangers: Race and American Literary Realism.* Chicago: University of Chicago Press, 1993.

Warren, Robert Penn. *All the King's Men.* San Diego: Harcourt Brace Jovanovich, 1982.

——. *Who Speaks for the Negro?* New York: Random House, 1965.

——. *Democracy and Poetry.* Cambridge, MA: Harvard University Press, 1975.

——. *Wilderness: A Tale of the Civil War.* New York: Random House, 1961.

——. *Flood: A Romance of Our Time.* New York: Random House, 1964.

——. *Robert Penn Warren Talking: Interviews 1950–78.* Floyd C. Watkins and John T. Hiers, eds. New York: Random House, 1980.

——. *Segregation: The Inner Conflict of the South.* In *Reporting Civil Rights.* New York: Library of America, 2003.

——. *Talking with Robert Penn Warren.* Floyd C. Watkins, John T. Hiers, and Mary Louise Weaks, eds. Athens: University of Georgia Press, 1990.

——. "The Briar Patch." *I'll Take My Stand: The South and the Agrarian Tradition, by Twelve Southerners.* New York: Harper, 1962.

——. *The Legacy of the Civil War: Meditations on the Centennial.* New York: Random House, 1961.

Washington, Booker T. *The Booker T. Washington Papers.* Vol. 3. Louis R. Harlan, ed. Urbana: University of Illinois Press, 1974.

Watts, Jerry Gafio. *Ralph Ellison: Heroism and the Black Intellectual.* Chapel Hill, NC: University of North Carolina Press, 1994.

Welty, Eudora. *The Collected Short Stories of Eudora Welty.* New York: Harcourt Brace Jovanovich, 1980.

————. *Conversations with Eudora Welty.* Peggy Whitman Prenshaw, ed. Jackson: University Press of Mississippi, 1985.

————. *More Conversations with Eudora Welty.* Peggy Whitman Prenshaw, ed. Jackson: University Press of Mississippi, 1996.

————. "Place and Time: The Southern Writer's Inheritance." *The Mississippi Quarterly* 50.4 (Fall 1997): 545.

————. *Stories, Essays & Memoir.* New York: Library of America, 1998.

West, James L. W. III. *William Styron, A Life.* New York: Random House, 1998.

Woodward, C. Vann. *The Strange Career of Jim Crow.* New York: Oxford University Press, 1966.

Zinn, Howard. *SNCC, The New Abolitionists.* Boston: Beacon Press, 1964.

Index

abolitionists, 29–30

Advertisements for Myself (Mailer), 45, 48, 49, 62, 115, 126

Agrarianism, 14–15, 17, 28, 90

All the King's Men (Warren), 38

American Dream, An (Mailer), 11, 68

Arendt, Hannah, 107, 108

Armies of the Night (Mailer), 49

As I Lay Dying (Faulkner), 110

Atlantic Monthly, 89

Baldwin, James, 19

Barbary Shore (Mailer), 10, 47–49

Barish, Phillip, 8

Barnett, Ross, 77

battle of Shiloh, 22

Beard, Fred, 75

Black Arts Movement, 42

blamelessness. *See* innocence

Blight, David, 4–5

Bloody Angle, 31

"Briar Patch, The" (Warren), 14, 15–19, 25, 37

Brotherhood of Sleeping Car Porters, 20

Brown, John, 37–38

Brown v. Board of Education, 8, 9, 20, 31, 59, 74, 103

Camus, Albert, 114

Canzoneri, Robert, 129

Carter, Hodding, 75

Carter, Jimmy, 137

Chaney, James, 87–89, 95

Citizens' Councils, 76

Civil Rights Act, 103

Civil War: battle of Shiloh, 22; Bloody Angle, 31; cultural memory of reasons for, 4–5; and evolution of American exceptionalism, 4–6; "Great Alibi vs. Treasury of Virtue," 30, 32; role of abolitionists in, 29. See also *Legacy of the Civil War: Meditations on the Centennial, The*

Clark, John Henrick, 105, 126

Clark, Kenneth B., 37–39

"cliche of fear," 22

"cliche of hate," 23

Clinton, Hillary, 133

Cold War, 46–53, 64, 107, 137

Confessions of Nat Turner, The (Styron), 12–13, 105, 108, 114, 121–32

conformity: Cold War–era, 46–53, 59, 63–64, 137; in military, 111–12; struggles against, 66–70. *See also* McCarthyism

conservative liberalism, 49

"Conversation Piece" (Warren), 39

cultural memory, 4–6, 8

Dabney, Robert Lewis, 26

Deer Park, The (Mailer), 10, 56–58, 70

Defense of Virginia, A (Dabney), 26

"Demonstrators, The" (Welty), 11, 73, 92, 93, 95–104

Du Bois, W. E. B., 34

Ellison, Ralph, 19, 42, 87

ethnic identity and ambiguity, 57

Evers, Medgar, 11, 74–86. *See also*

"Where Is the Voice Coming From?"
(Welty)
exceptionalism, 6–9, 11
Executioner's Song, The (Mailer), 69
existentialism, 48, 66–67, 106, 114,
121–24, 128–32

Faulkner, William, 89, 90, 91, 93, 94–95;
and Norman Mailer, 61–62, 68. *See
also individual works*
fiction, as persuasive speech, 91
Fiscus, Ronald, 6

Gillis, John R., 6
God that Failed, The, 55
Goodman, Andrew, 87–89, 95
Gray, Thomas, 127
Great Alibi, 31, 32
Great Gatsby, The (Fitzgerald), 110
Gwaltney, Francis Irby, 61

Harlem riots, 36
Harper's Magazine, 127
"Hip and the Square, The" (Mailer),
60
hipsters, 62–65; language of hip, 65–66.
See also "Hip and the Square, The";
"White Negro, The"
Hodgson, Godfrey, 47, 107
Holmes, Oliver Wendell, 28, 34
Howe, Irving, 62
Huckleberry Finn (Twain), 94

*I'll Take My Stand: The South and the
Agrarian Tradition,* 9, 14–15, 27, 28, 34,
35. *See also* "Briar Patch, The"
Independent (magazine), 60–61
innocence: and connection to
exceptionalism, 6–9; premise of, 4–9;
protection of, 11–13; southern, 24–26,
30, 32, 93
integration: Norman Mailer on, 60–61;

Robert Penn Warren on, 10, 16, 23–26,
40–42; Eudora Welty on, 91, 102
integrity, literary vs. social, 91

John Brown: The Making of a Martyr
(Warren), 14, 28, 38
Jones, James, 127

Kelvin, Norman, 113
Kennedy, John F., 137
King, Martin Luther, 25, 34–35, 39, 91,
99, 105
Korean War, 109
Ku Klux Klan, 87–89

*Legacy of the Civil War: Meditations on
the Centennial, The* (Warren), 9–10,
14, 27–35, 38
Lewis, R. W. B., 131
liberal intellectuals, 107–8
Lie Down in Darkness (Styron), 109–10
Life magazine, 27
Lindner, Robert, 50
Little Rock Nine, 31
Logan, Rayford, 5
Long March, The (Styron), 12, 106, 108,
109–14, 121, 122, 124
Look magazine, 35–36
Losing Battles (Welty), 73, 104
Lost Cause movement, 5–7, 9, 14, 22, 68,
79, 81, 87
Lucy, Autherine, 22

Mailer, Adele Morales, 45
Mailer, Norman, 3, 10–11, 44–71;
education and military service, 45–46;
and William Faulkner, 61–62, 68; on
integration, 60–61; New York jazz
scene interest, 58–59, 60, 62, 66–68;
at "Our Country and Our Culture"
symposium, 50; socialist views of,
46–48; on William Styron, 126–27;

Village Voice columns, 59–60. *See also individual works*

Malaquais, Jean, 46–47

"Man Who Studied Yoga, The" (Mailer), 51–56

Mansbach, Adam, 136

Mars, Florence, 88

Marxism, 55, 107

McCarthyism, 48, 51–55, 63–64, 107, 137

Millsaps College, 73, 75, 76

Minton, Walter, 58

Mississippi Burning investigation, 88–89, 95

Mississippi State Sovereignty Commission, 76

Montgomery bus boycott, 8, 10, 20, 25, 44, 59, 61, 123

"More Perfect Union, A" (Obama), 134–37

Morris, Willie, 127

Mrs. Dalloway (Woolf), 110

"Must the Novelist Crusade?" (Welty), 11, 73, 89–92, 94, 104

Naked and the Dead, The (Mailer), 10, 45, 46–47, 55

National Association for the Advancement of Colored People (NAACP), 10, 25, 75

"Negro Now, The" (Warren), 35–36

New Critics, 89, 90, 91

New Journalism, 20

New Republic, The, 35

New Yorker, The, 77–78, 86, 104

Obama, Barack, 133–37

O'Donnell, George Marion, 90

Optimist's Daughter, The (Welty), 73

organization of labor, 18

"Our Country and Our Culture" symposium, 50

Paine, Thomas, 7

Pease, Donald, 7

Plessy v. Ferguson, 5

pragmatism, 28–29

Prenshaw, Peggy Whitman, 90

race, and sexuality, 61–62, 66–69, 79–82, 119, 127, 130–31

Randolph, A. Phillip, 20

Ransom, John Crowe, 90

Reagan, Ronald, 137

Rebel, The (Camus), 114

Rebel without a Cause: The Hypnoanalysis of a Criminal Psychopath (Lindner), 50

reconciliationist vision, post–Civil War, 4

Reconstruction, 16; failure and consequences of, 4–6; racial intolerance after, 4–6; reasons for failure of, 32; southern resistance to, 16; Robert Penn Warren on, 16. *See also* Lost Cause movement

"Reflections on Little Rock" (Arendt), 108

Return of Nat Turner, The (Stone), 106

Russell, Diarmuid, 77

Salter, John, 76, 77

Schwerner, Michael, 87–89, 95

Segregation: The Inner Conflict of the South (Warren), 9, 14, 20–25, 38

self-interests, 42–43

Set This House on Fire (Styron), 12, 110, 114–22, 126, 131

sexuality: power and politics of, 10, 51–58, 71, 115–16; and race, 61–62, 66–69, 79–82, 119, 127, 130–31

slavery, 28–30. See also *Confessions of Nat Turner, The*

Sophie's Choice (Styron), 110

Sound and the Fury, The (Faulkner), 110, 127

South Today: 100 Years After Appomattox, The, 127

Southampton Rebellion, 123–31. See also *Confessions of Nat Turner, The*

Spano, William, 8

Stegner, Page, 129

Stuart, Lyle, 60–61, 62

Student Nonviolent Coordinating Committee (SNCC), 75

Students for a Democratic Society, 105

Styron, William, 3, 105–32; effect of military experiences on, 108–9; influence of Albert Camus on, 114; Norman Mailer on, 126–27. See also *individual works*

Szalay, Michael, 36

Tate, Allen, 26, 90

television, expansion and censorship in the South, 74–75

Ten Black Writers. See *William Styron's Nat Turner: Ten Black Writers Respond*

"This Quiet Dust" (Styron), 127–29, 130

Thompson, Allen, 74–75, 77

Till, Emmett, 59, 61, 66, 74

Tougaloo Southern Christian College, 75, 76, 77

transcendentalists, 29

Treasury of Virtue, 31, 32

Trilling, Lionel, 107

Turner, Nat. See *Confessions of Nat Turner, The*; *William Styron's Nat Turner: Ten Black Writers Respond*

Village Voice, 59–60

Warren, Robert Penn, 3, 44, 90, 95; "cliche of fear," 22; "cliche of hate," 23; early defense of segregation, 9–10, 14; on integration, 10, 16, 23–26, 40–42;

on northern liberals, 25–26. See also *individual works*

Washington, Booker T., 34

Welty, Christian, 74

Welty, Eudora, 3, 11–12, 72–104; on integration, 91, 102. See also *individual works*

"Where Is the Voice Coming From?" (Welty), 11, 73, 77–86, 92, 93, 98

"White Negro, The" (Mailer), 60, 62–70, 115

white supremacy, 4–5, 11, 12, 16, 64, 105, 106, 118–19, 121, 126

Whitehead, Margaret, 125–26, 128, 129

Who Speaks for the Negro? (Warren), 10, 14, 36–37, 38

William Styron's Nat Turner: Ten Black Writers Respond (Clark), 105, 126

Witness in Philadelphia (Mars), 88

Woodward, C. Vann, 131

World War II, 108–9

Wright, Jeremiah, 133–34

Wright, Richard, 91

writers, effects of success on, 44–45

"Yankee Phariseeism," 25–26

Young Man Luther (Erikson), 127

Printed in Poland
by Amazon Fulfillment
Poland Sp. z o.o., Wrocław

25583831R00098